Federalism, Subnational Constitutions, and Minority Rights

Federalism, Subnational Constitutions, and Minority Rights

Edited by G. Alan Tarr, Robert F. Williams, and Josef Marko

Westport, Connecticut
London

Library of Congress Cataloging-in-Publication Data

Federalism, subnational constitutions, and minority rights / edited by G. Alan Tarr, Robert F. Williams, and Josef Marko.
p. cm.
Includes bibliographical references and index.
ISBN 0–275–98023–5 (alk. paper)—ISBN 0–275–98024–3 (pbk. : alk. paper)
1. Minorities—Legal status, laws, etc. 2. Human rights. 3. Constitutional law. 4. Federal government. 5. Subnational governments. 6. Comparative government. I. Tarr, G. Alan (George Alan) II. Williams, Robert F. (Robert Forrest), 1945– III. Marko, Joseph, 1955–
K3242.F43 2004
342—dc22 2004044229

British Library Cataloguing in Publication Data is available.

Copyright © 2004 by G. Alan Tarr, Robert F. Williams, and Josef Marko

All rights reserved. No portion of this book may be reproduced, by any process or technique, without the express written consent of the publisher.

Library of Congress Catalog Card Number: 2004044229
ISBN: 0–275–98023–5
ISBN: 0–275–98024–3 (pbk.)

First published in 2004

Praeger Publishers, 88 Post Road West, Westport, CT 06881
An imprint of Greenwood Publishing Group, Inc.
www.praeger.com

Printed in the United States of America

The paper used in this book complies with the Permanent Paper Standard issued by the National Information Standards Organization (Z39.48–1984).

10 9 8 7 6 5 4 3 2 1

Contents

Preface

It has often been asserted, at least outside the United States, that federalism is the best instrument for protecting the rights of minorities. Countries throughout the world have adopted federal or quasi-federal arrangements, typically including a system of subnational constitutions, in order to accommodate racial, ethnic, cultural, or religious minorities within their borders. Examples can be found in Europe (e.g., Switzerland and Spain), in Africa (e.g., Ethiopia), in Asia (e.g., India), and in North America (e.g., Canada). Still other federal systems such as Australia, Brazil, Germany, and the United States have component units whose borders were not drawn to accommodate minority groups, but these countries still must deal with issues of pluralism and diversity. Finally, systems emerging from authoritarian rule (e.g., Nigeria and Russia) have experimented with federal arrangements as a way to deal with ethnic and cultural pluralism.

Thus far, however, rigorous single-system analyses of the connection between minority rights on the one hand and federalism and subnational constitutionalism on the other have been rare. The lack of such studies has precluded meaningful cross-country comparisons. In addition, no comprehensive analysis exists of how federalism and subnational constitutions have served to safeguard the rights of minorities, nor of the conditions under which they are likely to do so.

This volume is designed to address these important issues. The essays introducing the volume, in turn, provide an initial foray into the complexities of comparative constitutionalism. They are followed by case studies of constitutional arrangements and the protection of minority rights in a wide variety of settings, including mature federal systems, federal systems in transition, and emerging federal systems. These studies of systems from several continents, with diverse problems of pluralism and minority-group accommodation, offer the basis for a more thorough exploration of the connection between federalism/subnational constitutionalism and minority rights.

This volume had its genesis in a conference, sponsored by the Center for State Constitutional Studies and the European Academy, held in Seiseralm, Italy, in 2001. The quality of the discussions at that conference is reflected in the contributions to this volume. Likewise evident are the impressive contributions made by two scholars, Kristin Henrard and Anna Gamper, who were unable to attend the conference.

The volume brings together scholars from several continents, ensuring both a scholarly feast and a logistical nightmare. At the European Academy, Francesco Palermo and Jens Woelk played a crucial role in coordinating the volume. Without their energy and commitment, this volume would never have been published. At Rutgers University, Sylvia Somers of the Center for State Constitutional Studies and Deborah Canuso of Rutgers Law School displayed remarkable patience and unfailing good humor as they kept the manuscript on track as it was prepared for submission. Their support was invaluable. Our initial editor at Greenwood Publishing, Michael Hermann, was enthusiastic about the project from the outset and unfailingly helpful in negotiating the hurdles necessary to ensure publication of the volume. His successor at Greenwood, Hilary Claggett, provided just the right mixture of assistance and insistence to bring the volume to completion.

I

Overviews

1

Subnational Constitutional Space: A View from the States, Provinces, Regions, Länder, and Cantons

Robert F. Williams and G. Alan Tarr

Every federal system is structured by a national constitution that divides power, establishes central institutions, prescribes the rules for resolving disputes, and provides a procedure for its own alteration.[1] In some federal systems, the national constitution prescribes the political institutions and processes for the country's subnational units as well, thus providing the complete constitutional architecture for the federal system.[2] Former unitary countries that have decentralized into federal systems—that is, countries that exemplify devolutionary rather than integrative federalism—are particularly likely to include subnational constitutional arrangements in the national constitution.[3] However, in most federal systems the national constitution is incomplete as a governing constitutional document, in the sense that it does not seek to prescribe all constitutional arrangements. Rather, it leaves space in the federal nation's constitutional architecture to be filled by the constitutions of its subnational units.[4] This is not surprising, for as Cheryl Saunders has noted, "The characterization of subnational units as political communities suggests that they must have constitutions of some kind as well, although it does not necessarily prescribe what form they should take."[5]

Even federal systems that recognize a place for subnational constitutions differ substantially in the extent to which the national constitution is incomplete, that is, in the amount of space that they allocate to subnational units to establish their own goals and institute their own governmental institutions and processes. Typically the less detail the national constitution provides or requires of subnational constitutions, the greater the subnational constitutional space will be. For example, the South African Constitution, as shall be seen, both serves as a national constitution and provides a model provincial constitution that operates unless a province adopts its own constitution. Thus it is much more complete than many other federal constitutions.

Although the language of incompleteness is widely used, evaluating national constitutions as more or less complete may seem to reflect a value judgment that a more, rather than less, complete national constitution is somehow better. Such a judgment would reflect a national perspective on federal constitutionalism, and thus it is emphatically not our intent here. For present purposes, it may be more useful to think of the relationship of national and subnational constitutions in federal systems as interdependent. Thus, in analyzing American constitutional federalism, Louis Bilionis concluded that the federal and state constitutions should be evaluated together, as an interconnected whole:

> Each is a distinct force which helps shape our national constitutional environment. Each force, however, is also dependent upon, limited by, and to some extent the product of, that very same environment. Federal and state constitutions thus are interdependent features of a greater *American* constitutional structure, the web of social institutions and practices the American people employ, sometimes unwittingly, to articulate and effectuate their highest ideals.[6] [emphasis in original]

As will be seen, the quantity and quality of constitutional interdependence expands and contracts together with subnational constitutional space.

THE SUBNATIONAL PERSPECTIVE

The study of constitutional federalism is most often approached from the vantage point of the national constitution. Analyzing constitutional arrangements from this angle encourages thinking from the perspective of the national government: What powers does the national government have, what constitutional impediments stand in the way of it achieving its objectives, and to what extent does the national constitution mandate certain constitutional structures for the subnational units of the federal state? Other questions, such as whether the federal arrangements are devolutionary or integrative, may likewise be best evaluated from this national, top, or center perspective.[7] But important as it is, the national vantage point does not encompass the full range of constitutional questions in a federal system, in part because it encourages an understanding of federalism as a top-down or center-periphery arrangement rather than as one based on differing spheres of governmental authority.

Much less common is the view from the subnational, bottom, or peripheral polities—indeed, subnational constitutions have been, and generally remain, low-visibility constitutions.[8] Yet the subnational perspective can reveal a wealth of new information about a federal system's constitutional arrangements that would likely be ignored or slighted from the national perspective. The approach from the subnational "sphere" (the terminology South Africa has adopted for its system of constitutional federalism) focuses on two questions: What range of discretion (space) is available to the component units in a federal system in designing their constitutional arrangements, and to what extent have the subnational units occupied the constitutional space permitted them? These questions are best addressed from a unit-by-unit, subnational vantage point rather than from the national, top, or center view.

Before these questions can be answered, however, a crucial preliminary question must be addressed: What qualifies a document as a subnational constitution? In some federal systems—for example, Australia, Austria, Germany, and the United States—the question is easily answered: Each has distinct identifiable subnational constitutions. In other federal systems, such as Canada, the question is likewise easily answered, though for a different reason: There are no subnational constitutions independent of the federal constitution.[9] However, in some federal systems the answer is not so clear. For one thing, subnational constitutions can be different in kind from the national constitution. In Spain, for example, are the regional "Autonomy Statutes" constitutions or not? They do seem to exhibit some of the attributes of constitutions, but that term is studiously avoided in Spain.[10] In Italy, would part of the move toward decentralization, including even the possibility that the regions would participate in the drafting of their "Statuti," qualify as subnational constitution-making?

Asymmetrical federal systems pose a particular difficulty. Some federal systems allow only some component units to devise subnational constitutions—for example, as Arshi Khan in chapter 11 of this volume notes, the Indian Constitution permits only one state, Kashmir, to have its own subnational constitution.[11] Others, for historical reasons, have special arrangements for some component units. In Italy, for example, which seems to be moving toward some sort of federal arrangement, the province of South Tyrol already exercises a wider range of autonomy than other Italian regions based on the international agreement that brought this territory from Austria to Italy after World War I.[12]

Russia's asymmetrical federal system presents a particularly complex situation.[13] Six different types of subnational units—republics, oblasts, krais, autonomous oblasts, autonomous okrugs, and federal cities—comprise the Russian Federation. Although Russia's Federation Constitution asserts the equality of its 89 component units, the various types of units each have their own distinctive status and powers. Among the factors differentiating republics and oblasts is the fact that a republic has legal authority to devise its own (subnational) constitution, whereas an oblast can only adopt a charter (*ustov*). Yet these charters in many ways resemble constitutions, raising the question of whether for purposes of analysis, they should be treated as subnational constitutions. Beyond that, the president of the Russian Federation can enter into treaties with the executive of a component unit to reallocate powers between the national government and that unit. President Boris Yeltsin in particular entered into numerous such treaties, in part to consolidate his political support. Once again, should these treaties, which may alter in important ways the powers of a subnational unit, be accorded constitutional status? As one scholar asked,

> What sort of state is Russia becoming: a loose confederation of regional units, a true federation, or a unitary state? Or, are asymmetries between the 57 predominantly Russian *oblasts* and *krais* and the 21 "ethnic homeland" republics producing a state in which "23 million Russian subjects will live in a federation and another 124 will live in a unitary state"?[14]

Although the complexities of the Russian Federation may be extreme, the problem of determining what qualifies as a subnational constitution is likely to arise in all asymmetrical federal systems. Certainly, the picture of subnational constitutions that will develop from evaluating them on their own terms will differ substantially among federal systems.[15]

SUBNATIONAL CONSTITUTIONAL SPACE: LEGAL PARAMETERS

Approaching the analysis of subnational constitutionalism from the subnational perspective requires first an essentially legal assessment of the amount of subnational constitutional space, competency, or autonomy that the component units are allotted within the federal system. The quantity of subnational constitutional space available in various federal systems might be conceptualized in the form of a continuum, with, for example, the United States and Switzerland at one end as systems that permit component units considerable subnational constitutional space. Alan Tarr's chapter (6) in this volume explores the distinctive character and history of American state constitutions. Giovanni Biaggini's chapter (12) chronicles the extensive use the Swiss cantons have made of their subnational constitutional space.[16]

The other end of this quantitative continuum might be represented by South Africa, in which the subnational constitution-making space is very restricted.[17] South Africa's constitution, adopted in 1996, contains an entire chapter (chapter 6) on the government structure and competency of the provincial governments. To this extent, the new constitution serves as both a national and a subnational (provincial) constitution. Interestingly, however, section 142 of the constitution authorizes provincial legislatures to adopt or amend a provincial constitution by a two-thirds vote of its members. Such a provincial constitution, according to section 143, has to be consistent with the national constitution but can provide for "provincial legislative or executive structures and procedures that differ from those provided for in this chapter." Thus, the provincial legislature can, through the adoption of a provincial constitution, vary some of the mandated provincial structures. Nevertheless, the availability of a model for provincial constitutions within the national constitution is likely to encourage provinces to adopt the model, while the national constitution itself makes clear the range of local variation that is possible.[18]

POLICING SUBNATIONAL CONSTITUTIONAL SPACE: LEGAL CONSTRAINTS ON POLITICAL CHOICES

Once the scope of the subnational constitutional space is determined, the question arises as to how a federal system polices the outer limits of subnational constitution-making space allotted to component units. There are, for example, many cases in which the U.S. Supreme Court has declared provisions of American state constitutions to be unconstitutional under the federal Constitution.[19] This is true even though the federal Constitution contains very few express restrictions on the states' constitution-making powers. Examples of courts exercising this policing function are found in other federal systems as well. The Constitutional Court in South Africa rejected the entire draft provincial constitutions of Kwazulu-Natal[20] and the Western Cape Province.[21] Also, the Constitutional Court of Russia ruled in 2000 that the sovereignty provisions in the constitutions of several Russian republics were unconstitutional.[22] The Austrian Constitutional Court declared unconstitutional a provision of the Land Constitution of Vorarlberg, concerning direct democracy, as violating the national constitution's "homogeneity clause."[23] Thus many federal systems rely on courts to enforce legal limits when subnational units attempt to overutilize or expand their subconstitutional space.

One way to minimize conflict between national and subnational constitutions is for the national constitution to give the national government some control over the content of subnational constitutions at the time they are being created. This, of course, requires that the national government predate the creation of those constitutions, and this is not always the case. In Australia, for example, state constitutions were established prior to the adoption of the Commonwealth Constitution, and that constitution specifically provided for the continued operation of the existing state constitutions.[24] In the United States, the situation was even more complicated. The 13 states that declared independence from England in 1776 devised their initial constitutions prior to the adoption of the nation's first constitution—indeed, four states had drafted constitutions even prior to the Declaration of Independence. Thus, there was no possibility of a national authority imposing conditions on what would be contained in the constitutions of the original 13 states. Most of the other 37 states, however, were formed from territory governed by the United States, with Congress controlling the admission of states and the delineation of their boundaries.[25] This gave the national government an opportunity to exert direct influence on state constitutions at the point that the states were applying for admission to the Union.

The United States Constitution implicitly confers on Congress the power to do so: By empowering Congress to admit new states to the Union, it in effect gives Congress the power to establish the conditions under which they will be admitted.[26] Acting under this authority, Congress has imposed conditions on what state constitutions should contain in the acts by which it authorized prospective states to devise constitutions and apply for statehood. State constitution-makers know that they must meet those conditions in order to secure a favorable vote on admission.[27] If a proposed constitution contains provisions of which Congress or the president disapproves, either of them can refuse their consent to legislation admitting the state until the offending provisions are altered or removed. This congressional and executive power, together with the states' eagerness to attain statehood, has in several cases served a deterrent function. State constitution-makers have refrained from including provisions in their charters because they expected those provisions would likely excite opposition in Congress and might jeopardize or delay admission to the Union.

The system just described is not common to all federal countries.[28] Germany, for example, imposed no special requirements on the constitutions drafted by the five Länder that became part of the country following the collapse of the German Democratic Republic.[29] Russia has established no principles to guide constitution-making in the 89 constituent units that comprise the Russian Federation.[30] However, there are interesting parallels in the processes established in the United States and in South Africa for the approval of proposed constitutions. In both countries there are pre-existing standards to which proposed constitutions must conform in order to win approval. Whereas in the United States these standards are contained in congressional enabling acts (the acts authorizing prospective states to draft constitutions), in the South African case, these standards are the well-known 34 principles enunciated in the transitional constitution. In both countries as well, there is a supervisory authority empowered to scrutinize whether proposed constitutions comply with the applicable principles. In the United States, this supervisory authority is a political body, Congress; but in South Africa, a judicial body, the Constitutional Court, performs this function. Finally, in both countries the supervising body can require changes in a proposed constitution as a condition for its acceptance—indeed, in both the United States and South Africa, this has occurred.

But South Africa has introduced a distinctive element. Typically, the supervision of constitutional content is a one-time process: In the United States, for example, once a state is admitted, Congress no longer has authority over the content of its constitution, even if subsequent constitutional changes introduce departures from the principles that governed it initially.[31] In contrast, South Africa has established a continuing judicial scrutiny of constitutions and constitutional changes before they take effect. No amendment to a provincial constitution is valid until the Constitutional Court certifies that it complies with the guidelines of section 143 of the South African Constitution. The South African approach may be viewed as consistent with the judicial resolution of constitutional issues in that country more generally. The Constitutional Court has authority to exercise "abstract review," determining the constitutionality of acts of government before they take legal effect.[32]

The Spanish approach seems to fall somewhere between the American and the South African models. It is too early to reach any firm conclusions about its operation, but it is based on continuing political scrutiny—the National Parliament must approve any change on an Autonomous Region's Autonomy Statute before such change can be implemented at the regional level. Eduardo J. Ruiz Vieytez explores this process in chapter 8 of this volume.[33]

Given the similarities among the American, South African, and Spanish approaches, it might be worth considering what effect they have had on the substance of subnational constitutions. In the United States, where the system has been in operation the longest, congressional mandates have had a very limited effect on the substance of American state constitutions. Many of the conditions that Congress imposed on prospective states were noncontroversial and, most likely, superfluous.[34] Enabling acts of the late nineteenth century, for example, required that state governments be "republican in form" and "not be repugnant to the Constitution of the US or the principles of the Declaration of Independence."[35] Yet in the absence of these congressional directives, no prospective state would have adopted a monarchical or oligarchic constitution, nor one blatantly inconsistent with the national constitution. Even some more specific congressional requirements may have been unnecessary. For example, state constitutional conventions were instructed to secure a "perfect toleration of religious sentiment" and to provide for "the establishment and maintenance of systems of public schools . . . free from sectarian control."[36] Yet even without such mandates, the constitutions of most states by the late nineteenth century already provided for a system of public schools and banned sectarian influences in those schools. Whether the American experience is representative is, of course, a matter that requires further investigation.

Another possible way to minimize conflicts between national and subnational constitutions is to prescribe the contents of the subnational constitutions in the national constitution. Indeed, the national constitution may obviate the need for subnational constitutions altogether by prescribing in detail the form of government for subnational units, creating a complete federal constitution, with no subnational constitutional space. India and Canada have shown that federal systems can get along quite well without subnational constitutions. Belgium does not utilize subnational constitutions but, as indicated in Wouter Pas' chapter (9) on the complex system of Belgian federalism, there is serious talk of proposing one in the Flemish Parliament.[37] But even if a country has subnational constitutions, mandates in the national constitution can restrict the range of choice for subnational constitution-makers or can induce the subnational units to alter their constitutions to bring them into conformity with national requirements. Certainly the South African approach, discussed previously, illustrates this model. A less specific, though still important, kind of mandate is the "homogeneity clause" in the German and Austrian national constitutions. This concept is explored in the chapters by Norman Weiss on Germany (5) and by Anna Gamper on Austria (4).[38] Weiss explains that this concept "has been understood to require states and municipalities to adhere to basic principles of a democratic and social welfare state bound by the rule of law."[39]

In the United States, various federal constitutional provisions have had an effect on state constitution-makers, although typically their effect has been indirect. For example, under the so-called Supremacy Clause of the U.S. Constitution,[40] national law is superior to state law, so that in cases of conflict, valid national enactments—be they constitutional provisions, statutes, or administrative regulations—prevail over state constitutional provisions. This, of course, limits subnational constitutional space. This has led state constitution-makers to seek to avoid such conflicts, even if that has meant forgoing provisions they would have wished to adopt.

One must look beyond strategies for preventing competency disputes to mechanisms for policing or resolving them as well. As noted, in the United States and in most other systems of divided powers, the judiciary has the main responsibility for resolving competency disputes. But that is not the only possible approach. The constitution of the Russian Federation, for example, authorizes the president of the Federation to suspend the acts of subnational executives if he believes them to be in violation of the federal law or human rights. The Justice Ministry also has the power to revoke regional laws that are in violation of the Federation Constitution and, as of early 1998, it had used that power to revoke nearly 2000 regional laws.[41] Finally, in addition to the formal mechanisms for resolving competency disputes (not necessarily only about national and subnational constitutional competency) there are a wide variety of informal mechanisms for dispute resolution. For example, in Spain the prior formal, legal/litigation model of resolving competency disputes between the national government and the autonomous regions seems (perhaps in light of the need to exist within the supranational European Union) to have been transformed into a process of consultation and negotiation.[42] In Italy, by contrast, which is at a much earlier stage of creating and recognizing regional autonomy, the legal/litigation model prevails, as noted in Francesco Palermo's chapter (7) in this volume.[43] Perhaps the transition from the legal/litigation model of policing subnational constitutional space and competency to the consultation/negotiation model is one of the indices of a maturing federal system.

UTILIZATION OF SUBNATIONAL CONSTITUTIONAL SPACE: POLITICAL CHOICES

Legal assessments of available subconstitutional space and of how the boundaries of that space are policed must be followed by a political analysis of what the subnational units have actually done in exercising their constitution-making competency within the allotted space. Looking at this from a subnational perspective and focusing on individual subnational units, one may find important differences among those units. This would hold true both in symmetrical and asymmetrical federal systems. Indeed, from the subnational perspective, one may find aspects of asymmetry even in symmetrical federal systems, as various component units may have made more (or less) of their constitution-making opportunities. For example, when one examines the component units of the American and German federal systems from the subnational viewpoint and begins to ask what those units have actually done in creating constitutions, the systems do not look quite so symmetrical any longer. The subnational constitutions within each federal system are actually somewhat different from each other (although perhaps not nearly as different as they might be).

Documenting how subnational constitutions within a particular country are similar to, or different from, each other is a crucial first step. However, the really interesting inquiry is explaining the reasons for the differences among subnational constitutions—that is, why subnational units have made more or less use of the constitutional space available to them. Relatively little research has been undertaken addressing this question, but a variety of possible explanations suggest themselves. One factor that might explain similarities and differences among subnational constitutions could be the era in which they were written—G. Alan Tarr has documented that different models for state constitutions were dominant at various times in American history, and so the period in which a state adopted its constitution could affect what it contained.[44] Related to this is another factor, namely, the ease with which subnational units can either revise or amend their constitutions. Even if two constitutions were adopted at the same time, if one is easily changed and another is not, then over time their contents are likely to diverge. A third factor might be regional differences reflecting distinctive political or legal traditions—Daniel Elazar has identified and described such regional patterns and their influence on American state constitutions.[45]

A fourth factor might be the extent to which component units have copied their constitutional provisions from or modeled them on those of other component units within the federal system. This process of modeling or copying provisions from other constitutions is one of the most significant and—upon reflection—understandable features of subnational constitutionalism. Willard Hurst explained its role in the evolution of American state constitutions: "There was a sort of *stare decisis* about this making of constitutions; it was altogether natural in a country in which men moved about readily taking with them the learning and institutions of their former homes."[46] There is even evidence that the initiative and referendum provisions added to the Oregon Constitution in 1902 were based on an idea of direct democracy reflected in the constitutions of the cantons of Switzerland.[47] Such constitutional borrowing is not limited to the United States. Peter Quint's conclusions about the recent German experience with subnational constitution-making are particularly pertinent in this regard:

> Even the most modest of these new state constitutions reflect the lessons of the GDR past and the 1989 revolution, and—with all their similarities to the Basic Law—can still be said to represent a distinctly different, and distinctly eastern, constitutional consciousness. One important question of future constitutional development in Germany is the extent to which the consciousness . . . may ultimately make its way, through constitutional revision or judicial interpretation, into the constitutional consciousness of the unified nation and the west itself.[48]

Various essays in this volume analyze how individual subnational units have made use of their constitutional space. They also identify pertinent literature, most of it in the language of the country being studied. One may note that in recent years important material in English has also appeared for several countries: Australia,[49] Austria,[50] Brazil,[51] Spain,[52] Germany,[53] and Switzerland.[54] Research by Daniel Elazar[55] and James A. Thomson[56] has also begun to explore subnational constitutions in a comparative manner, but there remains relatively little cross-national research on subnational constitutions and on subnational constitutional space. For those interested in contributing to this literature, one can point to a range of inquiries that could be pursued usefully in studying subnational constitutions.

First, what is the theoretical function of subnational constitutions? Do they limit residual governmental power, or grant enumerated powers? Are there records of the debates on adoption, amendment, and revision of such constitutions? Is there anything in the national constitution that mandates certain provisions or matters be contained in the state constitutions? What is the role of popular sovereignty or constituent power in the process of adopting, amending, and revising the subnational constitution, and does constituent power (initiative, referendum, approval of borrowing, etc.) come into play in the operation of governmental systems under the subnational constitutions?

Second, how similar are the subnational constitutions to each other? Is there evidence that provisions in some constitutions have been modeled from others, either within the country or from outside? What have been the processes of evolution of subnational constitutions over the years, both within the subnational polity and, more generally, within each federal system? Are governmental institutions, rights protections, distribution of powers, and other matters different from or similar to those contained in the national constitution? Is there a standard set of matters and issues—a checklist—that should be dealt with in any subnational constitution? Which governmental institutions provide authoritative interpretation of the subnational constitutions? Is there a subnational judiciary that interprets the subnational constitution, and, if so, can such interpretations be reviewed by the national judiciary? Were there important proposals put forward during consideration of subnational constitutions that were not adopted and, if so, were they adopted later?

Third, what are the politics of subnational constitutional change? Is the constitution frequently amended or revised, as a normal part of the component unit's politics, or are constitutional politics outside the scope of "normal politics"?[57]

Fourth, how have the federal system's origins as integrative (leaving subnational constitutional space) or as devolutionary (creating subnational constitutional space) affected such issues as whether the component units' constitutions primarily limit or grant power?[58] Have preexisting subnational constitutions served as models or provided experience for drafting the national constitution[59] or for other, more recently admitted or created component units?[60]

SUBNATIONAL CONSTITUTIONALISM AND THE RIGHTS OF MINORITIES

Nicole Töpperwein's chapter (3) in this volume indicates the broad range of substantive and process provisions for the protection of minorities that could be included in a subnational constitution if constitution-makers were accorded the appropriate space.[61] The mechanisms created for Bosnia and Herzegovina, described by Jens Woelk in chapter 10, indicate the level of complexity to which substantive and process protections can be taken.[62] Arshi Khan's chapter (11) on India argues for the inclusion of such protections within the legal systems of the Indian states, even though those states do not have their own constitutions.[63] Kristin Henrard's chapter (2) provides a more rights-oriented approach, based on equality principles, for minority protections.[64]

CONCLUSIONS AND FUTURE DIRECTIONS

In contrast to situations in which subnational units go too far in constitution-making in a quantitative, legal sense, often subnational component units make political, qualitative decisions not to assert their subnational constitution-making competency, not to occupy fully the space legally allotted to them. In fact, it may be that subnational units in federal systems more often underutilize their constitution-making competency than they overutilize it. They may refrain from developing subnational constitutions altogether. For example, despite express constitutional authorization to do so, seven out of the nine provinces in South Africa have chosen not to engage in subnational constitution-making at all. This reflected a political decision in keeping with the policy of the African National Congress in those provinces in which it attained a political majority. Alternatively, subnational units may proceed in lockstep with the national constitution or with the constitutions of other subnational units, never considering what might be most appropriate for their time and circumstances. Thus, American state constitutions, despite some minor differences, are quite similar to each other although they do not have to be, and this pattern is replicated in many other federal systems.[65]

If correct, this tentative finding about the tendency of subnational units to underutilize even legally available subnational constitutional space within federal systems has important implications. The development or reawakening of political awareness and regional identity among previously politically powerless and unorganized peoples in various countries has increased the urgency of finding mechanisms for according these peoples recognition and opportunities for self-government. The creation of separate countries for these peoples is typically not an option. Neither is secession; the Ethiopian national constitution is the only one recognizing a right of secession by subnational units.[66] However, these groups may find greater opportunities for political success at the subnational rather than the national level in federal systems, and the allocation of power to subnational units, including the power to determine their own constitutional arrangements, might provide a form of self-determination that can serve as an alternative to illegal movements for secession.[67]

From this perspective, then, underutilized subnational constitutional space offers interesting possibilities. It is often true that the opportunities for opening up participation in the decision-making process for ethnic and language minorities may be greater at the subnational than the national constitutional level. This realization seems to have been present in the ultimately unsuccessful campaign for a state constitution in Australia's Northern Territory,[68] and it is clear in the recommendations of Arshi Khan in his chapter (11) on India.[69]

Granting extensive constitutional space to subnational units, including in the field of rights protection, may also be crucial for minorities, who might find it easier to gain recognition of their rights at the subnational constitutional level.[70] As John Kincaid has observed concerning rights protections, based on the American experience,

> The new judicial federalism, however, suggests a model that would enable rights advocates to continue pressing for vigorous national and even international rights protections, while also embedding in regional constitutions and local charters rights that cannot be embedded in the national constitution, effectively enforced by the national government, or enforced only at minimal levels. Such an arrangement would produce peaks and valleys of rights protection within a nation, but this rugged rights terrain is surely preferable to a flat land of minimal or ineffectual national rights protection. The peak jurisdictions can function, under democratic conditions, as rights leaders for a leveling-up process. In an emerging democracy culturally hostile to women's rights, for example, such an arrangement could embolden at least one subnational jurisdiction to institutionalize women's rights, thus establishing a rights peak visible to the entire society without plunging the nation into civil war or back into reactionary authoritarianism.[71]

This is not to suggest that subnational constitutions offer a panacea for minority groups. The chapters by Alan Tarr (6) on the United States, by Wouter Pas (9) on Belgium, and by Arshi Khan (11) on India all underscore the difficulties of subnational constitutional protections where language and religious minorities are dispersed throughout the country rather than concentrated in the territories of component units. Nonetheless, on balance, the conclusion to be drawn from this volume is that federal arrangements, in which subnational units are granted broad constitutional space, can make a significant contribution to the protection of the rights of minorities.

NOTES

1. Cheryl Saunders, "The Relationship Between National and Subnational Constitutions," Seminar Report: Subnational Constitutional Governance (Konrad-Adenauer Foundation: Johannesburg, 1999), 21.

2. The use of the term "subnational" is intended to distinguish the constitutions of component units in federal systems from the constitution of the nation state. The authors recognize that many federal systems contain various nationalities, or nations, within them. This may be said in some sense about Bosnia and Herzegovina, as they are analyzed by Jens Woelk in chapter 10 of this volume.

3. Ronald L. Watts, "Forward: States, Provinces, Lander, and Cantons: International Variety Among Subnational Constitutions," *Rutgers Law Journal* 31 (summer 2000): 945.

4. Donald S. Lutz, "The United States Constitution as Incomplete Text," *Annals American Academy of Political and Social Sciences* 496 (March 1988): 23, 26; Donald S. Lutz, "From Covenant to Constitution in America Political Thought," *Publius: The Journal of Federalism* 10 (fall 1980): 101–2.

5. Saunders, "Relationship Between National and Subnational Constitutions," 21.

6. Louis D. Bilionis, "On the Significance of Constitutional Spirit," *North Carolina Law Review* 70 (September 1992): 1805.

7. A leading expert on federalism, Daniel Elazar, insisted that a top-down perspective was inappropriate because federalism is not hierarchical.

> Nor is it a different point on a hierarchical continuum, that is to say, partially decentralist or something similar. Federalism is on an entirely different continuum, one that values both unity and diversity and constitutionalizes both. Rather than a power pyramid, which is the approximate conceptual scheme for a hierarchy, federalism is based on a matrix of arenas, some smaller, some larger each with its own framing institutions.

Daniel J. Elazar, "A Response to Professor Gardner's 'The Failed Discourse of State Constitutionalism' " *Rutgers Law Journal* 24 (summer 1993): 23–37.

8. "Students of federal systems have tended to focus their attention on the federal constitutions that frame the entire polity while neglecting the constitutional arrangements of the constituent polities. . . . In fact, the constitutions of constituent states are part and parcel of the total constitutional structure of federal systems and play a vital role in giving the system direction." See Daniel J. Elazar, "The Principles and Traditions Underlying State Constitutions," *Publius: The Journal of Federalism* 11 (winter 1982): 18–22.

9. See James T. McHugh, "The Quebec Constitution," *Quebec Studies* 28 (fall 1999/winter 2000). For a listing of those federal systems that have subnational constitutions and those that do not, see Daniel J. Elazar, *Exploring Federalism* (Tuscaloosa: University of Alabama, 1987): 178, Table 5-1.

10. For example, see Luis Moreno, *The Federalization of Spain* (Portland, Ore.: F. Cass, 2001). The Autonomy Statutes in Spain, at least for Catalonia and the Basque Country ("Euskadi"), share many of the characteristics of written, subnational constitutions. They set forth the structure of government in the autonomous region and delineate its competencies. To the extent these differ among the autonomous regions, Spain reflects a system of "asymmetrical federalism." Finally the Autonomy Statutes of both the Basque Country (Article 46) and Catalonia (Article 56) require a favorable vote of the electorate in a referendum in order for the Autonomy Statute to be amended.

Jaoquim Solé-Vilanova has referred to the Spanish Autonomy Statutes as "internal constitution[s]." Jaoquim Solé-Vilanova, "Regional and Local Finance in Spain: Is Fiscal Responsibility the Missing Element?" in *Decentralization, Local Governments, and Markets: Towards a Post-Welfare Agenda,* ed. Robert J. Bennett (New York: St. Martin Press, 1990). See also Jaoquim Solé-Vilanova, "Spain: Developments in Regional and Local Government," in *Territory and Administration in Europe,* ed. Robert J. Bennett (New York: St. Martin Press, 1989), 205, 209–13.

11. Arshi Khan, "Federalism and Nonterritorial Minorities in India."

12. For example, see Melissa Magliana, *The Autonomous Province of South Tyrol: A Model for Self- Government* (Bozen/Bolzano, Italy: European Academy of Bozen/Bolzano 2000); Francesco Palermo, "Self-Government (and Other?) Instruments for the Prevention of Ethnic Conflicts in South Tyrol," in *The Constitutional and Political Regulation of Ethnic Relations and Conflict*, ed. Mitja Zagar, Boris Jesih, and Romana Bester (Ljubljana: Institute for Ethnic Studies, 1999); and Jens Woelk, "From Minority-Protection to Governance of Cohabitation? The

Case of South Tyrol" in *Essays on Regionalism,* ed. Agency of Local Democracy Subotica (Subotica, Yugoslavia: Agency of Local Democracy, 2001).

13. G. Alan Tarr, "Creating Federalism in Russia," *South Texas Law Review* 40 (summer 1999): 689. More recent developments, particularly President Putin's creation of super-regions has further complicated the situation. See Cameron Ross, *Federalism and Democratisation in Russia* (Manchester, U.K.: Manchester University Press, 2002), chapter 8; and Mark A. Smith, "Putin: An End to Centrifugalism?" in *Russian Regions and Regionalism: Strength Through Weakness,* eds. Graeme P. Herd and Anne Aldis (London: Routledge Curzon, 2001).

14. Steven L. Solnick, "Federal Bargaining in Russia," *East European Constitution Review* 5 (fall 1995).

15. See Ann L. Griffiths, ed., *Handbook of Federal Countries 2002* (Montreal: McGill-Queens University Press, 2002) for up-to-date information on constitutional arrangements in various federalist systems.

16. Alan Tarr, "American State Constitutions and Minority Rights"; Giovanni Biaginni, "Federalism, Subnational Constitutional Arrangements and the Protection of Minorities in Switzerland."

17. Watts, "States, Provinces, Lander, and Cantons," 945. See also Bertus de Villiers, ed., *Birth of a Constitution* (Kenwyn: Juta & Co., 1994); Robert A. Licht and Bertus de Villiers, eds., *South Africa's Crisis of Constitutional Democracy: Can the U.S. Constitution Help?* (Washington, D.C.: American Enterprise Institute, 1994).

18. This approach was also taken in the Interim Constitution, in section 160. See Dion A. Basson, *South Africa's Interim Constitution: Text and Notes* 214 (Kenwyn: Juta & Co., 1994) and de Villiers, *Birth of a Constitution.*

19. For example, see *Reitman v. Mulkey,* 387 U.S. 369 (1967); *Hunter v. Underwood,* 471 U.S. 222 (1985); *Romer v. Evans,* 517 U.S. 620 (1996). More generally see G. Alan Tarr, "Controlling Competency Conflicts: Subnational Constitutions, National Constitutions and the Allocation of Authority," Seminar Report, 77.

20. Robert F. Williams, "Comparative Subnational Constitutional Law: South Africa's Provincial Constitutional Experiments," *South Texas Law Review* 40 (summer 1999): 648–54.

21. Dirk Brand, "The Western Cape Provincial Constitution," *Rutgers Law Journal* 31 (summer 2000): 961, 966; Williams, "Comparative Subnational Constitutional Law," 654–59.

22. M. Faroukshin, "The New Trends in the Russian Federalism, Back to Unitary States?" Paper delivered at the International Political Science Association Comparative Federalism Research Committee Conference in Javea, Spain, December 4–7, 2001.

23. Anna Gamper, "The Principle of Homogeneity and Democracy in Austria." Paper delivered at the International Association of Centers for Federal Studies and the International Political Science Association Comparative Federation and Federalism Research Committee Joint Conference, Innsbruck, Austria, November 13–16, 2002.

24. Christine Fletcher and Cliff Walsh, "Comparative Fiscal Constitutionalism in Australia and the US—The Power of State Politics," in *Evaluating Federal Systems,* ed. Bertus de Villiers (Dordrecht: Martinus Nijhoff Publishers, 1994), 348.

25. Six states are exceptions to this statement. Texas was an independent republic before its annexation by the United States, and five states—Vermont, Kentucky, Tennessee, Maine, and West Virginia— were carved out of the territory of existing states.

26. The main provision dealing with the admission of new states is Article IV, section 3 of the U.S. Constitution. Further constitutional support for congressional conditions on admission is provided by Article IV, sect. 4 of the U.S. Constitution, which directs the federal government to "guarantee to each State in the Union a Republican Form of Government."

In addition to imposing conditions on prospective states, Congress also supervised the constitutions that Southern states adopted in the aftermath of the Civil War, requiring an acceptable constitution as a condition for "readmission" to the Union. However, the effects of these congressional efforts were short-lived. Most Southern states repudiated their Reconstruction constitutions as soon as they could, typically replacing them with documents that by the late nineteenth century entrenched white political control, and Congress did nothing to prevent this undermining of republican government. See Don E. Ferenbacher, *Constitutions and Constitutionalism in the Slaveholding South* (Athens: University of Georgia Press, 1989); Kermit L. Hall and James V. Ely, Jr., eds., *An Uncertain Tradition: Constitutionalism and the History of the South* (Athens: University of Georgia Press, 1989).

27. Some prospective states—for example, Wyoming in 1889—called conventions and drafted constitutions even without congressional authorization. In such circumstances, however, Congress had to approve the proposed constitution and confer statehood. On the Wyoming example, see Robert B. Keiter and Tim Newcomb, *The Wyoming State Constitution: A Reference Guide* (Westport, Conn: Greenwood Press, 1993): 4–5.

28. For a discussion of somewhat similar processes in other countries, such as Switzerland and Spain, see Bertus de Villiers, "The Constitutional Principles: Content and Significance," in de Villiers, *Birth of a Constitution.*

29. For a discussion of this process of reunification and constitution-making, see Peter E. Quint, *The Imperfect Union: Constitutional Structures of German Unification* (Princeton, N.J.: Princeton University Press,1997), 73–99.

30. See Tarr, "Creating Federalism in Russia."

31. Of course, such supervision can occur through judicial review, if state constitutional changes conflict with national law, but legal conflict and not political disagreement is the operative criterion.

32. On the distinction between abstract and concrete review in constitutional adjudication, see Carlo Guarnieri and Patricia Pederzoli, *The Power of Judges: A Comparative Study of Courts and Democracy* (New York: Oxford University Press, 2002).

33. Eduardo J. Ruiz Vieytez, "Federalism, Subnational Constitutional Arrangements, and the Protection of Minorities in Spain."

34. For more detailed discussion of this point, see G. Alan Tarr, *Understanding State Constitutions* (Princeton, N.J.: Princeton University Press, 1998), 39–41.

35. See, for example, the Enabling Act of 1864 (13 Stat. 30), which authorized the people of Nevada to form a constitution and apply for admission; and the Enabling Act of 1889 (25 Stat. 676), which authorized the Dakotas, Montana, and Washington to form constitutions and apply for admission. These enabling acts are reprinted in William F. Swindler, ed., *Sources and Documents of United States Constitutions* VI (Dobbs Ferry, N.Y.: Oceana Publications, 1976), 261 and 264.

36. Ibid.

37. Wouter Pas, "A Dynamic Federalism Built on Static Principles: The Case of Belgium."

38. Norman Weiss, "The Protection of Minorities in a Federal State: The Case of Germany"; Anna Gamper, "Austrian Federalism and the Protection of Minorities."

39. Weiss, "Protection of Minorities."

40. Article VI, Clause 2 of the United States Constitution—the Supremacy Clause—provides:

> This Constitution, and the Laws of the United States which shall be made in Pursuance thereof, and all Treaties made, or which shall be made, under the Authority of the United States, shall be the supreme Law of the Land; and the Judges in every State shall be bound thereby, any Thing in the Constitution or Laws of any State to the Contrary notwithstanding.

U.S. Constitution, Article VI, clause 2. Some American state constitutions, themselves, recognize the supremacy of federal law. See West Va. Const. Art. I, sec. 1; Michael J. Brodhead, "Accepting the Verdict: National Supremacy as Expressed in State Constitutions, 1861–1912," *Nevada Historical Society Quarterly* 13 (1969): 3.

41. Constitution of the Russian Federation, Article 85, section 2. The estimate of subnational laws invalidated was supplied by State Prosecutor Yuri Skuratov, quoted in "Constitution Watch," *Eastern European Constitutional Review* 7 (winter 1998): 32. Indeed, President Putin identified harmonization of the constitutions and laws of the Federation's constituent units with those of the Federation as a major element in his federalism initiative. See Smith, "Putin: An End to Centrifugalism," 27–28.

42. See Tanja A. Bürzel, "From Competitive Regionalism to Cooperative Federalism: The Europeanization of the Spanish State of the Autonomies," *Publius: The Journal of Federlism* 30, no. 2 (spring 2000): 17; Tanja A. Bürzel, "Toward Convergence in Europe? Institutional Adaptation to Europeanization in Germany and Spain," *Journal of Common Market Studies* 37 (1999): 573; Tanja A. Bürzel, *States and Regions in the European Union: Institutional Adaptation in Germany and Spain* (Cambridge: Cambridge University Press, 2002): 103–47.

43. Francesco Palermo, "Asymmetric, 'Quasi-Federal' Regionalism and the Protection of Minorities: The Case of Italy."

44. See Tarr, *Understanding State Constitutions*, chs. 3–5.

45. Elazar, *Exploring Federalism*, 18–22.

46. James Willard Hurst, *The Growth of American Law: The Law Makers* (Boston: Little, Brown, 1950): 224–25.

47. David Schuman, "The Origin of State Constitutional Direct Democracy: William Simon U'Ren and the 'Oregon System,'" *Temple Law Review* 67 (fall 1994): 947, 950.

48. Peter E. Quint, *Imperfect Union*, 99. Professor Quint has recently surveyed the judicial interpretations of the new German subnational constitutions in Peter E. Quint, "The Constitutional Guarantees of Social Welfare in the Process of German Unification," *American Journal of Comparative Law* 47 (1999): 303, 310–21, 325. See also Igna Markovits, "Reconcilable Differences: On Peter Quint's *The Imperfect Union*," *American Journal of Comparative Law* 47 (1999): 189, 194–97, 206–9.

49. R. D. Lumb, "Methods of Alteration of State Constitutions in the United States and Australia," *Federal Law Review* 13, no. 1 (1982): 1, 3. "In Australia the 'State Constitution' is not located in one Act with its amendments. It is located in other legislation besides the so-called basic Constitution Act." See also R. D. Lumb, *The Constitutions of the Australian States*, 5th Ed. (St. Lucia: University of Queensland, 1991); James A. Thomson, "State Constitutional Law: American Lessons for Australian Adventures," *Texas Law Review* 63 (March/April 1985): 1225; "State Constitutional Law: Gathering the Fragments," *Western Australia*

Law Review 16 (1985): 90; Cheryl Saunders, "Constitutional Arrangements of Federal Systems," *Staatswissenschaften und Staatspraxis* (no. 1, 1992), 228, reprinted in *Publius: The Journal of Federalism* 25 (winter 1995): 61; "State and Territory Constitutional Law: A Symposium," *Public Law Review* 3 (March 1992): 1.

50. For example, see Friedrich Koja, "Instruments of Direct Democracy in the Austrian Federal State and in its Länder," *Austrian Journal of Public and International Law* 45 (1993): 33. Dr. Koja has written extensively in German about the Austrian Länder constitutions.

51. Wayne A. Selcher, "A New Start Toward a More Decentralized Federalism in Brazil? *Publius: The Journal of Federalism* 19 (summer 1989): 167, 179–80; "Further, the states will all rewrite their constitutions during 1989. Whereas the former state constitutions tended to be replicas of the national one, the Constitution of 1988 does allow a bit more leeway to state framers." Both in a conversation with Dr. Selcher and in discussions with knowledgeable people in Sao Paulo in August of 1995, one of the authors was told that the Brazilian states made little use of the "leeway" because they were required to model their governments on the national example. This seems to be similar to the German and Austrian concept of homogeneity for subnational constitutions. The usual citation given for this proposition is Article 25 of the 1988 Constitution of Brazil. The text, however, does not seem to support that conclusion. Article 25 states, "The states are organized and governed by the Constitutions and laws they may adopt, in accordance with the principles of this Constitution." Paragraph 1 of that Article states, "All powers that this Constitution does not prohibit the states from exercising shall be conferred upon them."

52. Francisco Rubio Llorente, "The Writing of the Constitution of Spain," in Robert A. Goldwin and Art Kaufman, eds., *Constitution Makers on Constitution Making* (Washington, D.C.: American Enterprise Institute, 1988): 263–64. "Although the Constitution provided for a state made up of autonomous regions, it did not determine precisely how that autonomy would be organized. . . . The constitution did not define autonomous communities or limit their number. . . . The final solution distinguished two levels of autonomy, and called for a formal state law to define statues of each autonomous region. . . . Some lower-level autonomous communities would be able to assume only the powers that the constitution enumerated (Article 148); others, the higher-level bodies, would assume all the powers that the constitution did not reserve for the state." See also César Enrique Diaz López, "The State of the Autonomic Process in Spain," *Publius: The Journal of Federalism* 11 (summer 1981): 193, and Robert W. Kern, *The Regions of Spain: A Reference Guide to History and Culture* (Westport, Conn.: Greenwood Press, 1995).

53. See Arthur B. Gunlicks, "State (Länd) Constitutions in Germany," *Rutgers Law Journal* 31 (summer 2000): 971, and Quint, *The Imperfect Union*.

> Constitutional creativity at the state level is much more important in those fields where there is a certain abstention at the federal level. If one compares the Basic Law with the constitutions of the Länder, in particular the so-called new Länder, it is striking that the Länder constitutions contain a number of provisions in the social, economic and cultural field where the Basic Law is completely silent. While it has proven to be very difficult to introduce into the Federal Constitution new elements, such as the protection of the environment as being a fundamental principle of state policy, the constitutional processes at the level of the Länder have been very open for such innovations.

From Michael Bothe, "The Limited Role of Judicial Federalism: Comparison and Comparative Lessons," in *The American Federal System: Federal Balance in Comparative Perspective,* eds., Franz Gress, Dellef Fechtnerod, Matthias Hannes (Franfurt: Peter Lang, 1994): 88. See also Arthur B. Gunlicks, "German Federalism after Unification: The Legal/Constitutional Response," *Publius: The Journal of Federalism* 24 (spring, 1994): 81, 93–94; Charles Jeffery and Peter Savigear, *German Federalism Today* (New York: St. Martin's Press, 1991); Gunter Krings, "Structure and Governmental Status of Local Government in Germany," *The Federalism Report* 20 (spring 1995): 10.

A major contribution to the comparative study of subnational constitutions has been made by the Konrad Adenauer Foundation with respect to publications in English about the Länder constitutions in Germany. See Christian Stack, *The Constitutions of the German Lander and Their Origins: A Comparative Analysis* (Konrad Adenauer Foundation Occasional Papers, June 1995); *The Constitution of the Free State of Bavaria, The Constitution of Land Brandenburg, The Constitution of Land Schleswig-Holstein* (Konrad Adenauer Foundation Occasional Papers, January 1995). These materials were prepared for use in the South African constitutional process. See also *Implementing Federalism in the Final Constitution of the Republic of South Africa* (Konrad Adenauer Foundation Occasional Papers, September 1995).

54. See Hanspeter Tschaeni, "Constitutional Change in Swiss Cantons: An Assessment of a Recent Phenomenon," *Publius: The Journal of Federalism* 12 (winter 1982): 113.

55. Elazar, *Exploring Federalism.* See also Norman Dorsen, Michael Rosenfeld, Andras Sajo, and Suzanne Baer, *Comparative Constitutionalism: Cases and Materials* (St. Paul, Minn.: Thomson/West, 2003), ch. 4.

56. James A. Thomson, "State Constitutional Law: Some Comparative Perspectives," *Rutgers Law Journal* 20 (summer 1989): 1059.

57. See G. Alan Tarr, ed., *Constitutional Politics in the States: Contemporary Controversies and Historical Patterns* (Westport, Conn.: Greenwood Press, 1996).

58. The situation may be even more complicated. In chapter 12 of this volume, Giovanni Biaggini notes that although the Swiss federal system was integrative, it exhibited a devolutionary feature when it created the new Canton of Jura.

59. For example, see Robert F. Williams, "Experience Must Be Our Only Guide: The State Constitutional Experience of the Framers of the Federal Constitution," *Hastings Constitutional Law Quarterly* 15 (fall 1988): 403.

60. Several years before he gained his place in history with his controversial economic analysis of the American federal constitution, Charles A. Beard wrote an article analyzing the 1908 Oklahoma Constitution. He concluded that, despite widespread criticism, the Oklahoma Constitution was not a radical departure from American principles and practice. He stated, "The American people are not given to sailing the ship of state by the stars or to deducing rules of law from abstract notions; and every important clause of the Oklahoma Constitution has been tried out in the experience of one or more of the older commonwealths." Charles A. Beard, "The Constitution of Oklahoma," *Political Science Quarterly* 24 (1909): 95, 114. See also Christian G. Fritz, "More Than Shreds and Patches: California's First Bill of Rights," *Hastings Constitutional Law Quarterly* 17 (fall 1989).

61. Nicole Töpperwein, "Participation in the Decision-Making Process as a Means of Group Accommodation."

62. Jens Woelk, "Federalism and Consociationalism as Tools for State Reconstruction? The Case of Bosnia and Herzegovina."

63. Khan, "Federalism and Nonterritorial Minorities in India."

64. Kristin Henrard, "Equality Considerations and Their Relation to Minority Protections, State Constitutional Law, and Federalism."

65. Robert F. Williams, "State Constitutional Law Processes," *William & Mary Law Review* 24 (winter 1983): 169, 172–73; G. Alan Tarr, *Understanding State Constitutions;* Robert F. Williams, *State Constitutional Law: Cases and Materials,* 3rd ed. (Charlottesville, Va: Lexis 1999).

66. See Minasse Haile, "The New Ethiopian Constitution: Its Impact upon Unity, Human Rights and Development," *Suffolk Transnational Law Review* 20 (winter 1996); T. S. Twibell, "Ethiopian Constitutional Law: The Structure of Ethiopian Government and the New Constitution's Ability to Overcome Ethiopia's Problems," *Loyola L.A. International & Comparative Law Journal* 21, no. 1 (March 1999): 399; Bereket Habte Selassie, "Self-Determination in Principle and Practice: The Ethiopian-Eritrean Experience," *Columbia Human Rights Law Review* 29 (fall 1997): 91.

67. A full consideration of these issues is beyond the scope of this book. For an introduction to the literature, see Margaret Moore, ed., *National Self-Determination and Secession* (New York: Oxford University Press, 1998); Michael J. Kelly, "Political Downsizing: The Re-Emergence of Self-Determination, and the Movement Toward Smaller, Ethnically Homogeneous States," *Drake Law Review* 47 (1999): 209; Alemante G. Selassie, "Ethnic Identity and Constitutional Design for Africa," *Stanford Journal of International Law* 29, no. 1 (fall 1992). Professor Kelly observed,

> The principle of self-determination has become a tool used by sub-groups within nation-states to ensure their continued existence as diverse and uniquely different cultures. While the world today contains about 200 nation-states, there are about 3000 different linguistic groups and easily 5000 distinct national minorities. Continued diversity is their goal, and self-determination is the banner under which they march to realize that goal, whether independently from the unified state in which they exist or within it. (211–12)

From this he concluded,

> Ironically, devolution, and other internal self-deterministic moves like increased federalism, could be the salvation of the nation-state. Acquiescing to internal self-determination provides the recognition, sovereignty, and identity that homogenous groups crave without breaking apart the country so those groups can achieve independence in what might prove to be unviable nation states of their own. "All over the developed world, devolution is a fact of life. In the dictum of Daniel Bell, an American sociologist, 'the nation-state has now become too small for the big problems of life and too big for the small problems.'" So, utilizing internal self-determination to avoid external self-determination is a path to continued viability for the multi-ethnic nation-state today. (275–76)

68. See Cheryl Saunders, "Australian State Constitutions," *Rutgers Law Journal* 31 (summer 2000): 1014–18. See Alistair Heatley and Peter McNab, "The Northern Territory Statehood Convention 1998," *Public Law Review* 9 (1998): 155, 157:

> The Constitution, which emerged from the Convention, was very different from the Final Draft prepared by the Sessional Committee. Significant in

> the material deleted from the draft were the Organic Law provisions and those relating to the protection of certain Aboriginal rights.

See also Alistair Heatley and Peter McNab, "The Northern Territory Statehood Referendum 1998," *Public Law Review* 10 (1999): 3; Garth Nettheim, "Aboriginal Constitutional Conventions in the Northern Territory," *Public Law Review* 10 (1999): 8.

69. Arshi Khan, "Federalism and Nonterritorial Minorities in India."

70. Robert F. Williams, "The New Judicial Federalism in the United States: Expansive State Constitutional Rights Decisions," Seminar Report, 71–73.

71. John Kincaid, "Foreword: The New Federalism Context of the New Judicial Federalism," *Rutgers Law Journal* 26 (summer 1995): 944–47. See generally Ellis Katz and G. Alan Tarr, eds., *Federalism and Rights* (Lanham, M.D.: Rowman and Littlefield, 1996); Michael E. Solimine and James L. Walker, "Federalism, Liberty and State Constitutional Law," *Ohio Northern University Law Review* 23 (1997): 1457.

2

Equality Considerations and Their Relation to Minority Protections, State Constitutional Law, and Federalism

Kristin Henrard

This chapter focuses on certain developments of the equality paradigm of special relevance to the protection of minorities. Some attention is also given to the implications of the equality principle for subnational constitutions and the concomitant autonomy of the subnational units. In view of this focus, it seems appropriate to start by setting out the general framework concerning the close, intricate relationship between equality (considerations) and minority protection. By way of introduction to that discussion, a couple conceptual remarks concerning the equality principle need to be made so as to facilitate the ensuing analysis.

THE EQUALITY PRINCIPLE

Several dimensions of the equality principle can be distinguished, including equality before the law and equal protection by the law, but the most well-known ones are the prohibition of discrimination and affirmative action (or positive discrimination). Furthermore, a crucial distinction needs to be made between formal or mathematical equality on the one hand and substantive or real, concrete equality on the other.[1]

Regarding the prohibition of discrimination, a number of clarifications and further distinctions need to be made. First, one should distinguish between so-called open and closed models of nondiscrimination. The former, which are generally found in international human rights treaties like the European Convention on Human Rights, are open in two respects, firstly as regards the grounds on the basis of which discrimination is prohibited but more importantly in the sense that a differentiation is said not to amount to a discrimination when it fulfills certain general criteria. The typical formula that is used is that the differentiation (of comparable situations) should have a reasonable and objective justification, implying a legitimate aim and a relation of proportionality between the means (the differentiation) and that aim.[2] This open model thus conceives a flexible, not predefined arena of possible differentiations that are justified and that do not constitute prohibited discriminations, implying always a certain balancing process.

A closed model, on the other hand, can be closed in two respects: firstly by enumerating an exhaustive list of prohibited grounds of discrimination, and secondly (and more importantly) in the sense that differentiations on these grounds are prohibited full stop, except and only insofar as the text (act, treaty, etc.) provides for explicit exceptions. A typical example of such a closed model can be found in the European Communities, as will be discussed.

Insofar as an open model of nondiscrimination is used, two further points need to be made. First, when assessing whether a differentiation complies with the criteria, the general formula so as not to amount to discrimination, it is possible to use different levels of scrutiny. Different levels of scrutiny are particularly connected to the case law of the U.S. Supreme Court, but can also be perceived, albeit less explicitly, in the jurisprudence of the European Court of Human Rights (Council of Europe) and of the European Court of Justice (EC).[3] When courts assess differential treatment by public authorities for compatibility with the prohibition of discrimination, they tend to undertake a rather marginal scrutiny, granting a wide margin of discretion to the authorities. However, for differential treatment on certain suspect grounds, a higher level of scrutiny is adopted. Considering that there are innumerable forms of differential treatment and innumerable grounds of differentiation, it is virtually self-evident that not all the former are equally intrusive in the lives of people and not all of the latter are equally suspect. Typical characteristics of suspect grounds of differentiation are that they concern very personal issues, often immutable characteristics, that the differentiations are based on prejudices while there is a history of disadvantages for and prejudices against the disadvantaged, vulnerable group.

Roughly speaking, the jurisprudence of the U.S. Supreme Court reveals that whereas the normal review test is rational basis review, merely requiring the absence of arbitrariness, strict scrutiny is adopted for differentiations on the basis of race and intermediate scrutiny for gender. The strict scrutiny test requires a compelling government objective for the differentiation, which needs to be also necessary and precisely drawn (neatly tailored) to reach that objective. Although this test is often fatal in effect, the intermediate scrutiny test can sometimes be passed as it (merely) requires an important governmental objective for the differentiation, which needs to be substantially related to the achievement of that objective.[4]

Although the European Court of Human Rights does not adopt this language of strict and intermediate scrutiny, its jurisprudence does reveal that it departs from its general marginal review, granting the states a margin of discretion, and demands that states provide "very weighty reasons" for differentiations on certain suspect grounds. Gender is a clear example of the latter, but race and religion arguably also qualify as suspect grounds. Similarly, when contemplating the jurisprudence of the European Court of Justice and the secondary legislation focused on eradicating discrimination, discrimination on the basis of gender ostensibly leads to enhanced scrutiny.[5] The recent inclusion of article 13 in the EC Treaty considerably broadens the scope of differentiation of concern to the EC, by including discrimination on the basis of race or ethnic origin, religion or belief, disability, age, and sexual orientation. The so-called Race Directive[6] adopted on its basis clearly places race at the apex of the EC's equality hierarchy.

Especially when such different levels of scrutiny are used, a crucial question is whether a symmetrical or an asymmetrical approach to nondiscrimination is adopted. In the case of a symmetrical conception of discrimination, the heightened scrutiny for a suspect classification would be used irrespective of the group in whose favor the norm works. Conversely, in the case of an asymmetrical approach to discrimination, the heightened scrutiny would be adopted only when the suspect classification was used to the (further) detriment of the historically disadvantaged group. This asymmetrical approach thus acknowledges that harm caused by measures that disadvantage further vulnerable groups is a greater evil, which merits more suspicion than measures disadvantaging powerful groups.[7] Most international and several national jurisdictions adopt a (rather) symmetrical approach.

Reference should also be made to the possibility of acknowledging and sanctioning so-called indirect discrimination, in addition to direct discrimination. Direct discrimination concerns a differentiation expressly, explicitly on one of the enumerated grounds in nondiscrimination clauses, which is not justified. When an apparently neutral criterion is used to differentiate but has a disproportionate impact without reasonable and objective justification on a group defined in terms of one of the enumerated grounds, this differentiation actually amounts to an indirect discrimination on the enumerated ground.[8] It should be underlined that there is no need to establish intent to discriminate against the group concerned.

Acknowledging indirect discrimination is obviously important when different levels of scrutiny are used. The apparent neutral criterion of differentiation would only attract the basic, marginal review, whereas redefining it as indirect discrimination on one of the suspect grounds would make the review stricter.

Finally, one must address the relation between nondiscrimination and affirmative action. Despite or perhaps because of its highly contentious nature, the exact meaning of the term "affirmative action" is not clear. A helpful distinction is that between forward looking and backward looking affirmative action. Whereas the latter is primarily concerned with compensation and remediation of wrongs suffered in the past, the former is geared toward the realization of the multicultural society more broadly, which would be inter alia reflected in the composition of the workforce of companies, the public administration, and so on.[9] As the emphasis of affirmative action schemes in most jurisdictions is on backward looking affirmative action, this receives most attention here. It is important to underline that affirmative action implies a form of differential treatment that ultimately aims at achieving full, real, substantive equality, thus clearly exposing the paradox of the equality principle. Still, the ambit of affirmative action is restricted by the prohibition of nondiscrimination. Indeed, "where the non-discrimination principle removes factors such as race, gender, nationality, etc. from the society's decision-making processes, affirmative action seeks to ensure full and substantive equality by taking those factors into account." Nevertheless, affirmative action measures must be carefully devised so as not to undermine the principle of nondiscrimination.[10]

According to the criteria developed in the open models of non-discrimination, there should be a reasonable and objective justification for the differential treatment involved in the affirmative action measures, implying a legitimate aim and a relationship of proportionality between the differential treatment and that legitimate aim. Although it is clear that affirmative action has as a legitimate aim the realization of substantive equality, redressing disadvantages from the past, the proportionality principle demands that the specific affirmative action measures should not go beyond what is demanded by substantive equality. This would exclude extreme measures, like very rigid quotas, and tends to imply that affirmative action measures are meant to be temporary.[11] Proportionality also involves inter alia the difficult issues of under- and overinclusiveness of the group of beneficiaries, which are not developed further here.

THE EQUALITY PRINCIPLE AND MINORITY PROTECTION: THE GENERAL FRAMEWORK

A comprehensive system of minority protection consists of a set of rules and mechanisms enabling an effective integration of the relevant population groups, while allowing them to retain their separate characteristics. Such a system is arguably based on two pillars, namely the prohibition of discrimination on the one hand and measures designed to protect and promote the separate identity of the minority groups on the other.[12] Although the relationship between nondiscrimination and substantive equality is not unequivocal (the former being at least conducive to the latter), the second pillar is actively geared towards realizing substantive equality.[13] Both pillars are closely intertwined and are intrinsically related to the equality principle.

It can thus be said that, overall, minority protection is inherently geared toward substantive equality, whereas nondiscrimination is generally recognized to be a necessary but insufficient condition for an adequate system of minority protection. It remains important to track substantial changes in the domain of nondiscrimination, and certainly its intersection with affirmative action measures and with substantive equality more generally. Affirmative action's focus on redressing disadvantages suffered by a population group in the past implies that the beneficiaries are vulnerable groups that can often be qualified as minorities. At the same time it should be emphasized that minorities require more then just affirmative action measures as these are inherently temporary. Indeed, more long-term special measures might be required to protect and promote the minorities' right to identity adequately, which would still be constrained by the goal of substantive equality.[14]

In any event, several factors can be identified as having an impact on the extent to which nondiscrimination actually can be favorable for substantive equality/minority protection. In principle the use of an open system of nondiscrimination should be more favorable toward substantive equality as the general balancing act it implies makes it much easier for arguments to be made in terms of achieving substantive equality. A more important and more direct contribution to substantive equality would be offered by the acceptance of indirect discrimination, as that clearly looks beyond the surface and sets out to identify and eradicate more covert forms of discrimination by critically examining possible disproportional impacts of apparently neutral differentiations.[15] Of course, substantive equality requires more than the eradication of indirect discrimination. Here, as in the case of the establishment of direct discrimination, the burden of proof that needs to be discharged by the claimant is crucial, which is in turn closely related to the two other issues. When using an open system of nondiscrimination, it is important to know whether different levels of scrutiny are applied when assessing the criteria to establish whether a differentiation amounts to a discrimination. In view of the fact that race, ethnic origin, and religion are often considered to be suspect grounds, differentiations on those bases meet with a stricter level of scrutiny, hence providing a greater protection for population groups defined on those bases, often minorities.[16] Finally, an asymmetrical approach to discrimination is obviously also in favor of minority protection because minorities tend to be vulnerable, disadvantaged groups and that approach adopts a stricter level of scrutiny when differentiations have negative consequences for disadvantaged groups.

In view of the theme of this book, it should be pointed out that constitutional provisions and jurisprudence in federal states on equality in general do not preclude subnational units from adopting different rules as compared to one another as this would be implicit in having a certain measure of autonomy. Indeed, within their spheres of competencies, federal and federated governments act on their own, and equality is measured (only) within each jurisdiction. However, as is clarified by the German Bundesverfassungsgericht, that autonomy is not unlimited, also due to the principle of federal comity, implying limitations to the scope of differential treatment that can be enacted by substate entities. Preferential treatment for inhabitants of the subnational unit concerned, as compared to inhabitants of the other subnational units, is in any event prohibited.[17]

RECENT DEVELOPMENTS AND THEIR IMPLICATIONS FOR MINORITY PROTECTION

Several potentially important developments concerning the equality principle can be noted that are of relevance for the extent to which equality considerations can have positive implications for minority protection. These developments both at the level of the European Convention on Human Rights (Council of Europe) and the EU are undoubtedly worth studying, as these arguably reflect and forestall developments at the national level. In this respect reference can be made to the use of "common European standards" by the European Court of

Human Rights and "constitutional traditions" at the EU level (article 6 EU and the jurisprudence of the European Court of Justice).

The European Convention on Human Rights

At the level of the European Convention of Human Rights, the jurisprudence of the European Court used to reflect a clear preference for formal equality. In terms of the Court's jurisprudence, a differential treatment is allowed insofar as it is reasonably and objectively justified. Admittedly, this implied an opening toward substantive equality, but it did not go as far as establishing an obligation for states to treat things differently when they are not analogous. Furthermore, the Court was very reluctant to acknowledge instances of indirect discrimination. The focus on formal equality was also visible in its asymmetrical approach to nondiscrimination, resulting in strict scrutiny for all kinds of measures differentiating on the basis of suspect classes, like gender, including those favoring women in comparison to men.[18]

Recent case law of the European Court of Human Rights (ECHR) clearly shows that it is gradually opening up toward substantive equality, while still numerous criticisms can be formulated as regards the way the Court interprets and applies article 14 ECHR.[19] In *Thlimmenos v. Greece* (2000), the Court significantly expanded its nondiscrimination jurisprudence in favor of substantive equality by acknowledging that

> The Court has so far considered that the right under Article 14 not to be discriminated against in the enjoyment of the rights guaranteed under the Convention is violated when States treat differently persons in analogous situations without providing an objective and reasonable justification. . . . However, the Court considers that this is not the only facet of the prohibition of discrimination in Article 14. The right not to be discriminated against in the enjoyment of the rights guaranteed under the Convention is *also violated when States without an objective and reasonable justification fail to treat differently persons whose situations are significantly different.* [emphasis added]

In other words, the prohibition of discrimination can in certain circumstances entail an obligation for states to treat differently, which is clearly geared toward substantive equality. It is exactly this opening toward the attempt to achieve substantive equality that brings the recognition of this dimension of the prohibition of discrimination close to the acknowledgment of indirect discrimination.[20] Indeed, indirect discrimination recognizes the fact that a formal equal application can lead to a material, de facto inequality. Furthermore, the *Thlimmenos* rationale might influence the European Court on Human Rights to adopt a more asymmetrical approach to nondiscrimination.

Traditionally, the case law of the ECHR demonstrated a strong reluctance to accept instances of indirect discrimination. The Court's reasoning—for example, in the *Abdulaziz, Cabales and Balkandali* case (series A, no. 94)—implied the virtual impossibility of claiming indirect discrimination, as it basically classified as irrelevant disparate effects on certain groups of facially neutral rules. Typical cases where this denial of indirect discrimination was particularly alarming are the host of (older) cases brought by Gypsies against the United Kingdom. The general laws of the use of territories in the United Kingdom de facto entail that Gypsies could not live in their caravans on their own land. The disproportionate impact on the Gypsies of these apparently neutral rules was several times claimed to amount to prohibited discrimination. The Court, however, ignored the broader impact of the legislation on the Gypsies as a group (refusing to transcend the individual case before it) and in this way failed to establish indirect discrimination (assuming that the justification given would not have been reasonable and objective).[21]

It seems that the Court is now becoming more receptive to the idea of indirect discrimination, albeit very hesitantly. In *Kelly v. UK* (2001), the Court explicitly acknowledged for the first time (and repeated it in 2002 in *McShane v. UK*) that "where a general policy or measure has disproportionately prejudicial effects on a particular group, it is not excluded that this may be considered as discriminatory notwithstanding that it is not specifically aimed or directed at that group" (par 148). Nevertheless, the Court requires at the same time a very heavy burden of proof and will (still) not easily accept that indirect discrimination is established. In both cases, the Court pointed out that it is not sufficient merely to demonstrate disparate impact, and that further proof is needed, though not identifying what that should be exactly. It seems, however, that a wrongful or illegitimate exercise of power or competence should be involved.[22]

Another interesting development, albeit not mainly concerning article 14 ECHR but still denoting a further opening toward concerns of substantive equality, can be noticed in more recent case law pertaining to Roma. The Court decided in January 2002 on five similar Roma cases, all dealing with the problems regarding caravans mentioned earlier, *Chapman v. UK* being the pilot case. A first important innovation was that the Court for the first time explicitly recognized that respect for a distinct, separate way of life is covered by article 8 ECHR (par 73). Furthermore, in its assessment whether the interference with this right was in conformity with paragraph 2 and thus proportional to the legitimate aim, the Court pointed to an emerging international consensus recognizing the special needs of minorities and an obligation to protect their security, identity, and lifestyle, which confines the usual deference to states (par 93). The Court was not persuaded that the consensus is sufficiently concrete to derive specific rules on what kind of action is expected from the States in any particular situation (par 94) and did not interpret article 8 to involve a far-reaching positive obligation of general social policy, such as providing sufficient number of adequate housing and camping facilities for the Roma (par 98). Nevertheless, the Court did underscore that there is a positive obligation imposed on the Contracting States by virtue of article 8 to facilitate the Gypsy way of life (par 96).

More directly relevant to equality concerns, the claim of a violation of article 14 (in combination with article 8) was formulated as a failure to make a distinction between qualitatively different situations in that the application of the general laws and policies did not take into account the special needs of the Roma flowing from their tradition of living a nonsedentary life and traveling in caravans (being very close in kind to a claim of indirect discrimination). The majority of the Court did explicitly refer to its *Thlimmenos* reasoning but found that there was an objective and reasonable justification for the absence of this differential treatment because the proportionality requirement would be fulfilled, for which it referred back to its reasoning in terms of the legitimate limitations to article 8. The application of the *Thlimmenos* reasoning thus remains rather restrictive. The seven dissenting judges, however, relying on the *Thlimmenos* case, found a violation of article 14 in combination with article 8, because the authorities had failed to take the specific circumstances and needs of Roma into account in the application of the planning regulations.

It seems clear that this area of law is indeed in the process of development.[23] It could be that the Chapman case signals a development in the ECHR's jurisprudence that would give more prominence to belonging to a national minority as a ground of prohibited discrimination, possibly leading to another instance of heightened scrutiny.[24]

Developments at the Level of the European Union

Although there is a considerable continuity in the approach to the equality principle pre- and post-Amsterdam, the Amsterdam Treaty (1997) undoubtedly signified an important landmark, announcing new developments. Traditionally, the focus of EC nondiscrimination law was on nationality and especially gender, as was reflected in the EC Treaty (articles 6 and 141 respectively). In view of the host of directives pertaining to the prohibition of gender discrimination,[25] the closed model for direct discrimination on the basis of gender—allowing only very few explicitly named exceptions—and the stricter review by the European Court of Justice in this respect, it was generally accepted that gender—as a ground of differentiation—attracted a higher level of scrutiny. Hence it stood at the apex of the equality hierarchy in the EC/EU.

Early on, the ECJ accepted the concept of indirect discrimination, which was later also explicitly taken up in Council Directive 97/80 on the burden of proof in cases of discrimination based on sex (article 2,2). This openness toward concerns of substantive equality, however, is not reflected in the ECJ's attitude toward affirmative action, as demonstrated in its interpretation of article 2(4) of the Equal Treatment Directive. Even though that article provides an opening for "measures to promote equal opportunity for men and women, in particular by removing existing inequalities which affect women's opportunities," the ECJ has consistently interpreted that language very strictly, leaving little scope for affirmative action. In other words, the ECJ clearly adopted a symmetrical approach to nondiscrimination, implying that heightened scrutiny is also used for positive discrimination.[26]

The adoption of article 13 EC gave a new impetus to nondiscrimination in EU law by placing discrimination against new groups on the agenda, implying a shift in the primary rationale from enhancing the common market and economic integration to broader, purely human rights concerns. Article 13 indeed provides the basis to adopt legislative measures aimed at combating discrimination on the basis of race or ethnic origin, religion or belief, age, disability, and sexual orientation.[27] On the basis of article 13, two directives have been adopted so far,[28] namely Directive 2000/43 EC implementing the principle of Equal Treatment between persons irrespective of racial or ethnic origin (the Race Directive) and Directive 2000/78 EC establishing a general framework for Equal Treatment in employment and occupation. In view of its obvious relevance for the protection of racial or ethnic minorities, the Race Directive is focused upon here.

Several features of that directive seem to lead to the conclusion that a change has taken place in favor of race as the nondiscrimination ground of greatest concern, so that racial equality now seems to be at the peak of the equality hierarchy at the EU level.[29] The directive expressly distinguishes between direct and indirect discrimination, while giving a broad definition of both (article 2), especially of indirect discrimination, and making it considerably easier to establish cases of discrimination by facilitating the burden of proof (article 8). As regards direct discrimination, a strict and closed model of nondiscrimination is used, providing virtually no exceptions to the prohibition of direct race discrimination (articles 4 and 5). Furthermore, the directive has a conspicuous focus on making the prohibition of race discrimination effective by (among other things) providing strong protection against retribution for filing a complaint, by creating an obligation for states to establish bodies for the promotion of equal treatment, and by providing for effective and dissuasive sanctions in the event of noncompliance (articles 7, 13, and 15).

Although article 13 EC does not explicitly create openings toward affirmative action or more generally aim at achieving substantive equality, the Race Directive in article 5 demonstrates that states are allowed, not obliged, to adopt certain affirmative action measures in favor of previously disadvantaged groups, in order to further the goal of substantive equality. In view of the differences in formulation between article 5 of the Race Directive and article 2(4) of the Equal Treatment Directive, it is not entirely clear how this will transform the jurisprudence of the ECJ. On the one hand, the Court could indeed have regard to the different social context of each ground of prohibited discrimination, possibly justifying a change in the scope of permitted affirmative action on the basis of race/ethnic origin. On the other hand, reference should be made to the ECJ's initial interpretation of article 141(4) EC, an article included by the Treaty of Amsterdam that is very close in formulation to article 5 Race Directive, in *Katarina Abrahamsson and Leif Anderson v. Elisabet Fogelqvist* (C-407/98 [2000]), which arguably indicates that the ECJ will not significantly enhance the scope of affirmative action and will stick to the existing principles developed in its case law so far.

In any event, the equality paradigm in EU law is obviously also in the process of transformation, possibly leaning toward substantive equality. Indeed, the Court might still opt to shift to a more asymmetrical approach to the prohibition of discrimination in its case law.[30]

IMPLICATIONS OF THE PROHIBITION OF DISCRIMINATION FOR SUBNATIONAL CONSTITUTIONS

Finally, it should be acknowledged that, as is illustrated by the rulings of the constitutional courts in South Africa and Germany, the prohibition of discrimination does not stand in the way of subnational units adopting constitutions that have their own additional measures pertaining to human rights and minority protection, as long as these do not fall below the national standards.[31] In the certification process of the Constitution of Kwazulu-Natal,[32] the South African Constitutional Court was confronted with a provincial Bill of Rights and formulated certain guidelines about the extent to which provincial constitutions can actually include a Bill of Rights. Although the Court acknowledged that the national Bill of Rights was not "intended to deal completely, exhaustively or exclusively with fundamental rights at all levels of government," a provincial Bill of Rights should be completely consistent with the national constitution.[33] This would imply not only that no provision of a provincial Bill of Rights can be inconsistent with the corresponding provisions of the national Bill of Rights but also that the provincial Bill of Rights should not deal with matters falling outside the province's legislative or executive powers. Whereas the latter is not likely to happen because the mainstreaming function of human rights is widely accepted, it seems clear that the equality provision of the national Bill of Rights does not stand in the way of divergences among the various provincial Bills of Rights. The Court formulated the following test under which a provincial Bill of Rights could confer greater rights and even other rights on individuals than those conferred by the national Constitution: "a provision in a provincial Bill of Rights and a corresponding provision of Chapter 3 [Bill of Rights in the national constitution] are inconsistent when they cannot stand at the same time or cannot stand together or cannot both be obeyed at the same time" (par 24). Because provisions aimed at the accommodation of ethnic, linguistic, and religious population diversity, and hence minority protection, are often found in the Bill of Rights, this seems to allow provinces to go further in this regard, as long as they would not violate other fundamental rights enshrined in the national Constitution, including the equality provision. A province could, for example, provide for financial support for cultural organizations or be more specific about the kinds of rights available to members of minority communities.

CONCLUSION

The equality paradigm appears to be moving to substantive equality considerations and hence, not only toward special measures for members of minorities but also to some extent toward an asymmetrical approach to the prohibition of discrimination, which would open possibilities for states to adopt affirmative action measures in favor of previously disadvantaged groups. It has also been pointed out that the equality principle does not prevent one subnational unit from adopting different rules than another subnational unit, as this would be inherent in their necessary degree of autonomy. Similarly, the constitutions of the subnational units could provide human rights and minority rights in addition to those found in the federal constitution, as long as this would not lead to inconsistencies with the latter constitution. Consequently, the ongoing developments pertaining to the equality paradigm will also open up possibilities for the subnational units to adopt, maintain, and develop further minority protection measures as well.

NOTES

1. See inter alia K. Wentholt, "Formal and Substantive Equal Treatment: The Limitations and the Potential of the Legal Concept of Equality," in *Non Discrimination Law: Comparative Perspectives*, ed. T. Loenen and P. R. Rodrigues (Martinus Nijhoff, 1999), 53–64.

2. Inter alia P. Lemmens, "Gelijkheid en Non-discriminatie in het Internationale Recht: Synthese," in *Gelijkheid en Non-discriminatie*, ed. A. Alen and P. Lemmens (Kluwer, 1991), 88–89.

3. For an excellent overview, see A. W. Heringa. "Standards of Review for Discrimination," in *Non Discrimination Law: Comparative Perspectives*, ed. T. Loenen and P. R. Rodrigues (Den Haag, Martinus Nijhoff, 1999), 25–37.

4. For an excellent overview of the reasoning of the U.S.A. Supreme Court in its identification of "suspect grounds," see J. H. Gerards, *Rechterlijke Toetsing aan het Gelijkheidsbeginsel* (Sdu, 2002), 387–98.

5. Ibid., 307–15 and 357–58.

6. Council Directive 2000/43/EC of 29 June 2000 implementing the principle of equal treatment between persons of racial or ethnic origin.

7. T. Loenen, "Indirect Discrimination: Oscillating Between Containment and Revolution," in *Non Discrimination Law: Comparative Perspectives*, ed. T. Loenen and P. R. Rodrigues (Den Haag, Martinus Nijhoff, 1999), 205.

8. Ibid., 196–98.

9. Inter alia M. C. Kaveny, "Discrimination and Affirmative Action," *Theological Studies* (1996): 291–92.

Note in this respect the South African Employment Equity Act of 1998, which in chapter III deals with affirmative action measures, defined as "measures designed to ensure that suitably qualified people from designated groups have *equal employment opportunities* and are *equitably represented* in all occupational categories and levels in the workforce of a designated employer" (article 15(1)). The designated groups are enumerated in article 1 as being blacks (African, Indian, and Colored), women, and people with disabilities. One can assume that this is a case of backward looking affirmative action in view of the fact that all these designated groups are historically disadvantaged, but there could also be some degree of forward looking perspective involved.

10. M. Bossuyt, *The Concept and Practice of Affirmative Action: Preliminary Report*, UN, E/CN.4/Sub.2/2000/11, 19 June 2000, Par. 44.

11. The requirement that affirmative action measures need to be temporary can be found in article 1(4) CERD and article 4(1) CEDAW as these stipulate that affirmative action measures may not as a consequence lead to the maintenance of unequal or separate standards and they shall be discontinued after the objectives for which they have been taken have been achieved.

12. K. Henrard, *Devising an Adequate System of Minority Protection: Individual Human Rights, Minority Rights and the Right to Self-Determination* (Kluwer, The Hague, 2000), 8. See also G. Alfredsson, "Minority Rights: A Summary of Existing Practice," in *The UN Minority Rights Declaration*, ed. A. Phillips and A. Rosas (Turku, Abo Akademi Tryckeri, 1993), 62; J. P. Humphrey, "Preventing Discrimination and Positive Protection for Minorities: Aspects of International Law," *Les Cahiers de Droit* (1986): 24–25.

13. Inter alia K. Henrard, *Devising an Adequate System of Minority Protection*, 59–60; K. Wentholt, "Formal and Substantive Equal Treatment," 53–64.

14. Inter alia J. Duffar, "La Protection Internationale des Droits des Minorites Religieuses," *Revue de Droit Public et de Science Politique en France et a l' etranger*

(1995): 1525; W. Kymlicka, *Multicultural Citizenship: A Liberal Theory of Minority Rights* (Oxford, Oxford University Press, 1995): 120–23.

15. See inter alia T. Loenen, "Indirect Discrimination," 198–200. See also B. Vizkelety, "Adverse Effect Discrimination in Canada: Crossing the Rubicon from Formal to Substantive Equality," in *Non Discrimination Law: Comparative Perspectives,* ed. T. Loenen and P. R. Rodrigues (Den Haag, Martinus Nijhoff, 1999): 233–34.

16. J. H. Gerards, *Rechterlijke Toetsing aan het Gelijkheidsbeginsel,* 87–91 and especially at 465, referring to the Carolene products rational in terms of discrete and insular minorities.

17. W. Heun, "Der allgemeine Gleichheitssatz des Art. 3.1 GG," in *Grundgesetz Kommentar,* ed. H. Dreier (Mohr Siebeck, 1996): 252–53.

18. This symmetrical approach was clearly visible in the following cases: Karlheinz Schmidt (18 July 1994, Series A no. 291-B); Burghartz (22 February 1994, Series A no. 280-B) en Van Raalte (21 February 1997).

19. See S. Spiliopoulou-Akermark, "The Limits of Pluralism—Recent Jurisprudence of the European Court of Human Rights with Regard to Minorities: Does the Prohibition of Discrimination Add Anything?" *Journal of Ethnopolitics and Minority Issues in Europe* 3(2002): 5–20.

20. T. Loenen and A. Hendriks, Case Note with Thlimmenos, *NJCM Bulletin* (2000): 1102. See also S. Spiliopoulou-Akermark, "The Limits of Pluralism," 5.

21. *Buckley v UK* of 25 September 1996 is a paradigmatic case of this restrictive attitude of the Court as regards claims by Gypsies. See also O. de Schutter, "Le Droit au Mode de Vie Tsigane devant la Cour Européenne des Droits de l' Homme," *Revue Trimestrielle des Droits de l'Homme* (1997): 84–85.

22. See also J. H. Gerards, *Rechterlijke Toetsing aan het Gelijkheidsbeginsel,* 115.

23. See also S. Spilopoulou-Akermark, 'The Limits of Pluralism," 20.

24. In *Conka v Belgium* (5 February 2002), the ECHR similarly demonstrated special attention for the particularly vulnerable situation of Roma, qualifying for the first time an action of a state as a prohibited case of collective expulsion in violation of article 4 of additional protocol 4. Arguably this also reflects substantive equality reasoning in the sense that because of their vulnerable situation, the authorities should pay even greater attention to not creating conditions that could be interpreted as amounting to collective expulsion.

25. To name only a few: directive 76/207 on Equal Treatment for Men and Women as regards access to Employment, Vocational Training and Promotion, and Working Conditions; and directive 79/7 on Equal Treatment between Men and Women in matters of Social Security.

26. Two of the key cases here are C-450/93, *Kalanke v Freie Hansestadt Bremen* and case c-409/95 *Marschall v Land Nordrhein—Westfalen.* See also A.G. Veldman, "Preferential Treatment in European Community Law: Current Legal Developments and the Impact on National Practices," in *Non Discrimination Law: Comparative Perspectives,* ed. T. Loenen and P. R. Rodrigues (Den Haag, Martinus Nijhoff, 1999): 280–88.

27. For an extensive discussion of article 13 EC and its possible impact, see L. Waddington, "Testing the Limits of the EC Treaty Article on Non-Discrimination," *Industrial Law Journal* (1999): 133–51.

28. For an in-depth discussion of both, see L. Waddington and M. Bell, "More Equal Than Others: Distinguishing European Union Equality Directives," *Common Market Law Review* (2001): 587–611.

29. See also M. Bell, *Anti-discrimination Law and the European Union* (Oxford: Oxford University Press, 2002): 75–79; G. Von Toggenburg, "The Race Directive:

A New Dimension in the Fight Against Ethnic Discrimination in Europe," in *European Yearbook on Minority Issues* (2002).

30. See also L. Waddington and M. Bell, "More Equal Than Others," 601–3.

31. See inter alia Constitutional Court of South Africa, Ex parte Speaker Kwazulu-Natal Provincial Legislature: In Re Certification of the Constitution of the Province of Kwazulu-Natal, CCT 15/96, 6 September 1996, paragraphs 17–18.

32. Note that the Constitution of the Western Cape, which was duly certified by the Constitutional Court of South Africa, does not contain its own Bill of Rights but does contain other provisions with clear minority protection potential. One of the directive principles of provincial policy, for example, is "the promotion of respect for the rights of cultural, religious and linguistic communities in the Western Cape" (section 81 d).

33. Ex parte Speaker Kwazulu-Natal Provincial Legislature: In Re Certification of the Constitution of the Province of Kwazulu-Natal, CCT 15/96, 6 September 1996, 1996 (4) *SA* 1098, paras 17–18.

3

Participation in the Decision-Making Process as a Means of Group Accommodation

Nicole Töpperwien

INTRODUCTION: THE PROMISE OF PARTICIPATION RIGHTS

Today developing countries and countries in transition, as well as the so-called developed world, are challenged by the quest of different ethnic or cultural groups for political relevance. With nation-state building and a renewed importance for the local levels of government, there are growing demands by self-conscious groups to be recognized and to have political relevance at the state and local levels. The new trend toward the self-consciousness of groups can be at least partly explained by the difficulties and legitimacy crises encountered in transition processes that give heightened attractiveness to ethnic and cultural arguments and by the phenomenon normally called globalization or "glocalization" that increases the relevance of the local level and therefore of local groups as well.[1]

Citizens demand that they can influence politics not only as individuals but also as members of a group. They desire that politics be the expression of individual and group interests. They oppose majority rule because majority rule primarily takes the interests of the majority into account and smaller groups face the risk of being continuously outvoted and their interests ignored. More often than not, these groups want to be recognized as equally state-constituting parts of the population and not as minorities. They do not aim at individual or formal equality but demand an attributive and distributive differentiating understanding of equality. In other words, they do not demand equal rights but the right to be equal as groups.[2]

Autonomy can sometimes satisfy the demands of self-conscious groups because autonomy can increase the self-determination of groups at the subnational level, especially when these groups are territorially concentrated. When, however, local autonomy is introduced and the local entity is not culturally homogeneous, then political integration of local minorities into the political process through participation rights at the subnational level can become relevant. Participation rights at the state and the local level can render states able to respond to the multicultural challenge. Participation rights are here understood as a guaranteed and institutionalized special influence on the decision-making process of the state. The special influence can be obtained either by the requirement of special majorities for decisions and/or through a guaranteed representation of groups in state institutions.[3] Participation rights of different groups promise to promote the democratic integration of these groups.[4] Participation rights as means of group accommodation can be instituted because of group membership or group status and are therefore attributive and distributive differentiating.

Having a guaranteed influence on the decision-making process promises to enhance the loyalty to and identification with the state and prevents the alienation inherent in the feeling of being a perennial loser.[5] The inclusion of self-conscious groups in the political process promises to avoid fragmentation and violent conflict. Because the groups can pursue and realize their interests within the political process, they do not have to rely on extrapolitical means. Participation rights can lead to a sharing of political responsibilities and finally to the enhancement of the unity of the state.

Participation rights can be a means for group accommodation. However many nation-states remain reluctant to accord these rights at the state or the local level because they are regarded as being in contradiction with the nation-state principle. Even when participation rights are accepted and are introduced, problems can arise in defining what groups shall receive participation rights and what kind of participation rights shall be accorded. These concerns are addressed in the following analysis.

PARTICIPATION RIGHTS AND THE NATION-STATE

The modern nation-state is ill equipped to accommodate self-conscious groups through special political representation. In order to give special participation rights to groups as means of group accommodation, groups must be recognized and must be deemed as relevant.[6] It is due to these two prerequisites that participation rights are often contested, because recognizing the political relevance of groups can be regarded as opposed to the nation-state principle.

The two main liberal traditions, the American and the French, both do not recognize subgroups in their population as relevant. For both, the only relevant and recognized unit is the nation. According to these traditions, all citizens belong to the nation as equal individuals. Whereas in the American perception, culture is deemed irrelevant for the political process, in France the population is supposed to assimilate willingly to a state-created culture. In the United States, different cultural groups are recognized but taken as politically irrelevant.[7] In France, cultural homogeneity of all citizens in the French Republic is assumed.[8] Different cultural groups other than the nation or within the nation are constitutionally nonexistent and are therefore not deemed relevant.[9]

Countries relying on an ethnic perception of the nation exclude from the nation all those who do not share the common ethnicity. Therefore these countries normally recognize the existence of groups other than the nation. Although the state recognizes these groups, the groups can be, but need not be, deemed as relevant for the state, and they are hardly ever recognized as equally constituting the state, because this would question the nation-state principle, which defines the nation-state as the state of and for one nation.[10] Because different groups can be recognized, they can as well be accorded some special rights including participation rights.[11] However the quest of self-conscious groups to be accepted as state-constituting or, in other words, as equally relevant as the nation will be seen as threatening not only the regime but the ethnic nation-state as such.[12]

Granting special political rights to cultural groups in systems like France and the United States, whether on the national or the subnational level, questions the nation concept. In France, the nation concept is questioned because it would give rights to groups that constitutionally do not exist. In the United States, the nation concept would be questioned because it would grant political relevance to culture in a system that deems culture as irrelevant for the public sphere.[13] In ethnic nation-states, participation rights question the nation-state principle because they question the exclusivity of the nation, unless these rights are conferred only to small minorities with little political impact. Both states that are still in the process of nation-state building and traditional nation-states tend to resist political group accommodation. Special rights for groups will face resistance when they are viewed as questioning the state or the nation.

Nevertheless more and more states and subnational units have relied on federal elements in state organization and have accorded special participation rights to various groups.[14] Federal elements can be introduced for efficiency and effectiveness reasons or for bottom-up democratization. In these cases, federal elements are seen as being in accordance with the interest of the nation and therefore as in accordance with the nation-state principle. In many cases, however, federal elements and especially participation rights are suggested or introduced at least partly as pragmatic answers to demands from factually existing groups who seek political relevance. In these cases, participation rights are accepted as a necessity but are viewed as being in tension or even in contradiction with the values of the nation and the nation-state.[15]

Participation rights as group accommodation will only be seen as in accordance with the nation-state principle when diversity is viewed as a value. For instance, Charles Taylor argues in favor of the value of diversity based on the equal value of all groups, the importance of group identity for the individual,[16] and finally the enrichment of society through the influence of different cultures.[17] When diversity is viewed as enriching society, it will be considered within the interest of society to actively protect and promote diversity. In such a case, participation rights as group accommodation can become a legitimizing state feature.[18]

Because participation rights give special relevance to some groups, two questions inevitably arise. First, what groups shall receive special relevance, and second, what kind of participation rights shall be accorded?

WHO SHALL RECEIVE PARTICIPATION RIGHTS?

The question of what groups shall receive participation rights will be answered differently depending on the reasons why participation rights are introduced. When participation rights are introduced as a response to group demands but are not accompanied by accepting diversity as a value, then most likely groups that are viewed as too small to be dangerous or groups that are seen as too influential to be disregarded will receive participation rights. In the latter case, it will probably depend on the degree of identity assertion and the amount of pressure that the group is able to generate. Most likely, participation rights will be negotiated on a case-by-case basis.

When diversity is regarded as a value and participation rights as a legitimating factor, then a more general or normative stand toward participation rights will be pursued. Some countries might view only the given diversity as a value—as is the case with Switzerland. In this case, the traditional diversity will be promoted.[19] It is, however, also possible that a state might endorse a more general notion of cherishing diversity or, in other words, adopt a policy of normative diversity. According to this understanding, every kind of diversity would merit accommodation and promotion. Therefore, every kind of difference would qualify for special treatment. Brought to its logical conclusion, the promotion of all diversity would lead to the promotion of individual difference, or (in different words) individualism. The only difference to the classic liberal state would be that such a state would base individualism on universal difference instead of on universal equality.[20]

States that want to accommodate groups will not be able to avoid distinguishing some diversity as relevant for promotion while neglecting other diversities. The criteria for distinguishing and the processes for doing so can create conflicts. There are at least two different mechanisms for deciding what groups shall receive special participation rights. One could either establish fixed criteria like, for instance, the size of the group, the way or degree of identity expression, and cultural distinctiveness; or one could foresee a procedure for group recognition. In such a procedure, fixed criteria could, but need not, have an influence.

The reliance on fixed criteria can pose a variety of practical difficulties because it will not be possible to define group belonging exclusively based on objective criteria. The conception and imposition of objective criteria can be coercive for the individual and for the group. Procedures that do not rely on fixed criteria can rely for instance on the self-definition of the group[21] or can substitute a territoriality approach insofar as certain areas, which can be defined through democratic procedures, are accorded participation rights.[22] The most relevant aspect for the definition of criteria and procedures would have to be their legitimacy for all concerned groups, including the population as such.

WHAT KIND OF PARTICIPATION RIGHTS SHALL BE GRANTED?

Participation rights should promote integration without paralysis of the system and without risking an ethnification of politics. In order to encourage integration, the groups need to have the feeling that they have an effective say. However, the influence given to the different groups must not be so strong that they can completely paralyze the system. In addition, participation rights ought not to lead to a situation in which political mobilization is based exclusively or primarily on ethnic arguments. Participation rights can enlarge legitimacy of governmental decisions, so that decisions do not only have an overall legitimacy but are additionally perceived as legitimate by the different concerned groups. In other words, participation rights should prevent the tyranny of the majority without introducing the tyranny of the minority or the continuous unsolvable confrontation of groups. Participation rights, therefore, should aim at establishing a system that generates viable compromises.

A compromise will be accepted as the best solution and as within the interest of the nation only when the reason for compromising is accepted as legitimate and desirable. The telos of compromising can render a compromise legitimate. When the telos is viewed in peace promotion, compromise is perceived as a tool for conflict prevention and management. The legitimacy of compromise will depend on the peace prognosis and will dissolve when conflict or effectiveness is viewed as unlikely. When diversity is understood as a value, the telos of compromise will be diversity promotion. In this case, compromise is not only legitimate under the threat of conflict but in general as a means for taking diversity into account. The compromise as such can turn into a legitimate and legitimizing form of decision-making.[23]

Most states today are still far from accepting diversity as a value. On the contrary, most states adopt policies of overcoming diversity. Compromising or participation rights will in such cases always remain the exception and will need a special justification.

When participation rights are introduced as a means of conflict prevention even though group accommodation is viewed as being in tension with the nation concept or the nation-state principle, then participation rights will be granted as restrictively as possible. When participation rights are introduced in order to promote diversity as a value, participation rights can be designed more extensively. In both cases, participation rights should not jeopardize but enhance the legitimacy of decisions.

Participation rights can be foreseen in every governmental institution on every governmental level. There can be participation rights in the national parliament, the national executive, and/or the national judiciary.[24] Participation rights can be introduced at the subnational level as well. It is vitally important for the different groups to be able to influence effectively issues that directly concern the life of their communities, and the lower levels of governments are generally assigned exactly those sensitive tasks that are of immediate concern for the groups.[25] Thus, effective participation in the decision-making of the subnational level will be at least as important for the groups as on the national level.[26]

When groups are effectively represented at the subnational level, they will most likely feel well represented at the national level in all cases in which the subnational level can participate in the decision-making of the national level. Effective participation rights at the subnational level promise therefore not only a better integration at the subnational but at the national level as well. However, these participation rights can, by the same mechanisms, influence the power balance at the subnational and at the national levels.[27] The weakening of the influence of the majority of the subnational unit due to the participation rights of other groups can jeopardize the loyalty of that majority to the federal system in those cases in which the participation rights are viewed as an imposed mechanism to restrict the influence of the subnational majority. The tensions will probably be even greater when the majority of the subnational unit is a minority at the national level and perceives its influence weakened unjustly. The more multifaceted participation rights are and the more levels that are involved, the more complex will be the influence on the power balance.

As the foregoing example suggested, participation rights must be regarded with a view to the balance between different groups. In addition, attention must be paid to the relation between groups and the state as such. When all institutions are constituted so as to represent the groups and there is not a counterweighing representation of the citizenry as a whole, there can as well only be direct legitimacy of decisions in respect to the groups.[28] In such a case, state legitimacy derives from and depends on group legitimacies. Disputes between groups can put the state as such in question because the state does not have legitimacy on its own to justify its existence and thus has no basis through which it could counterweigh, bridge, or mediate conflicts. Though participation rights aim at ameliorating legitimacy of groups, this must not be done in detriment to an overall legitimacy.

The constitutions of the countries of the world and of their component units show multiple forms of participation rights. Parliaments can be designed as two-chamber parliaments, with the second chamber of parliament representing subgroups.[29] The elections can be designed so as to give maximal representation to different groups. An election system based on the proportionality principle will assure a better representation of groups than the majority system. Additionally group interests can be taken into account, for instance, through gerrymandering or the designation of special constituencies,[30] through exceptions to a percentage barrier, or through a guaranteed minimum number of seats.[31] Parliamentary commissions can be constituted so as to represent different groups and interests. Consultations with different groups can help to avoid conflicts at the drafting stage in the decision-making process.[32] Special majority requirements and alarm-bell procedures can try to ensure that sensitive decisions are backed by a broad consensus.[33]

Participation and representation can be introduced in the executive branch, for instance, by providing for a presidency instead of a president.[34] The composition of the judiciary can either be influenced by the procedure of nominating, appointing, or electing the judges[35] or through the criteria for the qualification of judges.[36] It can as well be provided that group membership is taken into account for representation at the higher levels of courts.[37] What kind of participation rights are appropriate and acceptable on which level and in which institutions and who can introduce these rights will depend greatly on the specific context of the country. In the end, only participation rights that find the acceptance of all concerned groups and that are not in opposition to an overall or overarching legitimacy will have chances of being effective.

CONCLUSIONS

Participation rights are a promising tool for group accommodation. Nevertheless, for many states, participation rights are difficult to accept. The most important barrier to this kind of group accommodation is the self-understanding of most states as being a state of and for one nation and the definition of the nation as being composed of equal individuals or as a culturally homogeneous entity without subgroups. This understanding of the nation-state limits the legitimacy of participation rights at the very outset.

Effective participation rights will change the way politics are conducted. Participation rights have an impact on the outcome of decision-making. Decisions that are based on compromises are encouraged, even though such decisions are often regarded as compromising the interests of the dominant group. In this sense, participation rights go further than the right to self-government. Decisions of groups do not only influence their own destinies but also directly the destiny of the whole state. This influence of groups on the destiny of the whole state will be difficult to accept unless it is also accepted and supported that the groups shall have a common destiny in a common state. The notion of a common destiny in a common state necessitates that neither the borders nor the legitimacy of the state, nor the right of groups to pursue their interest within the state and through its institutions, are questioned.

Participation rights necessitate a mutual respect of groups. Participation rights ought not to be used to manipulate the decision-making process so as to institute the dominance of one group but should instead ensure that the interests of all groups are taken into account. In order to ensure this, it will be necessary to balance the influence of the different groups. Participation rights can be the first step toward a new way of living together. Participation rights can be the beginning or the expression of a rethinking of the state and of the nation. The rethinking can either lead to an understanding of the state as no longer the state of and for one nation but the state of and for all groups or to an understanding of the nation as no longer a homogeneous unity or the aggregation of equal individuals but as an aggregate of different groups. Due to this redefinition, the state or the nation can cherish diversity. The value of diversity can turn into a fundamental principle of the state.

NOTES

1. For the legitimacy crisis in postcommunist federations due to the illegitimacy of regime and state and the reliance on ethnic arguments, see, for example, Lidija R. Basta, "The Role of the Constitution in Central and Eastern Europe in Transition: From the 'politique constitutionnelle politisée' towards the 'politique constitutionnelle politisante,' in Beat Sitter-Liver (ed.), *Herausgeforderte Verfassung, Die Schweiz im globalen Kontext* (Freiburg i.Ue. 1999).

For globalization and the new relevance of the local level, see for example, Saskia Sassen, *Globalization and Its Discontents, Essays on the New Mobility of People and Money* (New York, 1998), 3–76; Niels Lange, *Globalisierung und regionaler Nationalismus, Schottland und Québec im Zeitalter der Denationalisierung* (Baden-Baden, 2000), 13–45.

2. For this trend, see for example, Charles Taylor, "The Politics of Recognition," in Amy Gutmann (ed.), *Multiculturalism: Examining the Politics of Recognition* (Princeton, 1994); Erhard Denninger, "Vielfalt, Sicherheit und Solidarität: Ein neues Paradigma für Verfassungsgebung und Menschenrechtsentwicklung?" in *Menschenrechte und Grundgesetz: Zwei Essays* (Weinheim, 1994); Will Kymlicka, *Multicultural Citizenship: A Liberal Theory of Minority Rights* (Oxford, 1998).

3. This could be proportional, overproportional, or equal representation of groups.

4. See Thomas Stauffer and Nicole Töpperwien, "Balancing Self-Rule and Shared Rule," in Lidija R. Basta Fleiner and Thomas Fleiner (eds.), *Federalism and Multiethnic States: The Case of Switzerland*, PIFF Etudes et colloques 16, 2nd ed. (Fribourg, 2000), 47–49.

5. See Thomas Fleiner, "Limiter les conflits, empêcher la violence, protéger les minorités," in *Swiss, made: La Suisse en dialogue avec le monde* (Geneva, 1998): 355–60, Wolf Linder, *Schweizerische Demokratie, Institutionen, Prozesse* (Bern, 1999): 26, 35.

6. See, for example, Jörg Paul Müller, *Der politische Mensch—Menschliche Politik* (Basel, 1999): 42–43.

7. See, for example, Thomas F. Pettigrew, "Ethnicity in American Life: A Social Psychological Perspective," in John Hope Franklin and Thomas F. Pettigrew (eds.), *Ethnicity in American Life* (New York, 1971): 22–23; Kenneth L. Karst, *Belonging to America: Equal Citizenship and the Constitution* (New Haven, 1989): 30–31.

8. France makes an exception for the peoples of the overseas territories. From them, complete assimilation is not expected.

9. See Article 2 of the French Constitution of 1958:

(1) France is an *indivisible*, secular, democratic, and social Republic (personal emphasis).

Because of the indivisibility, France made a reservation to Article 27 of the International Covenant on Civil and Political Rights of 1966 based on the explanation that there are no minorities in France.

Article 27 of the International Covenant on Civil and Political Rights of 1966: "In those States in which ethnic, religious or linguistic minorities exist, persons belonging to such minorities shall not be denied the right, in community with the other members of their group, to enjoy their own culture, to profess and practise their own religion, or to use their own language."

10. See Rogers Brubaker, "Myths and Misconceptions in the Study of Nationalism," in John A. Hall (ed.), *The State of the Nation: Ernest Gellner and the Theory of Nationalism* (Cambridge, 1998): 46. The nation-state is therefore used as a prescriptive term and not as a descriptive term that describes the congruence between nation and population of a specific state. The nation-state principle is mainly problematic because nations demand that the state is of and for a nation, even though the nation does not include the whole population.

11. See, for instance, the Danish and Sorbish minorities in Schleswig Holstein/ Germany.

12. See, for instance, the demands of the Albanian population in Macedonia. The fear that minorities want to be recognized as state-building groups and would therefore question the ethnic nation-state as such makes federalism a solution unacceptable to the political elites in most of the postcommunist countries in Eastern Europe.

13. The United States is nevertheless organized as a federation. Federalism is viewed as part of the checks-and-balance system as an antimajoritarian device to limit the majority and the national government.

14. See, for example, Ronald Watts, *The Relevance Today of the Federal Idea*, to be published on the Web site of the International Conference on Federalism 2002, http://www.federalism2002.ch.

15. See the debate in France concerning Corsica.

16. The protection of identity turned quasi into a human right.

17. See Charles Taylor, "The Politics of Recognition," in Amy Gutmann (ed.), *Multiculturalism: Examining the Politics of Recognition D* (Princeton, 1994).

18. For such a case, see Switzerland and the argument in Nicole Töpperwien, *Nation-State and Normative Diversity* (Diss, Fribourg, 2001).

19. See Article 2 Purpose of the Swiss Constitution of 1999: "The Swiss Confederation . . . shall promote . . . the cultural diversity of the country."

Even though this article is formulated in a general way, Switzerland promotes only traditional diversity—that is, the different national languages, religions, and cantonal cultures—and is reluctant to accommodate new diversities—for instance, the Spanish-speaking community or the Muslim community.

20. See Töpperwien, *Nation-State and Normative Diversity*, 300–305.

21. Such an approach can be coercive for the individual who is defined to belong but does not want to belong or vice versa.

22. This was the approach for the creation of the Canton of Jura. The Jurassian people wanted to have their own canton and therewith as well participation rights at the federal level in Switzerland. The borders of the canton were not drafted so as to include the Jurassian community, but the borders were defined

in a cascade of popular votes. The procedure was established in the constitution of the Canton of Bern to which the Jura region belonged. This amendment to the constitution and therefore as well implicitly the secession in accordance with this procedure was accepted in a popular vote in the Canton of Bern. Afterwards first the districts belonging to the Jura could vote, then each district separately, and finally each municipality at the border line. Eligible to vote was the concerned Swiss population and not only the people of Jurassian descent. According to this procedure, the border could be defined as closely to the wishes of the concerned population as possible. Finally the Federal Constitution was amended in order to include the new canton. This amendment needed a majority vote of the Swiss population and a majority of the populations of the cantons.

23. For the legitimacy of compromises in Switzerland, see Lidija Basta Fleiner, "Minority and Legitimacy of a Federal State: An Outsider Perception of the Swiss Model," in Lidija R. Basta Fleiner and Thomas Fleiner (eds.), *Federalism and Multiethnic States: The Case of Switzerland,* PIFF 16, 2nd ed. (Fribourg, 2000): 76–77.

24. For instance in Switzerland different groups are represented in the second chamber of the federal parliament through the equal representation of the cantons in the Council of States. Different groups are represented in the federal executive that is composed of seven members who are "head of state" and directorate of the ministries. In this federal council, the different regions of Switzerland are represented as well as the different parties, religious and linguistic groups. The composition of the Federal Court also reflects the diverse population. For further examples, see Thomas Stauffer and Nicole Töpperwien, "Balancing Self-Rule and Shared Rule," in Lidija R. Basta Fleiner and Thomas Fleiner (eds.), *Federalism and Multiethnic States: The Case of Switzerland,* PIFF Etudes et colloques 16, 2nd ed. (Fribourg, 2000): 56–59.

25. For instance, culture, education, and policing.

26. For instance, the Constitution of the Canton of Bern is according a special representation to the French speaking population of the Bernese Jura in order to maintain the loyalty of this group and to prevent their joining the Canton of Jura.

27. The most prominent example in this respect is probably the influence of the Province of Kosovo on national decisions through its special status at the subnational level.

28. This is normally the case in confederations, but it was the case as well in the Federal Republic of Yugoslavia under the 1974 Constitution.

29. This is the case in federal countries.

30. For instance, in New Zealand the Maori can decide whether to vote in a special extraterritorial constituency only for Maoris or in the ordinary territorial ones. Through the special constituency, they have a quasi-automatic representation in parliament.

31. See the Constitution of the Canton of Bern.

32. See for instance the consultation procedure in Switzerland, in which drafts of legislation are presented to different interest groups in order to find a compromise already at that stage.

33. Belgium not only relies on representation but also introduced additionally alarm-bell procedures to protect the interests of the different linguistic groups. Three quarters of the members of one linguistic group in parliament can sign a reasoned motion that declares the provisions of a draft bill or of a motion as destructive for the relations between the linguistic communities. In such a case, the parliamentary procedures are suspended and the motion is referred to the Council of Ministers. The Council gives recommendations to the implicated House of Parliament.

34. For instance, in Tanzania either the president or the vice president must be from Zanzibar. The president can hold office for only two terms, and afterwards the next president must be from the other community so that there is a rotation between Tanzanian mainland and Zanzibari presidents. In Switzerland, a seven member council is "head of state."

35. For instance, different groups can be given the right to nominate one or more judges.

36. See, for instance, the Constitution of the Canton of Fribourg of 1857 providing that the majority of the judges shall have knowledge of both German and French: Art. 61 Die Mehrheit der Mitglieder sowohl als der Ersatzmänner des Kantonsgerichtes soll der französischen und der deutschen Sprache mächtig sein.

37. For instance, the bilingual canton of Valais in Switzerland is represented by a German- and by a French-speaking representative in the second chamber of federal parliament. The Scotland Act foresees in Paragraph 7 (2) (b) Part I of Schedule 5 that Scottish ministers can assist their British counterparts in EC/EU relations.

II

Mature Federal Systems

4

Austrian Federalism and the Protection of Minorities

Anna Gamper

Ethnic minorities in Austria have been granted specific legal protection since the second half of the nineteenth century and have continued to be a political and legal issue after the end of the multination monarchy and both World Wars. The earliest of all relevant[1] constitutional provisions in the field of minority protection was Article 19 of the State Basic Law on the General Rights of Citizens.[2] Whereas this law, as a whole and in general, is in force today— being even part of Austrian federal constitutional law[3]—the question whether Article 19 became invalid when the State Treaty of St. Germain-en-Laye of 1919[4] and Art 8 B-VG[5] came into force has not been answered unanimously by the Austrian ruling doctrine and jurisdiction of the Constitutional Court.[6]

In addition to these provisions, Article 7 of the State Treaty of Vienna of 1955[7] grants specific minority rights to those Austrian nationals who belong to the Slovenian and Croatian minorities in the Länder Carinthia, Burgenland, and Styria. Finally, two Federal Acts determine the establishment of specific schools for children belonging to the minorities in Carinthia and Burgenland.[8] Although these Acts were enacted as ordinary federal laws, part of their individual provisions have been specifically given federal constitutional rank.

Ethnic minorities—or ethnic groups, as the Austrian terminology prefers them to be called— are thus protected by a variety of rather heterogeneous federal constitutional provisions. Not only have they evolved from a very different (historic, national/international) background, but they also protect (partly) different sets of minority aspects.

At the level of (ordinary) federal law, ethnic groups are protected by the Ethnic Groups Act.[9] According to section 1, paragraph 2 of this Act, ethnic groups are groups of Austrian citizens with their own non-German mother tongue and their own traditions populating part of the federal territory. The Ethnic Groups Act empowers the Federal Government to establish advisory councils[10] for each ethnic group by regulation and to determine in the same regulation which ethnic groups are to be officially treated as such. Accordingly, advisory councils have been established for the Croatian, Slovenian, Hungarian, Czech, Slovakian, and Roma minorities.[11] These six ethnic groups are therefore officially recognized as ethnic minorities in Austria. The criterion that determines affiliation to one of these groups—and that also is the key element of their specific protection—is language.[12] According to the nationwide census of 2001, the Slovenian minority consisted of 17,953 Austrian nationals; the Burgenland Croatian minority of 19,374 nationals; the Hungarian minority of 25,884 nationals; the Roma minority of 4,348 nationals; the Czech minority of 11,035 nationals; and the Slovakian minority of 3,343 nationals.[13] They traditionally live in the Länder Burgenland (Burgenland Croatians, Hungarians, Roma), Carinthia (Carinthian Slovenes), Lower Austria (Slovaks), Styria (Hungarians, Slovaks, Styrian Slovenes), Upper Austria (Slovaks), and Vienna (Czechs, Hungarians, Roma, and Slovaks).[14] Some of these Länder fall under particular legal obligations to protect minorities, which arise from Article 7 of the State Treaty of Vienna and the Carinthia and Burgenland Minority Schools Acts. However, minority protection in general is not restricted to specific Länder, as, for instance, Article 8 paragraph 2 B-VG demonstrates.

This chapter focuses not on the current status of minority protection at the federal level,[15] but instead on the legal possibilities that are left to the constituent states in order to protect these ethnic groups. To provide the necessary context, we begin with a short outline of the Austrian federal system.

THE AUSTRIAN FEDERAL SYSTEM—AN OVERVIEW

General Features

The Republic of Austria, together with Germany and Switzerland, belongs to the classic European federal systems.[16] Although it is difficult to define the key elements of a classic federal system—because legal comparison shows an impressive variety of deviations from any ideal standard—there is some common understanding as to the minimum institutional requirements of all federal systems,[17] and, at the first glance at least, the Austrian federal system meets all these demands:

- Both legislative and administrative competences are distributed between the federation and the Länder.[18]
- The Länder participate in the legislative process at federal level, as the Länder parliaments elect the members of the Federal Assembly ("Bundesrat"), which is the second legislative chamber at the federal level.[19]
- Under the Fiscal Constitutional Act[20] and the Fiscal Adjustment Act,[21] the Länder have some budgetary powers.
- The State Governors and Independent Administrative Tribunals—instead of federal administrative agencies—are mainly responsible for carrying out federal administration on the federation's behalf ("indirect federal administration").[22]
- There exist a number of formal and informal instruments of cooperative federalism as well as an umpire (Constitutional Court) that solves conflicts between the federation and the Länder.

This is only one side of Austrian federalism, however. The other is that the major part of competences—and the more important—belongs to the federation[23] and that the Federal Assembly has never yet vetoed a bill on account of its centralizing tendency at the expense of the Länder.[24] Furthermore, the federation is clearly predominant with regard to the levying of taxes and the spending of revenues. The system of "indirect federal administration," though it entitles the Länder to carry out a wide range of federal administrative matters, at the same time subjects them to the instructions and supervision of a Federal Minister or the Federal Government as a whole.[25] Given these characteristics, one must classify Austrian federalism as one of the most centralized systems of its kind.[26]

Both the distribution of competences and another key element of Austrian federalism—the so-called "relative" constitutional autonomy of the Länder—are briefly outlined in the following section, as they directly concern the question of minority protection at the Länder level.

The Distribution of Competences

The distribution of competences between the federation and the Länder is mainly embodied in Articles 10–15 of the Austrian Constitution (B-VG). In addition to this general distribution of competences, specific federal constitutional law[27] applies as well, but it is of less importance. Competences are divided according to the following types:

- Exclusive federal competences (federation responsible for legislation and execution of the same matter): Article 10 B-VG
- Exclusive state competences (states responsible for legislation and execution of the same matter): Article 15 B-VG (residuary Länder competence) and where stated by specific federal constitutional law
- Mixed competences
- Federation responsible for full legislation, states responsible for the execution of a matter (Article 11 B-VG)
- Federation responsible for framework legislation, states responsible for implementing legislation and execution (Article 12 B-VG)

If a competence is not explicitly enlisted as a federal competence (the so-called principle of enumeration), a matter falls into the Länder residuary competence (Article 15 B-VG). A residuary competence of the constituent states is a common feature to most federal constitutions[28] and is believed to favor the states, but its effect depends on which and how many competences have been enlisted as federal competences. In the case of Austria, only few and less significant powers are left to the Länder in this way.[29] Neither are the Länder's explicit competences (Articles 11 and 12 B-VG) of a more fundamental nature.

To a certain extent, the Länder are compensated for this lack of competences, as they are responsible for carrying out a major part of federal administrative tasks. Basically, the State Governors have been largely responsible for the administration of federal administrative tasks, but have now been replaced by the Länder Independent Administrative Tribunals in a wide range of matters.[30]

The Constitutional Court has developed certain interpretation rules, according to which competence disputes have to be resolved: The so-called "petrification theory" will be applied if the Court construes federal competences, which have to be enumerated explicitly.[31] According to this theory, a federal subject-matter is to be understood as it was understood when the subject-matter was enacted (objective historic construction). In order to understand exactly what a subject-matter historically stood for, one must consult the respective (ordinary) law ("petrification material") that was in force at that time ("moment of petrification").[32] In other words, the meaning of the subject matter must not extend the limits set by the pertinent substantive law of that time, comprising only "petrified contents." A wider meaning will only be admitted in exceptional cases, namely if there is a close relationship between the "petrified contents" of a federal competence and new matters (arising from developments after the "moment of petrification"—e.g., technological matters), which, being not covered by a federal competence, would otherwise fall into the residuary competence of the Länder.

According to the "rule of different aspects," the Court recognizes that a matter can fall into several competences and thus be regulated by the federation and the Länder under different aspects. In this case, both units have to take consideration of each other's interests and must seek not to contravene the legislation of the other when enacting their own legislation ("principle of consideration").

If, after all these interpretation rules have been applied, a doubt remains as to which competence a matter falls into, the "federalistic interpretation rule" will finally be applied—that is, the matter will fall into the Länder competence.

Constitutional Autonomy

The Principle of Homogeneity as a Framework for Subnational Constitutions. Every federal system seeks to combine unity and diversity.[33] In a constitutional context, this key definition of what federalism aims at particularly concerns the distribution of competences. In order to maintain a balance between these two polar positions and to prevent conflicts between the federation and the constituent states that could lead to the dissolution of the federal system, a minimum standard of homogeneity[34] between the federation and the states as well as between the constituent states themselves is required.

Federal constitutions usually provide a large number of legal instruments in order to secure homogeneity among the various units.[35] These include the determination of explicit constitutional rules that must neither be violated by the constitutions nor by the ordinary legislation or administration of the constituent states. The federal constitution may also determine that certain policies or law-making of the constituent units need the consent of the federation or an agreement between the units. It can bind state legislation to standards laid down by ordinary federal legislation, or it can itself provide explicit or implicit standards that bind both federal and state legislation. Typically, compliance with these concrete legal standards of homogeneity is secured by procedural instruments provided by the federal constitution, including arbitration procedures, veto rights, and instruments of cooperative federalism.[36]

The "Relative" Constitutional Autonomy of the Austrian Länder. The B-VG includes a specific provision that determines the relationship between federal constitutional law and Länder constitutional law: Article 99 B-VG states that the Land constitution, which is to be enacted by a Land constitutional act, may be amended by a Land constitutional act in as far as this does not affect the federal constitution. This rather cryptic formulation essentially means that Länder constitutional law must not violate federal constitutional law. In the hierarchy of Austrian law, therefore, Länder constitutional law is at the top of all kinds of Länder law, it is equal to ordinary federal law, but it is below federal constitutional law.

According to the older jurisprudence of the Constitutional Court, this provision left the Länder nothing but the right to enact "implementation laws" in conformity with the standards laid down in the federal constitution.[37] Influenced by doctrine,[38] however, the Court has meanwhile changed its view and now recognizes that the Länder are endowed with what is called "relative constitutional autonomy." Relative constitutional autonomy means that the Länder constitutions may contain provisions of all possible kinds as long as they do not violate federal constitutional law.

Of course, the crucial point in this context is When does a Land constitution violate federal constitutional law? If the Land constitution (or a provision of it) is in breach of a federal constitutional provision that explicitly concerns the states, the answer to this question will be relatively easy. However, if there is no explicit federal constitutional provision concerning the Länder, but a federal constitutional provision that explicitly concerns the federation or just embodies a general principle without differentiating between the federation and the Länder, it will be much more difficult.[39] It needs a very thorough analysis to grasp whether a rule intends to concern the federation only or whether it has to be applied by the Länder as well.

In cases of doubt—that is, when a rule cannot be construed as clearly as to know whether it concerns the Länder as well—the principle of federalism will have to be heeded. This principle is one of the fundamental principles of the Austrian constitution, which is programmatically indicated by Article 2 B-VG and given more substance by many other federal constitutional provisions. All fundamental principles are protected from amendment to a much higher degree than the other layers of Austrian law, including ordinary federal constitutional law.[40]

In accordance with this hierarchic structure, the Constitutional Court has permanently held that, in case of doubt, law—including (ordinary) federal constitutional law—had to be construed in conformity with the fundamental principles of the federal constitution.

As mentioned earlier, the constitutional autonomy of the Länder itself belongs to the key elements of the principle of federalism. It must be construed in the sense given by Article 2 B-VG, which calls the Länder "autonomous," and in the sense of Article 15, paragraph 2 B-VG, which indicates the historic autonomy of the Länder. Looking at the historic process leading to the enactment of the B-VG, one recognizes that some Länder constitutions had even been enacted before that date.[41] In the light of the principle of federalism,[42] therefore, constitutional autonomy must be construed in a way that reflects the historic autonomy of the Länder and thus leaves them as much constitutional space as possible.

MINORITY PROTECTION AS AN ISSUE OF THE LÄNDER CONSTITUTIONS

In 1958 the Constitutional Court held that national minority matters, including the affiliation to a national minority, were a federal competence.[43] It argued that the subject matter "federal constitution"[44] comprised all matters that had been understood to belong to the "federal constitution" when the distribution of competences had been enacted and that the law on national minorities had belonged to it.[45] Despite the general responsibility of the Länder to implement international law if it falls into their competence,[46] the international obligations regarding minority protection demanded to be implemented through a uniform federal law according to the Court's opinion.

However, Article 7 of the State Treaty of Vienna itself explicitly mentions the Slovenian and Croatian minorities "in the Länder Carinthia, Burgenland and Styria." The Court's tautological argument that "no different law (including measures taken in conformity with the Treaty obligations) can be in force in these three Länder" is not highly persuasive, as it just depends on the distribution of competences whether the Länder can enact minority protection law or not. Even assuming that a "petrified" understanding of the subject matter "federal constitution" comprises the historic minority protection provisions, the question may be raised whether this as well includes the protection provisions imposed on Austria by the State Treaty of Vienna, which, indeed, was enacted decades after the relevant "moment of petrification." As Article 7 of this Treaty specifically deals with the Slovenian and Croatian minorities in these three particular Länder, its nature seems to be different from the prevailing minority protection provisions, which do not refer to specific minorities or specific Länder. It could be argued, at least, that the specific reference to these Länder required a different treatment, rooted in the affiliation to a Land, and not a uniform federal solution, and that the specific protection of specific Land minorities did not belong to the federal competence, such as minority protection in general.[47] In fact, it is almost absurd that two nonidentical Minority School Acts—regarding Burgenland and Carinthia—have been passed by the federation instead of the concerned Länder themselves. Despite the existing federal competence "federal constitution," these School Acts include both federal constitutional provisions that specifically distribute minority school competences between the federation and the respective Land, and (ordinary) federal provisions enacted in exercise of this competence. This example shows that the federal competence "federal constitution" was obviously not seen as a sufficient basis for any federal laws related to minority protection. Nevertheless, it is easy to discern that federal constitutional law itself not only distinguishes between the Länder with different ethnic groups and those without, but also between the Länder that are populated by different ethnic groups, and even vests them with some small competences of their own.

The existence of "autochthonous" minorities—this term comprises those minorities that have traditionally and for a long time been settling in certain areas of the Austrian Länder—has also been recognized by the Constitutional Court.[48] Regarding Carinthia, the Court has even differentiated between the original South-Carinthian settling area of the autochthonous Slovene minority and the rest of the Land. Since the amendment of its Article 8,[49] even the B-VG uses the term "autochthonous" in conjunction with the term "ethnic groups."

Although the fact that the territorial roots of the ethnic groups are thus recognized by law does not constitute an overarching territoriality principle that would allow a general shift of minority protection competences from the federation to the Länder, it seems worth discussing whether and how the Länder could adopt minority protection law in addition to what is enacted at the federal level.

The "Principle of Mutual Consideration"

According to the "principle of consideration," which has been developed by the jurisdiction of the Constitutional Court, the federation and the Länder must heed each other's interests and not excessively neglect the legislation enacted by the other when enacting their own legislation. However, this is only one side of the coin, as the principle does not only impose obligations on the two entities, but also authorizes them to adopt law that would not primarily fall into their own competence. The federation and the Länder are thus empowered to consider each other's legal aims within their own legislation, even though they do not possess the original competence. Of course, two requirements will have to be fulfilled in order to make such consideration compatible with the distribution of competences. First, making use of the other's competence must not be the main purpose of the one's legislation, which primarily has to be enacted in exercise of its own competence. Second, it must be auxiliary to the other's legislation—that is, facilitate its purposes and not contradict or undermine it.

The principle of consideration could thus serve as a possible source of legitimacy if the Länder wanted to enact minority protection law on a broader basis. Within the existing system of competences, several Länder competences encompass possibilities of minority protection. For instance, it is up to Land legislation to regulate events,[50] to foster folklore,[51] or to regulate kindergartens and day nurseries.[52] On the basis of all these competences, the Länder could safeguard the minorities' position by specific provisions. This would also satisfy the demands of Article 8 B-VG, which explicitly mentions the Länder among those entities that are obliged to heed, safeguard, and foster the languages and cultures of the autochthonous ethnic groups.

A practical example of how the Länder could consider minority protection within their own ambit is section 29 of the Salzburg Youth Act,[53] which, notwithstanding the fact that, traditionally, the Land Salzburg is not populated by one of the ethnic groups that are protected by the Ethnic Groups Act, provides that theater performances and films must not be seen by children or youth if they involve the debasement of one of the ethnic groups.

Summing up, the Länder will be able to adopt minority protection law if it is in conformity with Article 8 B-VG and other relevant federal constitutional provisions, if it is further in conformity with the (ordinary) federal law that was enacted on the basis of the federation's general minority protection competence and if it finally is in conformity with the "principle of consideration." This means that the Länder could protect minorities when making use of their own competences, but only in the form of auxiliary law and only with the intention to serve the minority protection law passed by the federation. However, it is not possible for the Länder (i.e., both constitutional and ordinary Land law) to protect minorities as a main purpose of their own law nor to arrogate the federation's competences in order to do so nor to discriminate minorities in a negative sense, as this would be in breach of federal constitutional law.

Minority Protection as a Matter of "Non-governmental Administration"

Notwithstanding the distribution of competences, both the federation and the Länder are free to use their private law-capacities (Article 17 B-VG). In other words, the distribution of competences only relates to legal acts of public authority, but does not have any impact on private (law) dealings of the federation or the Länder. For instance, they can enter into private contracts, operate enterprises, or grant subsidies. This ambit of "non-governmental administration" of the federation and the Länder confronts their respective ambits of "governmental administration."

In principle, both the federation and the Länder are bound to observe fundamental rights when acting under private law. However, according to the ruling doctrine, neither the federation nor the Länder have to observe the principle of legality[54] when acting under private law. This means that the administrative organs of the federation or the Länder do not need to be authorized by a specific law when acting within the ambit of "non-governmental administration." Even though they do not need a law, however, a law may determine their private law dealings, if the federal or a Land parliament chooses to do so. If, in such a case, a law binds the administrative organs, this will not automatically grant any subjective rights to individuals.

It follows that, within the framework of "non-governmental administration," the Länder are free to exercise influence on minority issues, in particular by granting subsidies to relevant institutions or projects. In practice, several have made use of this possibility. For instance, according to section 1, paragraph 3 of the Carinthian Culture Promotion Act 2001,[55] cultural promotion is explicitly granted in order to preserve cultural pluralism in Carinthia, "which is based on a variety of ethnic influences, including the influence of the Carinthian Slovenes." Similarly, section 2, paragraph 3 of the Burgenland Youth Promotion Act[56] includes promotion for youth activities that help to preserve and strengthen the culture and language of the Burgenland ethnic groups. On a private law basis, Carinthia has also undertaken to finance the Carinthian Institute for Ethnic Minorities (CIFEM) at least for a couple of years, which is a practical example of how a Länd can allocate funds for minority-related issues.[57]

The Länder Constitutions as Minority Protection Guarantees

As has been shown, the Federal Constitution does not absolutely prevent the Länder from enacting provisions related to minority issues, albeit the Constitutional Court supposes the latter to fall into the federation's competence. They can either adopt law that takes account of these issues with the intention to make the relevant federal legislation more effective, if on an auxiliary basis. Or they can promote ethnic groups on a private law basis, which particularly, if not exclusively, includes financial subsidies.

The federal constitutional limits by which the Länder constitutions are restricted will neither prevent the Länder from adopting minority-related law, if it is in conformity with the Federal Constitution and if it simply intends to strengthen the relevant (ordinary) federal law. Thus, the Länder could either enact provisions that, at least as a side effect, seek to make existing federal minority provisions more effective or determine Länder "non-governmental administration," where they may take account of minority issues without competential restrictions. Additionally, Article 8 B-VG enshrines an explicit rule to respect, safeguard, and foster ethnic groups. Although this provision grants rights neither to the ethnic groups as a whole nor to their individual members, it obliges the federation, the Länder, and municipalities to protect minorities when enacting or executing law.

Thus, the Länder constitutions almost seem to be predestined to take account of ethnic groups, at least if a Land is populated by one of them. In a strict legal sense, however, a Land constitutional law would not be necessary, as, in principle, the legal difference between constitutional law and ordinary law has only formal character—that is, Länder constitutional law requires a qualified quorum and support[58] as well as the explicit name "constitutional act."[59] Although, the federal constitution provides a minimum of legal rules that need to be passed by a Land constitutional act, there is no general rule that would exhaustively determine the exact legal contents of such an act or that would demand to regulate minority issues on a constitutional basis.

Thus, the Länder have enacted minority-related law in the form of ordinary Land acts rather than in the form of Land constitutional law. There are only few examples where a Land constitution contains provisions related to minority issues: Article 5 of the Styrian Constitution, Article 6 of the Lower Austrian Constitution, and Article 6 of the Burgenland Constitution provide that the language of the respective Land is German, "notwithstanding the minority rights which are granted by federal law." However, these provisions do nothing but reflect Article 8, paragraph 1 B-VG with regard to the respective Land.

However, the absence of more specific minority provisions within the Länder constitutions does not necessarily imply that they could not contain provisions on a more minorities-oriented basis.[60] Relying on the "principle of consideration," such Land constitutional provisions would be bound to observe the relevant federal legislation and would thus be unconstitutional if they undermined the respective interests and intentions of the federal parliament. Any provision, however, that would help to make the respective federal legislation more effective or even to improve it and thus not violate the distribution of competences (which, being a violation of the federal constitution, would also violate the principle of homogeneity as formulated by Article 99 B-VG) could be adopted by the *Land* constitutions. The substantive standards of this kind of legislation would on the one hand be determined by the relevant (ordinary) federal law, and, on the other hand, by Article 8, paragraph 2 B-VG. The very existence of this latter provision indicates that the federal constitution—without, however, amending the distribution of competences—itself supposes the Länder as well to be responsible to respect, preserve, and promote the ethnic groups, their languages, and their cultures. Notwithstanding international obligations, both constitutional sources—the principle of consideration and Article 8, paragraph 2 B-VG—prevent the Länder from adopting law that would contravene the relevant federal law or contravene the obligation to respect, preserve, and promote ethnic groups. Accordingly, if they adopted such law it would be unconstitutional and struck down by the Constitutional Court.

CONCLUDING REMARKS

It is thus due to a rather complicated mechanism that the Länder may adopt constitutional legislation in order to protect their ethnic groups. Article 99 B-VG creates the general framework within which Länder constitutional law may be enacted. Accordingly, a Land constitution must not violate federal constitutional law. In this context, the standards are set by Article 8, paragraph 2 B-VG on the one hand and the distribution of competences on the other hand. Even assuming that minority protection in general is a federal competence, as the Constitutional Court has held it to be, this does not prevent the Länder from taking account of minority protection when enacting their own law—either in their constitutions or in (ordinary) Land law. However, Länder minority legislation must neither contradict the relevant federal law nor the obligations imposed by Article 8, paragraph 2 B-VG. Neither is it their primary competence to enact minority-related legislation, but it may be one of their goals to assist the federation in granting a highly developed system of minority protection. Further, the Länder have the power to choose whether to enact minority law relating to their "governmental administration" or to their "non-governmental administration." In the latter case, such laws would appear to be self-binding rules to be applied to Land private law dealings.

As of 2004, the Länder have enacted more ordinary law than constitutional law in order to protect minorities. This reveals a final consideration—namely that it is a political question for the Länder whether they will vest their existing minority law with the rank of Land constitutional law or make altogether more use of their legal possibilities. At present, it is not easy to discern whether all of them would be willing to do so. In this context, one particularly remembers the conflict that arose between the Constitutional Court and the right-wing Governor of Carinthia in 2001, when the Constitutional Court annulled a provision of the Ethnic Groups Act that had provided that a municipality's name had to be written down in a minority language if at least 25 percent of local citizens belonged to this minority.[61] According to the Court's opinion, the percentage number was too high to meet the obligations imposed on Austria by the State Treaty of Vienna. The Land Governor, however, felt strongly disinclined to grant the Carinthian Slovenes any stronger rights. Apart from this recent case, however, minority issues form no typical source of conflicts between the levels of government or within the population. Moreover, some Länder have recently shown a tendency to adopt so-called "state aim" provisions (e.g., regarding environmental protection or social issues) or to enlarge the existing catalogues of "state aim" provisions within their constitutions. Such "state aim" provisions, though not granting any subjective rights to individuals, have to be legally taken account of by all state organs and set standards for the interpretation of Land law. They may be also understood as tokens of Land self-consciousness and identity. Under these auspices, it would not be improbable if minority protection were to be recognized also as a Land "state aim" in the future.

NOTES

1. According to Article 7 of the *Bundes-Verfassungsgesetz* (B-VG, which is the main, but not sole document of Austrian federal constitutional law) and Article 2 of the State Basic Law on the General Rights of Citizens, all Austrian citizens, including those belonging to non–German-speaking ethnic groups, are granted equality and the equal enjoyment of fundamental rights (cf. also Article 14 of the ECHR). In the following, only those provisions are mentioned that are specific minority protection safeguards (e.g., the right to use the ethnic language in private, in public life and regarding ethnic names; cf. Kolonovits, *Sprachenrecht in Österreich* [1999]) or the right to education [the ethnic language as an individually taught subject or general education in the ethnic language]; cf. idem, *Minderheitenschulrecht im Burgenland* [1995]).

2. Article 19 of the *Staatsgrundgesetz über die allgemeinen Rechte der Staatsbürger* (RGBl 1867/142 as amended by BGBl 1988/684) provides:

> All ethnic entities enjoy equal rights, and each ethnic entity has an inviolable right to the preservation and fostering of its nationality and language.

> The equal status of all customary languages in schools, administration and public life is recognized by the State. In the Länder populated by more than one ethnic entity, public places of learning should be so organized that, without making the learning of a second national language compulsory, each member of an ethnic entity should have adequate opportunity to receive education in his/her own language.

The original German text uses the term "Volksstamm," an archaic word that literally means "ethnic tribe." The official English translation of the Austrian Federal Chancellery, however, uses the term "ethnic entity." Cf. also Pernthaler, *Land, Volk und Heimat als Kategorien des österreichischen Verfassungsrechts* (1987) 31 et seq. and Pernthaler/Ebensperger, "Der rechtliche Status und die räumliche Verteilung von Minderheiten in den österreichischen Gemeinden im Geltungsbereich der Alpenkonvention," *Europa Ethnica* 3–4 (2000), 117 et seq. (122).

3. Cf. Article 149 B-VG.

4. Article 62–66 of this Treaty (cf. StGBl 1920/303) contain a number of minority protection provisions, which were given constitutional rank (cf. Article 149 B-VG). By contrast, both the European Charter for Regional or Minority Languages (BGBl III 2001/216) and the Framework Convention for the Protection of National Minorities (BGBl III 1998/120) have been ratified, but not given constitutional rank.

5. Article 8 para. 1 B-VG reads:

> Notwithstanding the rights which were given to language minorities by federal law, the German language is the official language of the Republic."

Article 8 para 2 B-VG, which was inserted by BGBl I 2000/68, reads:

> The Republic (federation, Länder and municipalities) is committed to its diversity of language and culture which has evolved in the course of time and finds its expression in the autochthonous ethnic groups. Language and culture, continued existence and protection of these ethnic groups is to be respected, safeguarded and promoted.

6. Cf. Pernthaler, *Land* 31 et seq.; Pernthaler/Ebensperger, *Europa Ethnica* 3–4 (2000), 122; Öhlinger, Der Verfassungsschutz ethnischer Gruppen in Österreich, in FS Koja (1998) 371 et seq. (373 et seq.). Cf. VfSlg 2459/1952; 4221/1962; 9224/1981.

7. BGBl 1955/152 (paras. 2, 3 and 4 of Article 7 have constitutional rank).

8. Strangely enough, these Acts, though being part of federal constitutional law, are limited to the territories of two of the nine Austrian Länder (Burgenland, Carinthia, Lower Austria, Salzburg, Styria, Tyrol, Lower Austria, Vienna, Vorarlberg), as these are the Länder with major presence of ethnic groups.

9. *Volksgruppengesetz* (BGBl 1976/396 as amended by BGBl I 2002/35).

10. Cf. Rautz, "Die Institution der Volksgruppenbeiräte und mögliche Formen der politischen Vertretung in Österreich," *Europa Ethnica* 3–4 (2000), 136 et seq.

11. BGBl 1977/38 as amended by 1993/895.

12. Article 7 of the State Treaty of Vienna regards language as the decisive factor of minority status and combines it with settlement in particular Länder. Article 8 para. 1 B-VG mentions the rights granted to "language minorities," and Article 8 para. 2 B-VG refers to the criteria of "language and culture."

13. Note that the census inquired for the colloquial language and not directly for the affiliation to one of the ethnic groups. The statistical problems in conjunc-

tion with the Austrian ethnic groups are referred to by Hilpold, *Modernes Minderheitenrecht* (2001) 51 et seq.

14. See Pan/Pfeil, *Minderheitenrechte in Europa* (2002) 314 et seq. (with further references). The remaining Länder (Salzburg, Tyrol, and Vorarlberg) traditionally are not populated by these ethnic groups.

15. For a general view, see the more recent works of Marauhn, "Die rechtliche Stellung der Minderheiten in Österreich," in Frowein et al. (eds.), *Das Minderheitenrecht europäischer Staaten,* Teil 1 (1993) 225; Sturm, "Der Minderheiten- und Volksgruppenschutz," in Machacek et al (eds.), *Grund- und Menschenrechte in Österreich,* Band II (1992) 77; Öhlinger, *Verfassungsschutz* 371 et seq.; Kolonovits, *Sprachenrecht*; Hilpold, *Minderheitenrecht* 240 et seq.; Pan/Pfeil, *Minderheitenrechte* 314 et seq.

16. This rigid definition, however, has undergone some modification. Since 1993 Belgium has adopted a federal system as well and been classified as one of the three EU federal states. Moreover, strongly decentralized states, such as Spain and, more recently, Italy and the United Kingdom, nearly approach the—very vague and controversial—standard of what is called a federal system.

17. Considering the plethora of literature on federalism, spread not only all over the world but also over the centuries and academic fields, it is not possible to give a complete list of concepts of federal systems. For instance, Wheare, *Federal Government* (1947) 1 or, more recently, Watts, *Comparing Federal Systems in the 1990s* (1996) 6 et seq. have gained international reputation. Even the Austrian doctrine is split: Cf. the complex theory of Ermacora, Pernthaler, Weber and Öhlinger (cf. e.g., Ermacora, *Österreichischer Föderalismus. Vom patrimonialen zum kooperativen Bundesstaat* [1976]; Pernthaler, "Der österreichische Bundesstaat im Spannungsfeld von Föderalismus und formalem Rechtspositivismus," *ÖZÖR* 19 [1969], 361 et seq.; Öhlinger, *Der Bundesstaat zwischen Reiner Rechtslehre und Verfassungsrealität* [1976] and Weber, *Kriterien* 78 et seq.), further Kelsen's three-circle theory (cf. Kelsen, *Allgemeine Staatslehre* [1925] 198 et seq. and idem, "Die Bundesexekution," in *Festgabe Fleiner* [1927] 127 [130 et seq.]) and the related decentralization theory (cf. again Kelsen, *Österreichisches Staatsrecht* [1923] 165; Walter, *Österreichisches Bundesverfassungsrecht* [1972] 108 et seq.; idem/Mayer, *Grundriß des österreichischen Bundesverfassungsrechts* [2000] 79 et seq.; Koja, *Bundesstaat* 61 et seq.; idem, *Allgemeine Staatslehre* [1993] 346 et seq.; Thienel, "Ein 'komplexer' oder normativer Bundesstaatsbegriff?," *AJPIL* 42 [1991], 215 et seq. and idem, "Der Bundesstaatsbegriff der Reinen Rechtslehre," in Walter [ed.], *Schwerpunkte der Reinen Rechtslehre* [1992] 123 et seq.).

18. Cf. particularly Article 10–15 B-VG (Bundes-Verfassungsgesetz, Austrian Federal Constitutional Act); see, for example, Pernthaler, *Kompetenzverteilung in der Krise* (1989); Schäffer, "Die Kompetenzverteilung im Bundesstaat," in Herbert Schambeck (ed.), *Bundesstaat und Bundesrat in Österreich* (1997) 65 et seq.

19. Cf. particularly Article 34–44 B-VG; see, for example, Walter, "Der Bundesrat," in Hellbling et al. (eds.), *Föderative Ordnung I: Bundesstaat auf der Waage* (1969) 199 et seq.; Koja, "Die Vertretung der Länderinteressen im Bund," in Hellbling et al. (eds.), *Föderative Ordnung I: Bundesstaat auf der Waage* (1969) 9 et seq.; Schambeck, "Der Bundesrat der Republik Österreich," *JÖR* 1977, 215 et seq.; Kathrein, *Der Bundesrat in der Ersten Republik* (1983); Kathrein, "Der Bundesrat," in Schambeck (ed.), *Österreichs Parlamentarismus* (1986) 337 et seq.; Walter, "Der Bundesrat zwischen Bewährung und Neugestaltung," in Schäffer/Stolzlechner (eds.), *Reformbestrebungen im österreichischen Bundesstaatssystem* (1993) 41 et seq.; Strutzenberger/Pointner, "Zur Reformdiskussion des Bundesrates," in Österreichische Parlamentarische Gesellschaft (ed.), *75 Jahre Bundesverfassung*

(1995) 685 et seq.; Schambeck, "Föderalismus und Parlamentarismus in Österreich," in Merten (ed.), *Die Stellung der Landesparlamente aus deutscher, österreichischer und spanischer Sicht* (1997) 15 et seq.; Palermo, *Germania ed Austria: Modelli federali e bicamerali a confronto: Due ordinamenti in evoluzione tra cooperazione, integrazione e ruolo delle seconde camere* (1997); Schambeck (ed.), *Bundesstaat und Bundesrat in Österreich* (1997).

20. *Finanz-Verfassungsgesetz 1948* (BGBl 1948/45 idF BGBl I 1999/194). See Ruppe, *Finanzverfassung im Bundesstaat* (1977); Pernthaler, *Österreichische Finanzverfassung* (1984); Schäffer, "Die österreichische Finanzverfassung," in *FS Weber* (1986) 87 et seq.; Pernthaler (ed.), *Reform der föderalistischen Finanzordnung* (1994); Ruppe, "F-VG," in Korinek/Holoubek (eds.), *Österreichisches Bundesverfassungsrecht. Textsammlung und Kommentar* (loose-leaf edition).

21. *Finanzausgleichsgesetz 2001* (BGBl I 2001/3 as amended by BGBl I 2002/115). See Schachner-Blazizek, *Finanzausgleich in Österreich* (1967); Pernthaler, *Finanzverfassung* 157 and 224; Hengstschläger, "Der Finanzausgleich im Bundesstaat," in Schambeck (ed.), *Bundesstaat und Bundesrat in Österreich* (1997) 181 et seq; Gamper, "Legistische Qualität und Verfassungskonformität des neuen Finanzausgleichs," *ÖJZ* 2001, 481 et seq.

22. Cf. 102–105 B-VG. See Weber, *Die mittelbare Bundesverwaltung* (1987).

23. For decades the Länder have thus claimed more competences, but only a few competences have been transferred to them so far (cf. the B-VG-Amendments in 1974, 1983, 1987, 1988, and 1992).

24. Under Article 44 para. 2 B-VG the Federal Assembly may veto a bill passed by the National Council if it restricts Länder competences. In practice, the Federal Assembly has never made use of this right for political reasons. In contrast to the right to veto (which cannot be overruled by the National Council), the right to objection (Article 42 B-VG) has been used, but has had little effect, because a mere objection can be overruled by the National Council.

25. See Pernhaler/Weber, *Theorie und Praxis der Bundesaufsicht in Österreich* (1979); Weber, *Die mittelbare Bundesverwaltung* (1987) 222 et seq.; Pernthaler, "Die Neuordnung der Bundesaufsicht im Zusammenhang mit der Abschaffung der mittelbaren Bundesverwaltung," in *FS Schambeck* (1994) 561 et seq.

26. Öhlinger, "Ein Bundesstaat auf dem Weg in die Europäische Gemeinschaft," in *FS Helmrich* (1994) 379 et seq. (381 et seq.) points out that Austria is a "borderline case of a federal system"; also on an international level, Austria is regarded as one of the most centralized federal systems (cf., e.g., Watts, *Systems* 25).

For decades the reform of the federal system has been strongly demanded, particularly in the context of the Austrian EU accession, which further diminished the ambit of the Länder parliaments. Up to now, however, the Länder have not been largely compensated for this loss of power, as had been agreed in 1994, although there have been several small steps of reform. The political suggestions for reform differ widely and include a further reduction of Länder competences or even their abolition.

27. Specific federal constitutional law primarily includes federal constitutional acts (apart from the B-VG) or single federal constitutional provisions (embedded in [ordinary] federal law). Within the general distribution system of the B-VG Article 14, 14a and 14b contain complex distribution systems of their own regarding schools and procurement policy. Article 13 B-VG only refers to the Financial Constitutional Act, which determines the distribution of fiscal competences.

28. In rare cases, the residuary competence belongs to the federation (cf. the drafted Scotland Act 1978 and Schedule 2 of the Government of Wales Act 1998;

Watts, "The Distribution of Powers, Responsibilities and Resources in Federations," in Griffiths [ed.], *Handbook of Federal Countries*, 2002 [2002], 448 et seq. [450] ascribes this phenomenon to those federal systems where the creation of a federation has involved a process of devolution from a formerly unitary state).

29. For example, (general) spatial planning, building law, nature protection, fisheries and hunting, agriculture, transfer of land. However, one must not overlook the dynamic aspect of a residuary Länder competence: Not only all recent but also future matters that may evolve will thus fall into the Länder competence, unless a federal constitutional provision claims them for the federation.

30. Cf. the *Verwaltungsreformgesetz 2001* (BGBl I 2002/65).

31. Otherwise, they would fall into the residuary competence of the Länder.

32. With regard to most subject matters, the "moment of petrification" is 1 October 1925, because this is the date of an important federal constitutional amendment, under which the general system of the allocation of powers came into force.

33. Cf. Watts, *Systems* 6 and 35 et seq.; idem, *Distribution* 448 et seq. Trager, "On Federalism," in Franck (ed.), *Why Federations Fail* (1968) formulated: "What we mean by federalism is not a fixed point on a map, but a tendency which is neither unitary nor separatist. In Aristotelean terms, it is the median between these two polar positions, and thus their true opposite."

Similarly, Pernthaler/Weber, "Landeskompetenzen und bundesstaatliches Homogenitätsprinzip im Dienstrecht," in *FS Schnorr* (1988) 557 et seq. (560 et seq.).

34. Cf., for example, Schäffer, "Dienstrechtliche Homogenität im Bundesstaat," in *FS Melichar* (1983) 371 et seq.; Novak, "Landesgesetzgebung und Verfassungsrecht—Stand, Tendenzen, Reformen," in Schambeck (ed.), *Föderalismus und Parlamentarismus in Österreich* (1992) 53 et seq. (54) and idem, "Article 99 B-VG," in Korinek/Holoubek (eds.), *Österreichisches Bundesverfassungsrecht. Textsammlung und Kommentar* (loose-leaf edition) 5.

35. Cf. Schäffer, *Homogenität* 372.

36. Cf. Schäffer, *Homogenität* 372.

37. These standards contain either explicit provisions concerning the states (e.g., Article 95 et seq., which determine the elections to the state parliaments, the legislative procedure at the state level, the status of members of state parliaments, etc.) or general provisions regarding both the federation and the states. Other provisions, such as Article 99 para 1 B-VG, do not themselves determine any material standards, but just the formal hierarchy between the different layers of law (Art. 99 para. 1 B-VG reads: "The *Land* Constitution to be enacted by a *Land* constitutional law can, inasmuch as the federal Constitution is not affected thereby, be amended by a *Land* constitutional law." This means that a Land constitution must not be in breach of federal constitutional law).

38. See Novak, "Bundes-Verfassungsgesetz und Landesverfassungsrecht," in Schambeck (ed.), *Das österreichische Bundes-Verfassungsgesetz und seine Entwicklung* (1980) 111 et seq.; Novak, "Die relative Verfassungsautonomie der Länder," in Rack (ed.), *Landesverfassungsreform* (1982) 35 et seq.; Pernthaler, "Die Verfassungsautonomie der österreichischen Bundesländer," *JBl* 1986, 478 et seq.; Koja, *Das Verfassungsrecht der österreichischen Bundesländer* (1988); Novak, *Landesgesetzgebung* 53 et seq.

39. Cf. VfGH 28 June 2001, G 103/00-22; Pernthaler, "Demokratische Identität oder bundesstaatliche Homogenität der Demokratiesysteme in Bund und Ländern," *JBl* 2000, 808 et seq. and Gamper, "The Principle of Homogeneity and Democracy in Austrian Federalism: The Constitutional Court's Ruling on Direct Democracy in Vorarlberg," *Publius* 33 2003 (forthcoming).

40. Namely, if a fundamental principle or one of its key elements is vitally changed, this amendment will require both qualified parliamentary majorities and the people's assent through a referendum.

41. Cf. Pernthaler, *Die Staatsgründungsakte der österreichischen Bundesländer* (1979).

42. It is admitted that the relevant framework consists not only of the principle of federalism but also of the other fundamental principles of the federal constitution. However, if it is unclear what the implications of one of the other principles are in a concrete case, the principle of federalism will serve as a residuary interpretation rule in favor of the Länder.

43. Cf. VfSlg 3314/1958.

44. Under Article 10 para. 1 lit 1 B-VG, this subject matter is a federal competence.

45. Because Article 8 (now: para. 1) B-VG, Article 19 StGG and Section V of Part III of the State Treaty of St. Germain-en-Laye were part of the "federal constitution" when this subject-matter was inserted into the B-VG as a part of the general distribution of competences in 1925, minority protection in general may be subsumed under it.

46. Article 16 B-VG.

47. Cf. Pernthaler, *Land* 33 et seq.

48. Cf. VfSlg 9224/1981; 12245/1989 and VfGH of 13 December 2001, G213/01, V62/01 et al. See also Unkart, "Ein Beitrag zur Auslegung des Article 7 des Staatsvertrages 1955," *ÖJZ* 1974, 94 et seq. and Pernthaler, "Personalitätsprinzip und Territorialitätsprinzip im Minderheitenschulwesen," *JBl* 1990, 613 et seq.

49. Cf. BGBl I 2000/68.

50. Cf. Article 15 para. 1 and 3 B-VG, as far as they do not concern the (federal) law regarding associations and assemblies (e.g., cinemas, theaters, sporting areas, shows, presentations).

51. Cf. Article 15 para. 1 B-VG (e.g., folk dances and costumes). See also section 5 of the Carinthian Land Museum Act (*Kärntner Landesmuseumsgesetz*, LGBl 1998/72).

52. Cf. Article 14 para. 4 lit b B-VG and the Carinthian Funding of Kindergartens Act (*Kärntner Kindergartenfondsgesetz*, LGBl 2001/74).

53. *Salzburger Jugendgesetz* (LGBl 1999/24).

54. Article 18 B-VG.

55. *Kärntner Kulturförderungsgesetz 2001* (LGBl 2002/45).

56. *Burgenländisches Jugendförderungsgesetz* (LGBl 1995/21).

57. Notwithstanding the fact that CIFEM research does not focus on the Carinthian Slovenes, but treats minority issues on a more general basis.

58. Cf. Article 99 para. 2 B-VG.

59. Cf. the ruling doctrine—for example, Mayer, B-VG (2002) 309 (with further references).

60. The suggestion to reserve one or more seats in the Land parliament to elected representatives of the ethnic groups of a Land (cf. Öhlinger/Pernthaler [eds.], *Projekt eines Volksgruppenmandats im Kärntner Landtag* [1997] and Öhlinger, *Verfassungsschutz* 384 et seq.) could serve as a politically significant example of how minorities could be considered by the Land constitutions within the relevant legal framework.

61. Cf. VfGH, 13 December 2001, G213/01, V62/01 et al.

5

The Protection of Minorities in a Federal State: The Case of Germany

Norman Weiss

This chapter examines the relationship between the protection of minorities in Germany and Germany's federal structure. It reveals that Germany has a long tradition of federalism and that the federalist distribution of powers and competencies affects the protection of minorities. But it should be emphasized that the protection of minorities is not an issue at stake in the German discussion of federalism. The more pressing question of how to deal with the high number of immigrants and their integration is being dealt with on the national level.

FEDERALISM IN GERMAN HISTORY—AN OVERVIEW

In Germany, even the premodern state was organized in a decentralized manner. In the Middle Ages, singular component entities (smaller or bigger monarchies and principalities, both secular and clerical, and free towns) had accepted—to some degree—the supremacy of the emperor who was elected out of the group of sovereign rulers. This constellation—the Holy Roman Empire being composed of 300 territories—

continued until 1806. After the victory over Napoleon I, the German states formed a confederation of sovereign governments (Deutscher Bund). In 1871 the German Reich was established as a confederation of sovereign monarchs and free towns following the structures developed earlier in the nineteenth century. Although the Reich was in fact dominated by Prussia, centralization was not intended. The entities' continuing sovereignty found its expression, for example, in their own monarchy, armies, postal services, and railway companies.

After World War I, the Reich became a federally organized republic. The state intensified the nation-building process, both from a social and a regional perspective. The republican constitution[1] began with the words: "[t]he German people, united in its tribes." As a consequence of the fact that the Reich was no longer a confederation, the constitution contained a catalogue of fundamental freedoms. Article 110, paragraph 2 guaranteed that every German has the equal civil and political rights in each German Land and should not be discriminated against on the ground of his origin. Explicit protection clauses for the members of minorities like Jews or the Polish did not exist on either the federal or state levels.

The Länder (the denomination for the states) continued to be strong and important factors in public life. Prussia, which had been the backbone of monarchy before, now became a pillar of the republic in the late 1920s and early 1930s. In 1932 the Reich's government undertook a coup d'état against the government of Prussia (Preußenschlag, 20 July 1932) in order to strengthen its own (no longer democratic) position. Subsequently, Prussia lost its sovereign government. In order to eliminate opposition, Hitler, who had become chancellor in the meantime, coordinated the Länder by the Act on the Co-ordination of the Länder with the Reich (Gleichschaltung der Länder mit dem Reich of 31 March 1933) and finally dissolved their parliaments by the law on the New Construction of the Reich (Neuaufbau des Reiches of 30 January 1934). The Länder continued to exist but lost their sovereign position and were governed by high-ranking party activists (Gauleiter, Reichsstatthalter). Federalism—understood and practiced as a safeguard for liberty and diversity—thus was eliminated.

During the last century in Germany, unitary states were modeled but stayed ephemeral. The so-called Third Reich lasted 12 years. The German Democratic Republic (GDR) ceased to exist after its 40th birthday. The GDR's beginning[2] and its last and revolutionary period[3] were nevertheless shaped by the existence of component entities and a federal structure. Those newly created entities were able to join the Federation by acceding to the Basic Law pursuant to its Article 23 (previous version).[4]

FEDERALISM IN THE FEDERAL REPUBLIC OF GERMANY

In Germany the subnational units today are still called Länder. The Federal Republic of Germany is composed of 16 Länder, each of which has a written constitution, a parliament, a government (an executive), and its own judiciary and administrative bodies. The principle of federalism is permanently incorporated into the Basic Law. Article 79, paragraph 3 prohibits any amendment of the Basic Law that would affect the division of the federal territory into Länder and their participation in the federal level. This provision together with Article 20, paragraph 1 is a clear and significant reaction to the explicit will of the Western Allies after World War II, especially the United States of America, which declared that

> [a] minimum of central government is necessary, but federalism and local self-government should be encouraged to the maximum in order to destroy the military potential of Germany and promote democracy. . . . No zonal government unit should be established but the political structure should be built upon the Laender.[5]

However, Article 79, paragraph 3 is not a guarantee for the original borders of the Länder, although they have proven remarkably stable even though they reflect historical boundaries only to a certain extent. Bavaria and the city-states of Hamburg and Bremen correspond to their historical borders. Saxony, Saxony-Anhalt, and Schleswig-Holstein contain much of their former territory. Brandenburg and the city-state of Berlin form together the core of the former Mark Brandenburg. However, the remaining Länder in the former Western part of Germany were carved out of the postwar zones of occupation allocated to France, the United Kingdom, and the United States.

Three southwestern states merged in the early 1950s, but this has been the only major change in the Federal Republic. This special case was due to French claims for a zone of occupation, which was not very popular. Therefore, it was likely to be dealt with soon after the constitution of the Federal Republic. Article 118 of the German Basic Law allows for a reorganization in a modified and easier way than the general provisions of Article 29. Plans currently exist for a merger of the Länder of Brandenburg and Berlin. Although this measure was already approved by the legislatures of both states, the population in Brandenburg voted against it. Article 29 specifies the procedure for such cases of reorganization of the federal territory; a sanction by federal law and the approval of the majority of the voters in the affected states are required.

The Länder are states as the federation is a state. Both have their own autonomous, constitutional power.[6] The sovereignty of the Länder does not derive from the federation's sovereignty; the federation has to respect the sovereignty of the Länder.[7] There exist separate constitutional spheres in the federation on the one hand and in the Länder on the other hand.[8] Each Land has the right to adopt its constitution and thereby structure its own political institutions.

With regard to the protection of minorities, it should be mentioned at this point that the few groups that have settled for a long time in Germany and are officially treated as minorities do not cause severe problems. The protection of minorities therefore is no issue for the so-called unitarian federalism that is established under the Basic Law.

The federal constitution provides the framework for the constitutions of the Länder in Article 28, paragraphs 1 and 3. The extent to which state and local governments must follow the constitutional order of the federation is an important issue of German federalism. This provision is often called the homogeneity clause, but it does not prescribe uniformity in governmental and institutional organization. The drafting history shows that the initial idea of strict and detailed homogeneity was abandoned in favor of the present solution: Article 28, paragraph 1 has been generally understood to require states and municipalities to adhere to basic principles of a democratic and social welfare state bound by the rule of law. Therefore representative political institutions and governmental structures are seen to be indispensable to the operation of the federal state. The principle of subsidiarity[9] is incorporated as well. The formalities of the governmental process must be organized in such a way as to make the social welfare state possible. The question is how much flexibility states and local governments have in establishing institutional procedures for the adoption of public policies. In the Startbahn West case from 1982, the Federal Constitutional Court held that the Länder

> are states vested with their own sovereign powers—even though limited as to subject matter derived not but rather recognized by the federation. . . . The basic law requires only a certain degree of identity between federal and state constitutions. To the extent that the basic law [does not provide otherwise] the states are free to construct their own constitutional orders. Their discretion [in this respect] most certainly extends to determining whether the legislature should reserve to accept the passage of the law or provide for its approval in a popular referendum.[10]

Due to the homogeneity clause in Article 28, the differences between the 16 constitutions are not so substantial. But of course there are different priorities. The Bavarian constitution, for example, states that

> [t]he paramount educational goals are reverence for God, respect for religious persuasion and the dignity of man, selfcontrol, the recognition of and readiness to undertake responsibility, helpfulness, receptiveness to everything which is beautiful, good and true, as well as a sense of responsibility for the natural world and the environment. (Article 131, paragraph 2)

Other constitutions do not contain this first goal of reverence for God. Also, the Bavarian constitution was the only state constitution that created a second legislative chamber, the Senate (although this body was abolished by popular referendum in 1998). Additional differences result from the fact that the constitutions in the western part of Germany were created in the late 1940s, whereas those on the territory of the former GDR were created in the early 1990s. Some of the early constitutions in the western part even preceded the Basic Law and the Universal Declaration of Human Rights.[11] The constitutions of Hessen (Article 21), Bavaria (Article 47), Rhineland-Palatinate (Article 3), Bremen (Article 121), and, originally, of Baden (Article 85) and Saarland (Article 95) contain the death penalty. After the adoption of the Basic Law and its Article 102 abolishing the death penalty, those provisions are no longer valid.

The constitutions of the so-called New Länder (in the territory of the former GDR) were modeled after the Basic Law. To a certain degree they are more similar to each other than to the older ones in the western part of the country that were understood as creative responses to the Nazi-regime and had no blueprint to follow. The five new constitutions all have a particular focus on social rights, mostly outlined as fundamental state goals such as a right to housing, a right to work, and a right to protection of the environment. This similarity has not, however, created some kind of eastern Sonderweg as was feared[12] in the early 1990s. Their constitutional framework is not extraordinary as such. Characteristics of the late and revolutionary period of the GDR, such as the omnipresent "round tables"[13] and the impetus of the civil rights movement, have faded away in the reality of the reunified country. The lasting success of the socialist party (PDS)—successor of the former state party (SED)—does not reflect a special constitutional consciousness and is not promoted by these constitutions. It is a political and even more a social phenomenon.

THE PROTECTION OF MINORITIES IN GERMANY

The Federal Constitution and the Protection of Minorities

The Basic Law—in contrast to the constitution of 1919[14]—does not contain an article dealing with the protection of minorities. There is only the antidiscrimination clause in Article 3, paragraph 3 that prohibits differentiation on grounds of, inter alia, language, religion, homeland, or origin. There is no reference to belonging to a minority.

After reunification, a specific article on the protection of minorities was discussed. This was initiated by the fact that the GDR constitution had contained a specific minority clause in its Article 40 dealing with the Sorbian minority.[15] This protection, it was argued, should be continued under the Basic Law as well and should be extended to other minorities in Germany.[16]

The Commission on the reform of the constitution[17] was of the opinion that minorities needed protection also by the Federation even though some of the constitutions of the Länder contain relevant articles.[18] The Commission made the following initial proposal for a state goal to be laid down in a new Article 20 b: "The State respects the identity of ethnic, cultural and linguistic minorities."[19] This draft would have been a mere basic policy clause of the constitution.[20]

After the commission delivered its final report, the procedure to amend the Basic Law under Article 79 was initiated. Any amendment to the Basic Law requires a majority of two thirds of the members of the Federal Parliament and a majority of two-thirds in the Federal Council (Article 79, paragraph 2). The amendment debate reflected the different attitudes of the conservative parties (Christian Democratic Union [CDU] and Christian Social Union [CSU]) on the one hand and of the left or liberal parties (Social Democratic Party [SPD], Free Democratic Party [FDP], the Green Party, and the Party of Democratic Socialism [PDS]) on the other. The conservative parties thought it unnecessary to provide for additional protection of minorities on the federal level, as the constitutions of those Länder where minorities settled already contained protection clauses. If an amendment was nevertheless deemed necessary, it should be restricted to those minorities who had settled for a long time in Germany and who are German nationals. The protection of the Roma and Sinti was rejected by the conservatives, as they feared that this might be interpreted as an invitation to Roma and Sinti to immigrate into Germany.[21] The other parties proposed again an amendment that was passed by the Legal Committee of the Federal Parliament[22] and that read: "The State respects the identity of ethnic, cultural and linguistic minorities."[23] However, this proposal was not approved by two thirds of the members of the Federal Parliament, so there is still no protection clause on the federal level.

The Protection of Minorities by the Federation

Despite the failure of this amendment, the Federation is obliged by public international law to protect national minorities. Upon ratification of the Council of Europe's Framework Convention on the Protection of National Minorities, Germany declared that the rights provided for in that convention shall be applied to the following groups: People of Danish origin living in the border area to Denmark, the Sorbs in Brandenburg and Saxony, the Frisian minority in Lower Saxony, and the group of the Sinti and Roma.[24] Thus, these four groups are the only officially recognized national minorities in Germany.

These international obligations may lead to law-making and law-executing activities. In a federal state both the federation and the states are involved. The pertinent distribution of authority[25] (division of responsibilities) derives from the Basic Law, which contains detailed provisions detailing the tasks for which the Federation has law-making power (either exclusive legislative power under Articles 71 and 73 or concurrent power with the Länder under Articles 72 and 74) and/or the tasks that are subject to federal administration. This follows the principle of enumerated powers.[26] For enacting legislation (laws and ordinances having the force of law) in today's constitutional reality, the primary responsibility lies with the Federation; for implementation of laws, or administration, primary responsibility rests with the Länder. The Länder execute federal laws as their own right, or according to their own responsibility. In addition, local governments (municipalities) are guaranteed the right to regulate all local affairs in their own right, within the limits prescribed by law. This includes, in particular, their own responsibility for staffing matters, organizational jurisdiction, fiscal jurisdiction/financial sovereignty, the right to make bylaws/ordinances, and local town and county planning.

Before dealing with the laws on minority protection of the Länder, one should mention what the Federal Republic has reported to the Advisory Committee acting under the Framework Convention.[27] In this report the Federal Government recalls its engagement for the protection of minorities as a matter of international cooperation and states that it has informed the German public on the Convention. The only reported legal activity on the federal level concerns a law on the changes of names of persons belonging to a minority (Minderheiten-Namens-Änderungsgesetz, 22 July 1997). This law, the "Act on Name Changes by Minorities" was passed in order to meet the obligations deriving from Article 11, paragraph 1 of the Framework Convention. Under this act every person belonging to a national minority has the right to adapt his/her former name, assigned to him/her under the national legal system, to the specific features of his/her minority language. Such adaptation may be effected by translation of the name into the minority language, if the name also denotes a specific term and thus is translatable from one into another language. If the name cannot be translated, it may be adapted to the phonetic particularities of the given minority language. Members of national minorities whose former name in the minority language had been given a German form or had been changed to another name, may again assume that original name. A pertinent declaration before the Registrar of the Civil Registry Office suffices for adapting a name to the special features of a minority language. No fees shall be charged for acceptance of a declaration to this effect and for its certification or authentication.

We may conclude that the protection of minorities is not a major task of the federation but rather falls within the authority of the Länder.

The Protection of Minorities by the Länder

The constitutions of 5 out of 16 Länder contain provisions on the protection of minorities. Whether or not they do largely depends on the presence of national minorities in the respective Länder. The constitutions of Schleswig-Holstein (Article 5),[28] Brandenburg (Article 25),[29] and Saxony (Articles 5 and 6)[30]—the Länder where the minority groups of the Danish, the Frisians, and the Sorbs live—have a special clause for the protection of minorities. In addition, the constitution of Sachsen-Anhalt offers the protection of the state and of the municipalities to (nonspecified) minorities (Article 37),[31] and the constitution of Mecklenburg-Western Pomerania offers protection to national minorities (Article 18).[32] Four out of the 5 constitutions presume that the members of the minority groups are German nationals. Those Länder with minorities living on their territory have more detailed protection clauses. In particular, Brandenburg and Saxony deal in depth with language rights.

This constitutional framework is implemented by laws concentrating on the issues falling into the competences of the Länder such as culture, school affairs, and administration of justice. We shall address some major areas.

Language and Religious Rights. The official language in courts and before public authorities is German.[33] The Länder Brandenburg and Saxony allow the use of Sorbian in the courts and before public authorities in the traditional area of settlement by statutory law. In Schleswig-Holstein no explicit law on this matter exists.

The Länder also regulate the matter of school education by statutory law. The State schools in Saxony, for example, are required to impart basic knowledge on Sorbian history and culture to all pupils (Article 2 Law on school education [Schulgesetz] of 1991). In areas in which Sorbians have settled, Sorbian schools are installed where enough pupils (25) constitute a class that is characterized by Sorbian being the teaching language. For these pupils Sorbian must be their mother tongue or second language. Mother tongue means that they only speak Sorbian, second language means that they speak Sorbian and German (Article 4 executive order 1992). The German classes are taught altogether in the German language, natural sciences from the 5th and 6th year onwards. The Sorbian language is taught from the 1st to 12th years and is equivalent to the teaching of a foreign language.

In areas in which minorities have settled, local names, street names, and other topographical indications as well as signs to public buildings are displayed in both German and Sorbian or Danish. Private displays in the minority language are also allowed. Schleswig-Holstein amended its law on children's day-care centers to enable national minorities to run such institutions as well.

Participation in the Decision-Making Process. In the case of the Danish minority in Schleswig-Holstein, the election act exempts their party from the general threshold of 5 percent usually required for representation in the Land Parliament. Thus, the party of the Danish minority (Südschleswigscher Wählerverband—SSW) needs fewer votes than other minority parties to have a member elected into the Land Parliament. This privilege was an issue at stake before the Federal Constitutional Court in two proceedings.[34] The Court had to find a balance between the individual right of all voters, the right of the minority party to equal competition, and the right of minorities to be represented in parliament. Regarded properly, the threshold is an exception from the principle of the equality of vote. It is justified by the intention to prevent political fragmentation and by the wish to have a parliament with the chance of building stable majorities. The nonapplication of the threshold with regard to a minority party enables their voters to be proportionally represented, which otherwise would probably not be the case because the minority people often settle in a specific area and would not reach the threshold all over the Land.

In Saxony and in Brandenburg, no such rule exists. In Brandenburg, the Sorbian minority is represented by a Council for Sorbian Affairs,[35] which gives advice to the Land Parliament on all matters concerning the minority. The election of the Land Parliament itself is, in the area of settlement of both Länder, as well as municipal elections, to be prepared and performed (election papers and ballot) in the Sorbian language.

Affirmative Actions. In some fields, minorities are not only protected against interference with their rights but also actively promoted. We mention the promotion of the science of the Sorbian language (Sorabistik), being part of the family of Slavic languages. Traditionally, the University of Leipzig has a chair in this field. At the University of Potsdam, there was a temporary possibility to train school teachers, but no special chair has been established. Nevertheless, research is done also at this university by experts on western Slavic languages.

The electronic public media[36] in those Länder where minorities live are obliged to broadcast special issues in the minority language and on the minority culture. A representative of the Sorbian and Danish minority is a member of the relevant broadcasting councils in Brandenburg, Saxony, and Schleswig-Holstein. Federalism in this field proves to be an advantage for the protection of minority rights. The Länder try to make private media respect those matters as well. In the minority languages, newspapers and books are published.[37] Thus, the media contribute to the preservation of the minority languages and the cultural heritage. What seems to be even more important is the fact that the use of Sorbian in everyday life keeps this language vital.

Miscellaneous. In actuality Germany has no minority question in the traditional sense, even though there are some minority groups present in the country, because most of the members of these groups are integrated into German society. On the other hand, Germany has a foreigner or immigrant question, as more than 7 million people live in Germany without being German nationals. Many of these people were born in Germany or have lived there over many decades. The newly amended act on the German nationality (2001) aims at increasing the number of nationalizations. In the future, citizens of Turkish origin might therefore claim minority status.

For the immigrants, none of the various minority rights clauses deriving from international law applies. Of course they are entitled to all basic rights, as long as these are not reserved to nationals, like the freedom of movement or the freedom to choose an occupation. These so-called German rights are guaranteed for foreigners by federal law and in a more indirect manner by Article 2.1 of the Basic Law, the clause that protects the general liberty of action. The most important guarantee for aliens is the nondiscrimination clause in Article 3 of the Basic Law. The ban on discrimination under Article 3.3 applies to immigrants as well as to German nationals. The principle of equal treatment and the prohibition of discrimination bind the legislative, the executive, and the judiciary as directly applicable law (Article 1.3).

Following a community directive[38] based on Article 13, ECT Member States are obliged to enact statutes prohibiting discrimination on grounds of national origin.[39] These statutes also bind private persons and thus, among others, are intended to improve the access of people belonging to a minority to clubs and restaurants. With respect to the situation in Germany, this statute will mainly affect aliens who have not been officially recognized as a national minority. As of May 2004, it is not clear when the statute will be enacted by the German legislature, although the directive had fixed a deadline for the implementation of the directive by 19 July 2003.[40]

CONCLUSION

There is a long tradition of federalism in Germany, and the Basic Law recognizes federalism as one of the fundamental structural principles. The obligation to protect minorities deriving from public international law reaches both the federal and state levels. However, due to the internal distribution of powers between the federation and the Länder, more issues relating to minorities fall within the latter's competences. Those Länder having settlements of German national minorities provide for protection clauses in their constitutions. In addition, their statutory law contains detailed rules for the use of the minority language and for the schooling of members of minority groups. Because these laws are the product of smaller governmental units that are closer to the people concerned, there tends to be a greater willingness to accept laws protecting and promoting minorities, as the population of the respective Land is acquainted with the local minority, its special situation, and its needs.

In sum, the legal framework for the protection of minorities corresponds with international standards, even though, except for minor amendments, international law has had no direct influence on the law of the federation or of the Länder.

NOTES

1. Verfassung des Deutschen Reiches (Weimar Constitution) of 11 August 1919, in RGBl (Reich Law Gazette) 1919, p. 1383 et seq.
2. Cf. Article 1 para. 1 GDR-constitution of 7 October 1949, Gesetzblatt (Law Gazette) I p. 5.
3. Law on the (Re-)Constitution of five Länder on the Territory of the GDR (Ländereinführungsgesetz) of 22 July 1990, Gesetzblatt (Law Gazette) I No. 51 p. 955.
4. Article s without further specification are those of the German Basic Law.
5. Decentralization of the Political Structure of Germany, Preliminary Report by the Special Advising Committee for Decentralization, US Group CC, 23 March 1945, reprinted in *Vierteljahreshefte für Zeitgeschichte* 24 (1976), p. 319 et seq. (p. 320).
6. BVerfGE [official series of the decisions of the Federal Constitutional Court] 36, 342 [360–61].
7. Wolfgang Graf Vitzthum, "Die Bedeutung gliedstaatlichen Verfassungsrechts in der Gegenwart," *VVDStRL* [publication series of the Association of the German Constitutional Law Professors] 46 (1988), pp. 7–56 (23–24).
8. BVerfGE 4, 178 [189]; 6, 376 [381–82]; 64, 301 [317]; 96, 345 [368].

9. The principle of subsidiarity—which can be traced back to Catholic Social Thought—says that no measure shall be taken by a higher or larger organization if it can be done as well or even better by a smaller or lower one. See the encyclical *Quadragesimo Anno* of 1931, para. 79.

10. BVerfG, Decision of 24 March 1982–2 BvH 1, 2, 233/82, in *Neue Juristische Wochenschrift* 1982, 1579 (1581). Translation by Donald P. Kommers, *The Constitutional Jurisprudence of the Federal Republic of Germany,* 1997, p. 79.

11. For example, the Constitution of the Land Hessen of 1 December 1946, the Constitution of the Free State of Bavaria of 2 December 1946, or the Constitution of the Free Hansestadt Bremen of 21 October 1947.

12. Cf. Wolfgang Graf Vitzthum, "Soziale Grundrechte und Staatszielbestimmungen morgen—Landesverfassungsgebung und Grundgesetzreform," in *Zeitschrift für Arbeitsrecht* 22 (1991), 695–711 (709f.). It was feared that the special experiences of the life in the former GDR might lead to a specific eastern type of democracy and a kind of policy not integrated into the traditional schemes of the Federal Republic. The term "Sonderweg" refers to a topic of German history when the country defined itself being neither a western democracy nor a communist state.

13. Fora of discussion and decision-making during the last year of the GDR, intended to allow the participation of all groups of the population.

14. Article 113 Verfassung des Deutschen Reiches (Weimar Constitution) of 11 August 1919, in RGBl (Reich Law Gazette) 1919, p. 1383 et seq. reads as follows: "Those parts of the Reich's people who are of a foreign language shall not be impeded by legislature and administration in their free native development, especially with regard to the use of their mother tongue in school as well as in court and before public authorities" (translation by the author).

This article clearly referred only to members of minorities being German nationals as did its ancestor (Article XIII, § 188 of the constitution of 1848 [Paulskirchenverfassung]), which never entered into force.

15. "Citizens of the German Democratic Republic of Sorbian nationality have the right to cultivate their mother tongue and culture. The exercise of this right is promoted by the state" (translation by the author).

The Treaty between the FRG and the GDR on the Creation of the Unity of Germany (Einigungsvertrag of 31 August 1990) also dealt with the question of culture (in Article 35). In a protocol to this treaty, the two governments declared with regard to this article, inter alia, that "(1) The profession of Sorbian nationality and Sorbian culture is free. (2) The preservation and development of Sorbian culture and Sorbian traditions are ensured."

16. Cf. Dietrich Franke/Rainer Hofmann, "Nationale Minderheiten—ein Thema für das Grundgesetz? Verfassungs- und völkerrechtliche Aspekte des Schutzes nationaler Minderheiten," in *Europäische Grundrechte Zeitschrift* 1992, pp. 401–9; and Markus Pallek, *Der Minderheitschutz im deutschen Verfassungsrecht,* 2001, pp. 397–467.

17. Established as the Joint Commission on the Constitution of the Federal Parliament and the Federal Council in order to implement Article 5 of the Treaty between the FRG and the GDR on the Creation of the Unity of Germany (Einigungsvertrag of 31 August 1990). The Commission started its work on 16 January 1992 and delivered its report on 28 October 1992 (BT-DrS 12/6000 of 5 November 1993). A Commission on the Reform of the Constitution was already established by the Federal Council in 1991. This Commission finally delivered a proposal for a minority protection clause (BR-DrS 360/92) that read: "The State respects the identity of ethnic, cultural and linguistic minorities." As the discus-

sions and the proposals were similar in both commissions, further reference is only made to the Joint Commission.

18. Those minorities who do not settle in areas might benefit from a safeguard for minorities on the federal level. Additionally, the proposed article should ensure a common standard even in those Länder where no traditional national minorities are settling and whose constitutions therefore do not contain protection clauses.

19. A second sentence that made a reference to public international law by introducing a differentiation between nationals and foreigners ([The state] protects and promotes ethnic groups and national minorities with German nationality) did not find approval by the commission itself. The drafting history does not really reveal why the second sentence was rejected but the more progressive first one was passed.

20. For details and references cf. Michael J. Hahn, "Die rechtliche Stellung der Minderheiten in Deutschland," in J. Frowein/R. Hofmann/S. Oeter (eds.), *Das Minderheitenrecht europäischer Staaten,* vol. 1, 1993, pp. 62–107 (69–73); Michael Kloepfer, *Verfassungsänderung statt Verfassungsreform, Zur Arbeit der Gemeinsamen Verfassungskommission,* 1995, pp. 49–58.

21. For details, cf. the report of the Joint Commission, BT-DrS 12/6000 of 5 November 1993, pp. 71–75; see also Karen Schönwalder, "Schutz ethnischer Minderheiten," in Norbert Konegen/Peter Nitschke (eds.), *Revision des Grundgesetzes? Ergebnisse der Gemeinsamen Verfassungskommission (GVK) des Deutschen Bundetsages und des Bundesrates,* 1997, S. 197–214.

22. No qualified majority was required.

23. Draft of Article 20 b, BT-DrS 12/6633, p. 2.

24. The group of Sinti and Roma has no special area of settlement and is spread all over Germany; their number is estimated from 50,000 to 80,000.

25. Compare Michael Fehling, "Mechanismen der Kompetenzabgrenzung in föderativen System im Vergleich," in J. Aulehner et al. (eds.), *Föderalismus—Auflösung oder Zukunft der Staatlichkeit?,* 1997, pp. 31–55.

26. Article 30: "The exercise of governmental powers and the discharge of governmental functions shall be incumbent on the Länder insofar as this Basic Law does not otherwise prescribe or permit."

Article 70: "(1) The Länder shall have the right to legislate insofar as this Basic Law does not confer legislative power on the Federation. (2) The division of competences between the Federation and the Länder shall be determined by the provisions of this basic Law concerning exclusive and concurrent powers."

27. First Report submitted by the Federal Republic of Germany under Article 25, paragraph 1, of the Council of Europe's Framework Convention for the Protection of National Minorities (1999), ACFC/SR (99) 17.

28. "(1) The profession to a national minority is free; it does not absolve from the general duties of a citizen.

(2) The cultural autonomy and the political participation of national minorities and ethnic groups are protected by the Land, the municipalities and the associations of local authorities. The Danish national minority and the ethnic group of the Frisians have a right to protection and promotion" (translation by the author).

29. "(1) The right of the Sorbian people to protection, preservation and cultivation of its national identity and its hereditary settlement area is guaranteed. The Land, the municipalities and the associations of local authorities promote the realization of this right, especially the cultural autonomy and the effective political participation of the Sorbian people.

"(2) The Land works towards the guarantee of the Sorbian's cultural autonomy across its borders.

"(3) The Sorbs have the right on preservation and promotion of the Sorbian language and culture in public life and on their imparting in schools and children's day-care centres.

"(4) The Sorbian language is to be used additionally for public displays in the area of settlement. The Sorbian flag has the colours blue, red, white.

"(5) The rights of the Sorbs are provided for by law. It has to make sure that Sorbian representatives can take part in matters concerning the Sorbs, especially the legislature."

30. "Article 5 (1) To the People of the Free State Saxony belong citizens of German, Sorbian and other origin. The Land respects the right to one's homeland.

(2) The Land ensures and protects the right of national and ethnic minorities of German nationality to the preservation of their identity as well as their right to exercise their language, religion, culture and heritage.

(3) The Land respects the interests of persons belonging to minorities not being German nationals who stay legally in the Land."

Article 6 (1) The citizens of Sorbian origin who live in the Land form an equally entitled part of the body politic. The Land ensures and protects the right to preservation of their identity as well as their right to exercise and develop their language, culture and heritage, especially through schools, preparatory and cultural departments.

"(2) The vital requirements of the Sorbian people are to be considered in the process of regional planning. The German-Sorbian character of the area of settlement of the Sorbian ethnic group shall be preserved.

"(3) The border-crossing cooperation of the Sorbs, especially in the regions of the Oberlausitz and of the Niederlausitz, are in the interest of the Land" (translation by the author).

31. "(1) The cultural individuality and the political participation of ethnic minorities are protected by the Land and the municipalities.

"(2) The profession to a cultural or ethnic minority is free; it does not absolve from the general duties of a citizen" (translation by the author).

32. "The cultural individuality of ethnic and national minorities and of ethnic groups of citizens with German nationality is especially protected by the Land" (translation by the author).

33. Cf. Article 184 GVG (Federal Judicature Act), Article 23.1 VwVfG (Federal Administrative Procedure Act), Article 87.1 AO (Federal Fiscal Code).

34. BVerfGE 1, 208 et seq.; 4, 31 et seq.

35. Law on the Rights of the Sorbs in the Land Brandenburg of 7 July 1993, Article 5:

"(1) Parliament elects for each electoral period a Council for Sorbian Affairs. This Council has five members. The Members of the Council for Sorbian Affairs shall be of Sorbian origin. The Sorbian Associations have the right of nomination. The Members of the Council for Sorbian Affairs exercise their function in an honorary capacity. They get an expense allowance.

"(2) The Council for Sorbian Affairs gives advice to parliament. Its task is to safeguard the interests of the Sorbian people in all matters that might affect their rights" (translation by the author).

36. In Germany, the competence for the broadcasting system lies with the Länder. To date, 10 public broadcasting corporations exist.

37. With regard to the Sorbian minority, seven newspapers exist, some appear daily, others weekly or monthly. Altogether, these publications are read by approximately 35,000 persons.

38. Council Directive 2000/43/EC of 29 June 2000 implementing the principle of equal treatment between persons irrespective of racial or ethnic origin, in *Official Journal L* 180, 19 July 2000, p. 22–26. The text can be found at http://europa.eu.int/smartapi/cgi/sga_doc?smartapi!celexapi!prod!CELEXnumdoc&lg=EN&numdoc=32000L0043&model=guichett (visited December 2002).

39. Article 1 reads: "The purpose of this Directive is to lay down a framework for combating discrimination on the grounds of racial or ethnic origin, with a view to putting into effect in the Member States the principle of equal treatment."

40. Cf. Andreas Haratsch, Die Anti-Diskriminierungspolitik der EU—Neue Impulse durch Article 13 EGV?, in Eckart Klein (ed.), *Rassische Diskriminierung—Erscheinungsformen und Bekämpfungsmöglichkeiten,* Berlin 2002, pp. 195–227.

The Federal Ministry of Justice proposed an Anti-Discrimination Act in 2001, but discussions with lawyers, pressure groups, and Members of Parliament revealed defects with it. In addition, it was assumed that many Germans did not want such an act. The Government made little progress on the issue prior to the parliamentary elections in 2003, and since then there has been very little public discussion of the issue. Cf. David Nii Addy, *Diskriminierung und Rassimus, Internationale Verplichtungen und Nationale Herausforderungen fur die Menschenrechtsarbeit in Deutschland,* Deutsches Institut fur Menschenrechte, 2003, pp. 56–58.

6

American State Constitutions and Minority Rights

G. Alan Tarr

In the United States, the connection between subnational constitutions and the advancement of minority rights has been viewed as problematic at best.[1] In Federalist #51 James Madison recognized that the nation's system of dual constitutionalism afforded a "double protection" for rights. However, he also observed in Federalist #10 that in smaller governmental units majority faction was more common and minorities therefore more vulnerable. Antebellum state constitutions in the South supported slavery; Northern constitutions restricted black voting and black civil rights.[2] Southern state constitutions of the late nineteenth century introduced racist provisions dealing with voting, education, and marriage; the constitutions in California and Oregon discriminated against Asian immigrants, and those of other states against Mormons.[3] During the late twentieth century, states have adopted constitutional amendments that critics have labeled anti-immigrant and antiminority—for example, provisions in Arizona and Florida mandating English as the official language, and a ban in California on benefits to illegal immigrants.[4] Given this record, it is small wonder that American minority groups have looked to the federal judiciary interpreting the federal Constitution as the main guarantor of their rights.

Nevertheless, since the 1970s proponents of expansive interpretations of rights have rediscovered state declarations of rights and have increasingly advanced claims in state courts based on state guarantees of rights. State courts have responded with rulings granting protections for rights beyond those afforded by the federal Constitution. The emergence of this new judicial federalism, as it has been called, marks a major shift in the role of state courts. It also raises anew the question of what contribution American state constitutions have made and can make to the protection of minority rights. Before addressing this question, however, it is appropriate to describe the system of subnational constitutionalism in the United States.

AMERICAN STATE CONSTITUTIONALISM

The States Within the Constitutional Framework

The position and powers of the 50 American states are safeguarded by the federal Constitution. The Constitution confers only limited powers on the federal government, and the Tenth Amendment confirms that all residual powers not prohibited to the states by the Constitution "are reserved to the States respectively, or to the People." Although the scope of federal power increased during the twentieth century, since 1990 the U.S. Supreme Court has displayed a renewed interest in safeguarding state power and curtailing federal overreaching.[5] In addition, the Constitution grants extraordinary protection to the territorial integrity of the states, forbidding tampering with state boundaries not only by congressional legislation but also by the normal processes for constitutional amendment (Article VI, section 3). The Constitution also secures to the states a role in the selection of federal officials and in the processes of the federal government. Initially, state legislatures selected senators, and even after the Seventeenth Amendment (1913) instituted popular election of senators, states still enjoy equal representation in the Senate. And as long as they do not discriminate on the basis of race, gender, or other factors, the states set eligibility requirements for voting in both national and state elections. Finally, constitutional amendments require ratification by three-quarters of the states (Article V).

Constitutional Creation and Constitutional Change

Even before the American colonies declared their independence from England, some states embarked on the task of constitutional creation.[6] By early in the nineteenth century, the process of constitutional creation had become standardized: Citizens would vote to hold a convention, elect those who would serve as convention delegates, and by referendum determine whether to ratify the convention's proposals. When states replace their existing constitutions, they employ the same procedure. Altogether, the states have held more than 240 constitutional conventions and adopted 146 constitutions. Only 19 states still retain their original constitutions, and a majority have established three or more.

During the twentieth century, the pace of state constitutional revision slowed, but the pace of state constitutional amendment increased. The states utilize various mechanisms for proposing constitutional amendments. States may call constitutional conventions to propose amendments, but the cost of conventions generally makes this unattractive. Most amendments are proposed by state legislatures. Eighteen states currently permit constitutional amendments to be proposed by a simple majority in each house of the legislature, five more by simple majorities in two sessions with an intervening election, and nine by a three-fifths vote in each house. In recent years, proposed amendments have often originated in constitutional commissions, groups of experts and notables appointed by the legislature or executive to develop proposals for consideration by the legislature or—in the case of Florida—for direct submission to the people for ratification. These commissions provide expert assistance to the legislature, while allowing it to keep control over what proposals are submitted for popular consideration.

Eighteen states employ the constitutional initiative, which empowers citizens to propose amendments directly to the voters (16 states) or to the legislature before submission to the voters (Massachusetts and Mississippi). To place an initiative on the ballot, supporters must collect signatures on petitions in support of the initiative. Although states differ as to the level of support that must be obtained, typically the level is a percentage of the turnout at the last election for governor or a percentage of the state population. Some states, in order to prevent one region of the state from dominating the process, require that a certain number of signatures be obtained from each county. Once the requisite number of signatures has been obtained and certified by the secretary of state, the constitutional initiative is placed on the ballot.

Regardless of the mode of proposing amendments, the mode of ratification remains the same—popular referendum. In 44 states, only a simple majority vote in a referendum is required to ratify amendments proposed by state legislatures. No state mandates a minimum turnout level to ratify an amendment. One state, Delaware, permits amendment of its constitution by an extraordinary majority in the legislature, without popular ratification. Of the 18 states that permit amendment by constitutional initiative, 13 permit ratification of proposals by a simple majority of those voting on the measures.

State Constitutional Design

Because state governments can exercise all residual powers not conferred on the federal government nor prohibited to them by the federal Constitution, it is common to distinguish the federal Constitution as a document granting powers and state constitutions as documents of limitation.[7] This function of state constitutions, not surprisingly, dictates their form. Generally speaking, because of the necessity to enunciate specific limitations, most state constitutions contain a high level of detail with respect to the structure and operations of government.

Other factors likewise promote uniformities among state constitutions. The federal Constitution does not mandate that state constitutions contain specific provisions or address certain matters.[8] But, federal constitutional provisions do affect the structure and operation of state governments by restricting the range of choice for state constitution-makers or by inducing states to alter their constitutions to bring them into conformity with federal requirements. Article IV, section 4 of the federal Constitution directs the federal government to "guarantee to every State in this Union a Republican Form of Government"; and Article VI, section 2 upholds the supremacy of federal law within its sphere over "any Thing in the Constitution or Laws of any State." Article I, section 10 imposes various restrictions on state power—for example, states cannot enter into treaties, impair the obligations of contracts, or coin money. Subsequent amendments have added to the federal constitutional restrictions on the states by imposing requirements relating to voting and to the apportionment of state legislatures, requiring that boundaries be drawn to ensure that legislative districts are equal in population (one person, one vote). Likewise important have been the incorporation under the Fourteenth Amendment of most provisions of the federal Bill of Rights, making those provisions applicable against state governments, and the more aggressive review of state constitutions by the federal judiciary. Thus, the U.S. Supreme Court has struck down a Colorado constitutional amendment infringing on the rights of homosexuals as a denial of equal protection of the laws, the Maryland Constitution's religious test for state officials as a violation of the First Amendment, and an Arkansas constitutional amendment limiting the consecutive terms that a member of Congress from Arkansas could serve under the Qualifications Clause of Article I.[9] Often the effects of such rulings on state constitutions have extended beyond the provisions that have been invalidated by rendering unenforceable analogous provisions in other state constitutions and by encouraging states to amend their constitutions to eliminate provisions inconsistent with federal constitutional law.

Finally, even in the absence of legal requirements to do so, state constitution-makers have borrowed extensively from other state constitutions. This is hardly surprising. It is natural for state constitution-makers to examine how other states have attempted to solve common problems and to emulate their (perceived) successes. This interstate borrowing (or horizontal federalism, as it has been called) has promoted uniformities both in the general design of state constitutions and in their specific provisions.[10] For example, structurally, all states have adopted presidential (rather than parliamentary) systems, instituted a separation of powers, and (with the exception of Nebraska) lodged law-making authority in bicameral legislatures. And all states have guaranteed a common set of fundamental rights.

Nevertheless, it is easy to overstate the commonalities among American state constitutions.[11] State constitutions reflect the reigning political perspective at the time of their adoption, and as these have changed over the 225 years of the nation's history, so too have state constitutions. Eighteenth-century state constitutions, for example, were short documents that placed few restrictions on the people's representatives. Late-nineteenth-century constitutions, in contrast, were lengthy documents containing numerous restrictions on state legislatures, based on the "belief that legislatures are by nature utterly careless of the public welfare, if not hopelessly corrupt."[12] Most twentieth-century state constitutions sought to eliminate excessive restrictions on legislative authority and to strengthen state executives in order to promote a more vigorous response to the problems confronting the states. However, in those states with the constitutional initiative, the last decades of the twentieth century witnessed a proliferation of amendments designed to restrict state legislatures and circumvent ordinary politics by constitutionalizing policy choices through "constitutional legislation."

In addition to changes in constitutional fashion, intrastate politics has promoted interstate differences in constitutions, affecting the subjects that state constitutions addressed and how they addressed them. For example, Idaho's Constitution has articles on water rights and on livestock, and California's on water resources development.[13] Moreover, general uniformities do not preclude important differences. For example, although all states have adopted a presidential system, they differ in the number of independently elected executive officers, as well as in the scope of budgetary, appointive, and veto powers vested in the governor.[14] Finally, the ease of constitutional change affects the frequency of constitutional change and thus the contents of state constitutions. States in which amendment is easy tend to contain provisions reflecting shifting political majorities, whereas those in which it is more difficult tend to have more stable and shorter constitutions.[15]

State Declarations of Rights

The same set of fundamental rights found in the federal Bill of Rights and the Fourteenth Amendment—the freedoms of speech and of the press, religious liberty, protections for defendants, and guarantees of equality—are likewise found in state declarations of rights. Nonetheless, there are important differences between state and federal guarantees, and these affect the interpretation of state constitutions. Many state guarantees are more specific than their federal counterparts. For example, in addition to prohibiting governmental establishment of religion, 19 states specifically bar religious tests for witnesses or jurors, and 35 prohibit expenditures for "any sectarian purpose."[16] In addition, many state declarations of rights contain additional protections that have no federal analogue. Thus, 39 states guarantee access to a legal remedy to those who suffer injuries, and 11 expressly protect a right to privacy.[17] Furthermore, in contrast to federal practice, states have not treated their declarations of rights as sacrosanct but have amended them with some frequency. Some amendments have expanded rights—several states added protections of gender equality during the 1970s and guarantees of victims' rights in the 1980s and 1990s.[18] Other amendments have curtailed rights. Since 1970, Texas has restricted the right to bail, Massachusetts and California have reinstated the death penalty, and Florida has circumscribed rights against unreasonable searches.[19] Finally, although the federal Bill of Rights only protects against governmental invasions of rights, some state guarantees expressly prohibit private violations of rights—Louisiana's ban on private discrimination is an example.[20] Other state provisions lend themselves to extension to private violations of rights. For example, the free-speech guarantees in 44 states affirmatively protect speech rights without specifying against whom, and these provisions have been interpreted in some states to protect speech rights on private property open to the public, such as shopping malls.[21]

This greater scope and specificity of rights protections extends to the rights of minorities as well. The federal Constitution secures religious liberty (First Amendment), guarantees the voting rights of African-Americans and of women (Fifteenth and Nineteenth Amendments), and mandates that no person should be denied the "equal protection of the laws" (Fourteenth Amendment). State protections are more capacious. State religion clauses do not simply forbid interference with the free exercise of religion, as the First Amendment does, but rather offer positive recognition of the right to worship God and delineate specific governmental actions that would infringe on religious liberty. State provisions also recognize that religious liberty encompasses freedom of action as well as freedom of belief, although some states stipulate that this does not "excuse acts of licentiousness" or justify "practices inconsistent with the peace and safety" of the state.[22] Finally, various state constitutions forbid discrimination on the basis of religion; outlaw religious tests for voting, testifying in court, or holding public office; and exempt believers from state military duty on the basis of their religious or conscientious scruples.[23]

Some state constitutions, like their federal counterpart, emphasize the protection of minority rights by guaranteeing the equal protection of the laws.[24] Other state equality provisions, however, are designed primarily to ensure that no special privileges should be reserved for a favored few. The Texas Constitution, for instance, decrees that "no man, or set of men, is entitled to exclusive separate public emoluments, or privileges."[25] Fifteen states specifically ban discrimination on the basis of race, color, or national origin; and 18 do so on the basis of gender. More recent provisions may expressly protect other groups as well. Thus, Florida forbids discrimination on the basis of handicap, and Louisiana on the basis of "physical condition" or "culture."[26] Finally, a few state constitutions specifically recognize and protect ethnic minorities within their borders. Thus the Montana Constitution "recognizes the distinct and unique cultural heritage of the American Indians and is committed in its educational goals to the preservation of their cultural integrity." The New Mexico Constitution encourages teachers to learn both English and Spanish, guarantees the education rights of students of Spanish ancestry, and provides for the publication of all legal enactments in both languages.[27] The Hawaiian Constitution mandates a "Hawaiian education program consisting of language, culture and history in the public schools," and the renewed interest in Hawaiian ethnic identity during the 1970s led to the addition of an entire article devoted to "Hawaiian Affairs."[28]

STATE CONSTITUTIONAL LAW AND THE RIGHTS OF MINORITIES

The state supreme court is the authoritative interpreter of a state's constitution. That is to say, if a case raises a matter of state constitutional law, the state supreme court's determination of that issue is final and not subject to review by any other court, not even the U.S. Supreme Court.[29] Since the early 1970s, as noted, state judges have shown an increased willingness to invoke state declarations of rights to secure rights unavailable under the U.S. Constitution. From 1950 to 1969, in only 10 cases did state judges rely on state guarantees to afford greater protection than was available under the federal Constitution. However, from 1970 to 2000, they did so in more than 1,000 cases.

The question remains, however, as to how important state constitutional guarantees have been in safeguarding the rights of minorities. A comprehensive response to that question would require consideration not only of judicial rulings under state constitutions but also of the effect such provisions have had on state legislation and the responses of governmental institutions and state electorates to those rulings. Nevertheless, one can observe that in general, state equality guarantees have not served as important sources of independent protection for minorities. A leading commentary on state constitutional law has concluded that "[s]tate constitutional litigation on behalf of minority or politically disfavored groups over rights to equal treatment remains largely dominated by fourteenth amendment equal protection doctrine."[30] A survey of state rulings found that equality claims before state supreme courts have focused less on "discrimination based on some kind of identifiable personal trait, such as race, gender, illegitimacy, or alienage" than on "less obvious kinds of distinctions."[31] Moreover, in challenges involving traits such as race or gender, litigants have tended to invoke the federal Equal Protection Clause in addition to state equality guarantees, and state courts have overwhelmingly based their rulings on federal rather than state law.[32] As a rule, then, federal constitutional law and statutory law (such as the Civil Rights Act of 1964 and the Voting Rights Act of 1965) have tended to dominate judicial decisions.

Race and Ethnicity

Nowhere is this federal dominance more evident than in the protection of the rights of racial or ethnic minorities. Nevertheless, two state initiatives are noteworthy. From 1963 to 1979, the California Supreme Court interpreted the state's equal protection clause to provide greater protection than its federal analogue, holding that segregation in public schools violated the state constitution, even if the segregation was not *de jure*, and imposed on districts an affirmative duty to integrate schools.[33] However, in 1979, California voters amended the state constitution to outlaw the use of busing to achieve integration unless that remedy was required by the federal Constitution, and the U.S. Supreme Court upheld the state's decision to conform to federal law rather than continue its enhanced protection.[34] More recently, the Connecticut Supreme Court concluded in *Sheff v. O'Neill* that the Connecticut Constitution required the Legislature to provide students with substantially equal educational opportunity, that the racial and ethnic isolation within Connecticut schools deprived students of such opportunity, and that the Legislature was therefore obliged to remedy this constitutional violation by ensuring all students with access to unsegregated education.[35] Finally—and more controversially—California voters endorsed by initiative Proposition 209, which provided that "[t]he state shall not discriminate against, or grant preferential treatment to, any individual or group on the basis of race, sex, color, ethnicity, or national origin in the operation of public employment, public education, or public contracting."[36] Whereas proponents of the measure hailed it as a victory for civil rights, opponents contended that by banning affirmative action, the amendment had in effect diminished the prospects of minority group members.

Mention should also be made of various state constitutional rulings that, although not framed in terms of racial discrimination, have attacked inequalities that disproportionately disadvantaged minorities. The New Jersey Supreme Court held that the state constitution forbade municipalities from using zoning regulations to exclude potential residents with low or moderate incomes and imposed on the municipalities an affirmative obligation to provide housing opportunities for the less fortunate.[37] And over the past three decades, supreme courts in 15 states have relied on their state constitutions to invalidate systems of public school finance that resulted in unequal education for students in poorer (usually urban) school districts.[38]

Gender

The U.S. Supreme Court does not recognize gender as a "suspect classification" under the federal Constitution and thus requires a less exacting scrutiny of governmental actions based on gender distinctions than it does for those based on race or national origin.[39] This, together with the inclusion of express guarantees of gender equality in 18 state constitutions, might have led to the development of a state constitutional jurisprudence of gender equality. Yet state constitutional rulings dealing with gender equality are quite limited. In part, the availability of federal statutes prohibiting gender discrimination in employment, housing, and other areas has encouraged litigants to bring their cases in federal rather than state courts and to rely on federal statutory law instead of state constitutions. In part, too, the limited litigation under state guarantees of gender equality reflects the success of legislative reform. Either simultaneous with the adoption of these state constitutional guarantees or immediately following their adoption, several states revised their laws to root out gender discrimination, thereby removing many bases for litigation. Thus, state guarantees of gender equality may have had a significant effect, even if they did not dramatically increase the number of rulings striking down gender discrimination.[40]

Sexual Orientation

In *Bowers v. Hardwick,* the U.S. Supreme Court rejected a challenge by a gay male plaintiff to Georgia's neutrally worded criminal sodomy statute, refusing to create a broad constitutionally protected zone of privacy for consensual sexual conduct.[41] Yet 10 years later, in *Romer v. Evans,* the Court struck down a Colorado constitutional amendment that banned local governments from prohibiting discrimination on the basis of sexual orientation.[42] Despite express protection for privacy rights in some state declarations of rights and the recognition of an implicit right to privacy by judges in other states, the states too have had a mixed record in dealing with sexual minorities. Beginning in the 1970s, some state courts relied on state constitutional privacy rights to strike down laws criminalizing consensual sexual activity between adults, although others have refused to do so.[43] Some states and localities have protected gays and lesbians against discrimination, but as the Colorado constitutional amendment illustrates, others have sought to deny such protection. Finally, after the Hawaii Supreme Court ruled in *Baehr v. Lewin* that the state constitution prohibited the state from limiting the right to marry to opposite-sex couples, Hawaii in 1998 amended its constitution to restrict marriage to opposite-sex couples, and four other states passed referenda limiting the marriage rights of same-sex couples.[44] But the Vermont Supreme Court in *Baker v. State* ruled that the Vermont Constitution mandated that same-sex couples were entitled to the same legal rights and benefits of marriage as opposite-sex couples.[45] The court directed the legislature to craft a law that would meet this constitutional obligation either by legalizing same-sex marriages or by creating an equivalent partnership structure. The Vermont Legislature chose the latter alternative.

Protections for Groups

Two states, Montana and New Mexico, have recognized constitutionally their obligations to Native Americans and to Americans of Spanish ancestry, respectively. However, these provisions have not become important independent protections for minority rights. In Montana, the "legal and practical effects [of the guarantee] have been minimal," and "there is an increasing sense of separation between the Montana tribes and the rest of the state."[46] In New Mexico, courts have ruled that neither the recognition of rights under the Treaty of Guadalupe Hidalgo nor the protection against discrimination for children of Spanish descent conferred a right to have the Spanish language and culture preserved and continued in public schools.[47]

Finally, as a result of an amendment to the Hawaiian Constitution in 1978, the state government is obliged to "protect all rights, customarily and traditionally exercised for subsistence, cultural and religious purposes and possessed by ahupua's tenants who are descendants of native Hawaiians who inhabited the Hawaiian Islands prior to 1778, subject to the right of the State to regulate such rights."[48] In its rulings interpreting the provision, the Hawaii Supreme Court has reaffirmed the state's obligation, while recognizing the need to balance traditional rights with the requirements of modern society.[49]

CONCLUSIONS AND QUESTIONS

Our survey of the protection of minority rights under state declarations of rights suggests that those guarantees have played a distinctly subsidiary role in the system of dual protection of rights. During the twentieth century, minority-group litigants overwhelmingly preferred to base their claims on federal law and to pursue them in federal forums rather than in state courts. Moreover, when arguing before state tribunals that their rights had been violated, they typically relied on the federal Constitution exclusively or on the federal Constitution and state constitution jointly. Despite the rise of the new judicial federalsim, state judges have only infrequently based their rulings exclusively on state guarantees of minority rights. Exceptions to this pattern of federal predominance have occurred primarily when federal courts have rejected the arguments of minority-group members, and they have been forced to rely on state courts and state guarantees to achieve their ends. Thus, state courts and state constitutions played the central role in school-finance litigation only after the Supreme Court in *San Antonio Independent School District v. Rodriguez* rejected a challenge to Texas's reliance on the local property tax as the primary basis for funding education, holding that Texas's system did not violate the Equal Protection Clause, even if it resulted in substantial interdistrict disparities in per-pupil expenditures.[50] Similarly, the New Jersey Supreme Court's aggressive role in exclusionary zoning litigation occurred in the face of federal disinterest, and the challenges to restriction of marriage to opposite-sex couples were filed in state courts and relied on state constitutions because the Supreme Court had demonstrated its lack of sympathy for gay rights claims in *Bowers v. Hardwick*.[51]

In part, historical factors account for this pattern. The policy of racial subordination in the Southern states, together with the failure of state courts to secure the protections of the law to black litigants and defendants even in egregious cases, produced well-founded skepticism about the commitment of state courts to equal rights. The record of state courts stood in sharp contrast to the leadership shown by the federal courts in the struggle for civil rights, and this leadership both instilled a trust in federal courts and federal law and created a habit of reliance on federal remedies. In part, too, tactical considerations have prompted litigants to pursue their claims in federal courts when they have a choice between federal or state forums. After all, recognition of a federal constitutional right by the U.S. Supreme Court would have national implications, whereas the results of a favorable outcome in a state court would be felt only within the borders of the state. In addition, it should also be noted that prior to the twentieth century, state courts and state law were sometimes more responsive to minority-group concerns than were their federal counterparts.[52]

Nonetheless, the fact that American federalism and American state constitutions have not played a central role in the protection of the rights of minorities raises important questions. Is the record of American state declarations of rights a product of unique historical factors, or is it indicative of a problem endemic to federal systems? Are the rights of minorities in federal systems more secure only if they comprise a majority within component units? If they do not, are their rights even less secure, because of the increased danger of majority faction? Only a cross-national comparison of subnational constitutions and minority rights can answer those questions.

NOTES

1. For overviews, see Ellis Katz and G. Alan Tarr, eds., *Federalism and Rights* (Lanham, MD: Rowman & Littlefield, 1996), and David L. Shapiro, *Federalism: A Dialogue* (Evanston, IL: Northwestern University Press, 1995).

2. See, for example, Ohio Const. of 1802, Art. 4, sec. 1; Mich. Const. of 1835, Art. 2, sec. 1; Mich. Const. of 1850, Art. 7, sec. 1; and Minn. Const. of 1857, Art. 7, sec. 1. For an overview of racial exclusion from the franchise, see Eric Foner, "From Slavery to Citizenship: Blacks and the Right to Vote," in Donald W. Rogers, ed., *Voting and the Spirit of American Democracy* (Urbana: University of Illinois Press, 1990).

3. The Southern disenfranchisement of African-Americans after Reconstruction is chronicled in J. Morgan Kousser, *The Shaping of Southern Politics: Suffrage Restrictions and the Establishment of the One-Party South 1890–1910* (New Haven, CT: Yale University Press, 1974). On the disenfranchisement of the Chinese and of the Mormons, see Calif. Const. of 1879, art. 2, sec.1; and Idaho Const. of 1889, art. 6, sec. 3. More generally, see David Alan Johnson, *Founding the Far West: California, Oregon, and Nevada, 1840–1890* (Berkeley: University of California Press, 1992), pp. 252–256; and Dennis Colson, *Idaho's Constitution: The Tie That Binds* (Moscow: University of Idaho Press, 1991), chapter 8.

4. On English as an official language, see Ariz. Const., Art. 28; Calif. Const., Art. 3, sec. 6; and Fla. Const., Art. 2, sec. 9. Proposition 187, which restricted benefits to legal residents, was adopted by California voters in 1994 but struck down by a federal court, and the state decided not to appeal the ruling. See *League of United Latin Am. Citizens v. Wilson*, 908 F.Supp. 755 (C.D.Cal. 1995).

5. See, for example, *Morrison v. Olson*, 120 S.Ct. 1740 (2000); *Alden v. Maine*, 119 S.Ct. 2240 (1999); *Printz v. United States*, 521 U.S. 898 (1997); *Seminole Tribe of Florida v. Florida*, 517 U.S. 44 (1996); and *Lopez v. United States*, 514 U.S. 549 (1995).

6. Four states actually devised their constitutions prior to the formal declaration of independence, and two employed slightly revised versions of their colonial charters as constitutions. See G. Alan Tarr, *Understanding State Constitutions* (Princeton, NJ: Princeton University Press, 1998), chapter 3; Donald S. Lutz, *Popular Consent and Popular Control: Whig Political Theory in the Early State Constitutions* (Baton Rouge: Louisiana State University Press, 1980); Willi Paul Adams, *The First American Constitutions: Republican Ideology and the Making of the State Constitutions in the Revolutionary Era* (Chapel Hill: University of North Carolina Press, 1980); and Gordon S. Wood, *The Creation of the American Republic, 1776–1787* (New York: Norton, 1969).

7. Provisions in modern state constitutions may be adopted to overcome earlier judicial interpretations of the constitution that prohibited the exercise of power in question. For example, the New York Constitution authorized the Legislature to create a system of workers' compensation to take the place of the tort liability system for workplace injuries after a court decision concluding that such a system was in violation of the state constitution. Such provisions are grants of power, or at least the removal of limitations. States also may insert grants of power in their constitutions to remove constitutional doubt or to ratify preexisting practices.

8. The only exception to this involves the admission of states to the Union. Article IV, section 3 of the U.S. Constitution, in empowering Congress to admit new states, in effect gives it the power to establish the conditions under which they will be admitted. In the enabling acts by which it authorizes prospective states to devise constitutions and apply for statehood, Congress can impose conditions as to the substance of state constitutions, and state constitution-makers must meet those conditions in order to secure a favorable vote on admission. Moreover, if a proposed constitution contains provisions of which Congress or the president disapproves, either can refuse to approve legislation admitting the state until the offending provisions are altered or removed. In practice, the impact of these congressional mandates has been minimal.

9. *Romer v. Evans*, 517 U.S. 620 (1996); *Torasco v. Watkins*, 367 U.S. 488 (1961); and *U.S. Term Limits, Inc. v. Thornton*, 514 U.S. 779 (1995).

10. See G. Alan Tarr and Mary Cornelia Porter, *State Supreme Courts in State and Nation* (New Haven, CT: Yale University Press, 1988), pp. 27–34.

11. See Tarr, *Understanding State Constitutions*, chapters 3–5.

12. Charles C. Binney, *Restrictions upon Local and Special Legislation in State Constitutions* (Philadelphia: Kay and Brother, 1894), p. 9.

13. Idaho Const., Arts. 15–16, and Calif. Const., Art. 10A.

14. See Thad Beyle, "Governors: The Middlemen and Women in Our Political System," in Virginia Gray and Herbert Jacob, eds., *Politics in the American States: A Comparative Analysis*, 6th ed. (Washington, DC: CQ Press, 1996).

15. Donald S. Lutz, "Toward a Theory of Constitutional Amendment," *American Political Science Review* 88 (June 1994): 355–70.

16. See G. Alan Tarr, "Church and State in the States," *Washington Law Review* 64 (winter 1989): 87–110. A useful compilation of state guarantees is Ronald K. L. Collins, Jr., "Bills and Declarations of Rights Digest," in *The American Bench*, 3d ed. (Sacramento: Reginald Bishop Forster and Associates, 1985–86).

17. On the state constitutional right to a remedy, see David Schuman, "The Right to a Remedy," *Temple Law Review* 65 (winter 1992): 1197–1227. On the state

constitutional right to privacy, see Ken Gormley and Rhonda G. Hartman, "Privacy and the States," *Temple Law Review* 65 (winter 1992): 1279–1323.

18. See G. Alan Tarr and Mary Cornelia Porter, "Gender Equality and Judicial Federalism: The Role of State Appellate Courts," *Hastings Law Quarterly* 9 (summer 1982): 953, Table A. On victims' rights provisions, see Jennifer Friesen, *State Constitutional Law: Litigating Individual Rights, Claims and Defenses*, 2nd ed. (Charlottesville, VA: Michie, 1996), pp. 813–14.

19. Tex. Const., Art. 3, sec. 11(a); Mass. Const., Part I, Art. 12; Calif. Const., Art I, sec. 27; and Fla. Const., Art. I, sec. 12.

20. La. Const., Art. 1, sec. 12.

21. See G. Alan Tarr, "State Constitutionalism and 'First Amendment' Rights," in Stanley Friedelbaum, ed., *Human Rights in the States* (Westport, CT: Greenwood Press, 1988).

22. See, for example, Wash. Const., Art I, sec. 11.

23. See, for example, Ala. Const., Art. I, sec. 3; Kan. Const. Bill of Rights, sec. 7; and Colo. Const., Art. X, sec. 2(a).

24. See Robert F. Williams, "Equality Guarantees in State Constitutional Law," *Texas Law Review* 63 (March-April 1985): 1195–1224.

25. Tex. Const., Art. I, sec. 3. See David Schuman, "The Right to 'Equal Privileges and Immunities': A State's Version of 'Equal Protection,'" *Vermont Law Review* 13 (Spring 1988): 221–45.

26. Fla. Const., Art. I, sec. 2; La. Const., Art. I, sec. 3.

27. Mont. Const., Art. X, sec. 1, para. 2; and N.M. Const., Art. XII, sec. 8, 10, and Art. XX, sec. 12.

28. Haw. Const., Art. X, sec. 4, and Art. XII. See Anne Feder Lee, *The Hawaii State Constitution: A Reference Guide* (Westport, CT: Greenwood Press, 1993), pp. 170–71.

29. The fact that state courts, rather than federal courts, render the authoritative interpretation of state constitutions should not obscure that other state actors also play an important role. In many states, the Attorney General of the state is authorized to render formal opinions, including those interpreting the state constitution, to state and local governmental officials. These opinions are not binding, but they do carry a good deal of weight in government deliberations. See Thomas R. Morris, "State Attorneys General as Interpreters of State Constitutions," *Publius: The Journal of Federalism* 17 (winter 1987): 133–52. Furthermore, the ease of state constitutional amendment means that state supreme court rulings may be the beginning of a dialogue rather than the end of a process. See Douglas S. Reed, "Popular Constitutionalism: Toward a Theory of State Constitutional Meanings," *Rutgers Law Journal* 30 (summer 1999): 871–932.

30. Friesen, *State Constitutional Law*, p. 146.

31. Susan P. Fino, "Judicial Federalism and Equality Guarantees in State Supreme Courts," *Publius: The Journal of Federalism* 17 (winter 1987): 58–59. Fino found that only 27 percent of equality challenges were based on such personal traits.

32. Ibid., pp. 60–61. Overall, only 6.7 percent of all decisions rested exclusively on state law, and these predominantly involved areas of traditional state concern—for example, bar regulation cases, Sunday closing cases, and zoning cases—rather than the protection of minority rights.

33. *Crawford v. Board of Education*, 551 P.2d 28 (1976); *Jackson v. Pasadena City School District*, 382 P.2d 878 (1963).

34. Calif. Const., Art. I, sec. 7, upheld in *Crawford v. Board of Education of the City of Los Angeles*, 458 U.S. 527 (1982).

35. *Sheff v. O'Neill*, 678 A.2d 1267 (Conn. 1996). This ruling went beyond the requirements of *Brown v. Board of Education*, 347 U.S. 483 (1954), which required states to remedy only *de jure* racial segregation—that is, segregation that resulted from actions of the state.

36. Calif. Const., Art 1, sec. 31.

37. *Southern Burlington County NAACP v. Township of Mount Laurel*, 336 A.2d 713 (1975); *Southern Burlington County NAACP v. Township of Mount Laurel*, 456 A.2d 390 (1983).

38. For a listing of courts that have invalidated state systems of school finance, see G. Alan Tarr, *Judicial Process and Judicial Policymaking*, 2nd ed. (Belmont, CA: Wadsworth, 1999), chapter 11.

39. See, for example, *Frontiero v. Richardson*, 411 U.S. 677 (1973); *Craig v. Boren*, 429 U.S. 190 (1976); and *United States v. Virginia*, 518 U.S. 515 (1996).

40. See Tarr and Porter, "Gender Equality and Judicial Federalism," 927–29.

41. 478 U.S. 186 (1986).

42. 517 U.S. 620 (1996).

43. Compare *Morales v. State*, 826 S.W.2d 201 (Tex. Ct. App. 1993) and *Commonwealth v. Wasson*, 785 S.W.2d 67 (Ky. App. Ct.1990), *aff'd*, 842 S.W.2d 487 (Ky. 1992) with *Christensen v. State*, 468 S.E.2d 188 (Ga. 1996).

44. 852 P.2d 44 (1993), overturned by Haw. Const., Art. I, sec. 23. For discussion of *Baehr* and its aftermath, see Reed, "Popular Constitutionalism." On developments in other states, see Mark Strasser, "Same-Sex Marriage Referenda and the Constitution: On *Hunter*, *Roemer*, and Electoral Process Guarantees," *Albany Law Review* 64 (2001): 949–81.

45. *Baker* v. *State*, 744 A.2d 864, (Vt. 1999).

46. Larry M. Elison and Fritz Snyder, *The Montana State Constitution: A Reference Guide* (Westport, CT: Greenwood Press, 2001), p.178.

47. *Lopez Tijerina* v. *Henry*, 48 F.R.D. 27 (D.N.M. 1969); appeal dismissed, 398 U.S. 922 (1970). See Chuck Smith, *The New Mexico State Constitution: A Reference Guide* (Westport, CT: Greenwood Press, 1996), pp. 33–34 and 139–40.

48. Haw. Const., Art. XII, sec. 7. An *ahupua* is a land division, usually wedge-shaped, and extending from the mountains at its narrowest to the sea at its widest.

49. See *Pele Defense Fund v. Paty*, 837 P.2d 1247 (Haw. 1992), and *Kalipi v. Hawaiian Trust Co.*, 656 P.2d 745 (Haw. 1982).

50. *San Antonio Independent Board of Education v. Rodriguez*, 411 U.S. 1 (1973).

51. The New Jersey Supreme Court's aggressive intervention in *Mount Laurel II* in 1983—*Southern Burlington County NAACP v. Township of Mount Laurel*, 456 A.2d 390 (N.J. 1983)—followed the U.S. Supreme Court's rejection of an effort to involve it in the issue in *Warth v. Seldin*, 422 U.S. 490 (1975). In *Bowers v. Hardwick*, 478 U.S. 186 (1986), the Supreme Court upheld a Georgia law that outlawed sodomy.

52. The plight of fugitive slaves in the era prior to the Civil War is a prime example; see *Prigg v. Pennsylvania*, 41 U.S. (16 Pet.) 536 (1842), and Paul Finkleman, "*Prigg v. Pennsylvania* and Northern State Courts: Anti-Slavery Use of a Pro-Slavery Opinion," *Civil War History* 25 (March 1979): 5–35. For an interesting general overview of the protection of rights in the nineteenth and early twentieth centuries, see John J. Dinan, *Keeping the People's Liberties: Legislators, Citizens, and Judge as Guardians of Rights* (Lawrence: University Press of Kansas, 1998).

III

Regional Systems in Transformation

7

Asymmetric, "Quasi-Federal" Regionalism and the Protection of Minorities: The Case of Italy

Francesco Palermo

MINORITIES AND REGIONALISM IN ITALY: TWO SIDES OF THE SAME COIN

Within Italy, approximately 2.5 million people (4.5 percent of the population) belong to—at least—12 minority groups, not taking immigrants into account.[1] This makes Italy the EU country in which the most minorities live.[2] The Italian Constitution of 1948 treats only language as a distinctive feature for identifying minorities, due to the basic assumption that all Italian citizens are members of the Italian nation, which is therefore a nation of nations. This does not mean that minority features other than language are not recognized, but only that in these cases the legal protection is different: for "other" minorities (racial, sexual, religious, etc.) the general provisions of the equality clause and the nondiscrimination principle of Article 3 of the Constitution apply,[3] whereas linguistic minorities are protected by means of "special measures" required by Article 6 of the Constitution.[4]

In addition, not even all linguistic minorities are officially recognized by the law, so that, in constitutional terms, it is correct to speak only about "protected" linguistic minorities. Moreover, the Italian "minority Constitution"[5] distinguishes not only between protected and unprotected minorities but also between different systems of protection: the intensity of protection varies from recognized minority to recognized minority.[6]

The criterion for allocation of minority rights is basically territorial.[7] Affirmative minority rights are connected primarily with the territory where minorities settle rather than with the inhabitants themselves. In the Italian constitutional system person-related minority rights are rarely recognized. This means, for instance, that a French-speaking inhabitant of the Aosta Valley can make use of his/her linguistic rights only within this Region, but cannot claim to speak French with the State authorities in Rome. Furthermore, individual membership in a minority group is generally based on the free will (and declaration) of each individual.

If territory is the basic reference for minority rights, it becomes evident that the territorial structure is closely linked with minority issues. In fact, the Italian regional system is deeply determined in its creation and evolution by the existence of strong minority groups, which in some cases even constitute the majority within their respective territory. The legal consequence of the linkage between regionalism and minority rights has been the establishment of strong asymmetries both in the regional system and in the machinery for minority protection.

This chapter analyzes the evolution and present shape of Italian regionalism and the most relevant features of its minority protection system in order to clarify the present and future relationship between national and subnational constitutional law in the asymmetric regulation of minority issues.

THE ITALIAN REGIONAL SYSTEM ON THE WAY TO A "DEVOLUTIONARY FEDERATION"

Establishment and Evolution

In spite of a multicentury history of regional division, Italian regionalism is legally quite a recent phenomenon. Since the achievement of national unity in the second half of the nineteenth century, the Italian constitutional and administrative system has been modeled on the French tradition of a unitarian, centralized, and bureaucratic form of government. Thus, no subnational entities were established after unification, although regional diversities (in economic, social, political, and even linguistic terms) have always been very strong. For a long time the sole form of decentralization was municipal self-government, but there the mayor used to be at the same time a locally elected figurehead and the representative of the State at the local level. Centralization reached its peak during the fascist regime (1922–1943), when even the mayor was appointed by the State. Surprisingly, however, the idea of the present Regions dates back to the 1930s, when regions were invented for statistical purposes, without following the borders of historical geographical units.

The republican constitution that entered into force on January 1, 1948, had to face a complex situation insofar as regional diversity was concerned. On the one hand, international obligations imposed by the peace treaty (such as the Degasperi-Gruber agreement on the protection of the German-speaking minority in South Tyrol[8]) had to be taken into account;[9] on the other hand, concrete fears for the secession of parts of the national territory,[10] as well as geographical reasons,[11] made the establishment of a strong subnational level of government in at least five areas inevitable: Trentino-South Tyrol, Aosta Valley, Friuli-Venezia Giulia, Sicily, and Sardinia. In order to avoid too strong an asymmetry between these areas and the rest of the country, and to experiment with a "third way" between a federal and a unitarian system, Regions were foreseen for the whole country, although the other Regions enjoyed much less autonomy than did the five just named.

The constitution thus establishes 20 Regions (Article 131), 5 of which enjoy a higher degree of autonomy (Article 116).[12] These 5 so-called "special" or "autonomous" Regions had their own basic law, approved as a constitutional law of the State; received much more legislative, administrative, and financial autonomy; and could negotiate their own bylaws directly with the national government, bypassing the national Parliament. In addition, the powers of each Region and, to some extent, even the governmental structure, were different in each special Region.[13] The remaining 15 —so-called "ordinary"—Regions had only a limited legislative power in specific fields listed by the national constitution (Article 117) and a very similar if not identical governmental structure. Moreover, they remained on paper for more than 20 years: Only in 1970 were the "ordinary" Regions established and only in 1972 were the first laws devolving some legislative power enacted.[14]

In the last 30 years, many things have changed. Apart from the special Regions, which were able to negotiate (in a more or less satisfactory way) their own destiny with the central government, big problems arose for the "ordinary" Regions immediately after their establishment. These Regions were lacking political culture as well as governmental experience, and the power-sharing between State and Regions designed by the constitution showed its inadequacy, especially in terms of the division of competencies. All this led to a profound cleavage between the constitutional provisions and the reality.[15] The more active Regions tried to "force" the central government toward a more benevolent interpretation and more autonomy, whereas the weaker Regions were left behind. Thus, the case law of the Constitutional Court became much more relevant in determining the real powers of the Regions than the laws and the wording of the constitution itself.

In other words, it became immediately clear that the real rules on the relationship between the levels of government were not to be found in the Constitution, but rather in ordinary legislation and administrative acts, and, primarily, in constitutional adjudication. As a consequence, regional interests could not be guaranteed by the constitution, and each Region actually had to negotiate them with the central State. On the one hand, this strengthened the asymmetrical features of Italian regionalism; on the other hand, it made a reform of the constitutional provisions on the regional system necessary.

In 1983 the first attempt was made to amend the constitution in a way that was more favorable to the development of regional self-government, but the *ad hoc* parliamentary commission did not reach any concrete result. This was followed by many other unsuccessful attempts. Not until 1990 were laws enacted that modified the general administrative structure and encouraged Regions to develop their potential of self-government. Also the political attitude toward decentralization changed radically, and the regional issue was brought to the fore on the political stage. After the failure of attempts to amend the constitution in 1992 and 1994, a different approach was taken in 1997. Instead of amendments, four ordinary laws (not requiring a qualified majority) were passed, reflecting a real revolution in the relationship between the State and the Regions. These laws constituted not a formal, but certainly a substantive constitutional change, especially because they redesigned the division of legislative and administrative competencies, enumerating the State's competencies and making the Regions responsible for all the rest. Also the fora for regional participation at the Central level and the cooperation between levels of government were regulated, and the principle of subsidiarity was established for the first time in the legislation. At the same time the last parliamentary commission for constitutional reform definitively failed, after having elaborated a text that was intended to enshrine these principles in the constitution.

The introduction of a *de facto* federal system by means of ordinary legislation bypassed some political problems, but obviously created legal ones. In particular, the constitutionalization of the new principles was necessary. Giving up—for political reasons—on attempts for an organic amendment of the constitution, single constitutional laws have been approved, modifying specific aspects of regional self-government. Constitutional law no. 1/1999 changed the regional form of government, introducing direct election of the Presidents of the Regions, and constitutional law no. 2/2001 did the same with regard to the autonomous Regions.[16] Finally, in March 2001, in a highly conflictive political atmosphere, constitutional law no. 3/2001 was approved, which succeeded in amending the entire part of the constitution dealing with the relationship between national and subnational levels of government. Because it was approved only by simple majority, the constitutional amendment could enter into force only on November 7, 2001, after having been approved by a nationwide referendum.[17]

The recent reform finally gives constitutional coverage to the principles already enshrined in the 1997 legislation as well as in the case law of the Constitutional Court: Most of the rules provided by the reform were already contained in the 1997 legislation, although some additional principles have been added. The new system limits the legislative and administrative powers of the national level, abolishes State control over regional legislation, and establishes a presumption of general regional legislative competence in the constitution. It also establishes a more cooperative regionalism, by creating new bodies for cooperation between Regions and States, although it does not transform the Senate into a Chamber of Regions, as advocated by most scholars. Regions are now also enabled to conclude international agreements (although with the consent of the State) and can freely determine their own form of government. In particular, they can decide how to appoint the President of the Region (in almost all Regions the President is now directly elected by the people and no longer nominated by the assembly) and can approve their own electoral law. As to competencies, the Regions not only received the general legislative competence in all the matters that are not explicitly reserved to the State, but they can also get some additional powers in the fields of culture and security by means of a new negotiation procedure with the State. Last but not least, ordinary Regions are now entitled to approve their own constitutions (while respecting the limits imposed by the national constitution and by EU law), which represents a decisive step, at least from the formal point of view, towards federalism.[18]

The new constitutional framework thus makes the Italian regional system so close to a federal system that it is almost impossible to draw a line between the two concepts. Nevertheless, the reform still contains many aspects that must be clarified in practice, will need to be specified by additional legislation and, above all, shall be interpreted by the Constitutional Court, which again will play the key role in determining the real contents of the new system.[19]

Current and Future Italian Regionalism: The Importance of Asymmetry

In brief, after the recent constitutional reform, Italian regionalism can be defined as "devolutionary asymmetric federalism in the making." Even though there seems to be no substantial difference between the present regional system and a more consolidated federal system, in the reformed constitution the term "federalism" never appears, thus indicating the self-perception of the Italian constitutional system as a transitional and open-ended one, which will need to be determined step by step, starting with the approval of the new "constitution" (*statuto*) of each Region.[20]

It will be up to the Regions to elaborate homogeneous constitutions or to differentiate among them. Under the present system, all the regional *statuti* are almost identical, and so are governmental structures, especially where ordinary Regions are concerned, whereas a higher degree of asymmetry can be observed between the special Regions, which already have different powers and different legitimization of the government (direct election of the governor[21] or its appointment by the assembly). Asymmetry in Italian regionalism is thus not only a consequence of historical developments, of political negotiations, and of the existence of more or less consistent minority groups, but also a constitutional "duty" for some Regions[22] and now an opportunity for all of them. One of the most innovative provisions of the reformed constitution, in fact, is enshrined in Article 116 al. 3, which provides the constitutional base for additional differentiation between ordinary Regions.[23] If Regions will take advantage of this asymmetrical opportunity, they could improve their own degree of self-government, especially in fields closely related to minority protection, like education, culture, and the environment.[24]

This opportunity will give rise to a very differentiated, asymmetrical regional system. At a first level there will be the special Regions, each of them different from the other in terms of powers, governmental structure, and capacity for self-government. At a second level there will be the ordinary Regions, making use of the new opportunity to achieve more powers in the mentioned areas (most probably the richer industrial Regions of the North). At a third level, there will be the ordinary Regions that will not acquire more powers but will nevertheless be able to accommodate their special needs by approving their own constitution.[25]

The near future of Italian regionalism will thus involve asymmetrical relationships. For our purposes, this has at least three fundamental constitutional and political consequences. First, most of the exclusive powers retained by the State are not competencies in the strict sense of the term. Issues like relations with the EU, competition protection, civil and criminal law, basic level of benefits relating to civil and social entitlements where civil and social rights are concerned (Article 117 of the constitution) are above all policy fields that, depending on the political development of Italian regionalism, can either limit in a substantive way the realm of regional self-government, or, on the contrary, accommodate the regional differences. The new system will be thus a very flexible one, distinguishing between macropolicies (reserved to the State and, even more, to the EU) and micropolicies, in which regional diversity can come to the fore. And it is self-evident that minority protection, showing both a macrodimension and a microdimension, will continue to be a typical cross-cutting issue, to be managed jointly by the different layers of government.

Second, the Italian case shows the importance of the political perception of the subnational self-government. Not all the Regions provided with more autonomy were able to take advantage of it, and not all the "ordinary" Regions are in fact weak political units. It can be said that one of the deficiencies of Italian regionalism has been (until now) the lack of true, locally developed regional policies. Apart from some special Regions—in particular, again, Trentino, South Tyrol, and Aosta Valley—the political discourse and the political careers of regional politicians were dominated by national politics. Thus, apart from small and peculiar realities (mostly determined by the very existence of ethnic minorities, as in South Tyrol, Aosta Valley, and to some extent Sardinia), the regional policy has been shaped by the national one: For example, many regional presidents resigned to become members of the national Parliament.[26] Direct election of the governors (if it is not repealed by the new regional constitutions)[27] is gradually making regional policy stronger and less dependent on national policy, thus transforming the perception of the role of Regions not only on paper but in everyday life. Such a self-consciousness of the importance of regional policy was, on the other hand, always a prerogative of some autonomous Regions, in particular those where minorities are settled. Thus, indirectly, the very existence of minorities contributed to the development of a regional political conscience.

Third, the newly acquired legislative powers in several crucial fields such as education, culture, and the like will certainly also play a role in minority-related legislation. The choice that each Region will make about the introduction of a regional bill of rights into its own constitution (which was not possible before the reform but seems not to be prohibited in the new system, provided that the national and the European fundamental rights are respected) will have a strong influence on the future shape of minority protection.

THE ITALIAN "MINORITY CONSTITUTION" AND ITS THREE LEVELS

The Italian "Minority Constitution" Is Based on Three Principles

1. Only linguistic minorities are considered to be minorities. According to the Italian constitutional tradition, based on the French-derived "citizenship approach" and avoiding the concept of ethnicity, the Italian nation is comprised of many linguistic groups. The concept of nation is thus to be understood as *demos* and not as *ethnos*.[28] Legally speaking, in Italy there are no ethnic, but only linguistic minorities;
2. The legal precondition for the protection of minorities is their legal recognition. Only officially recognized minorities can be protected by means of special legal instruments. Otherwise, only the equality principle and the principle of nondiscrimination can be applied;
3. Minority rights are related to the territory and not to the persons. Persons belonging to a (recognized) minority can enjoy their minority rights only within a certain territory (territorial principle instead of personal principle).[29] As a consequence, minorities are protected mainly through regional autonomy.

The most important criterion adopted by the Italian constitution for minority protection is thus territorial autonomy for the areas where such groups live. Obviously, the more developed the self-government, the easier the recognition and protection of minority groups at the local level, because small groups at the national level can become, in a local governance perspective, numerically more significant, or even the majority in their territory, such as in South Tyrol and in Aosta Valley. This criterion is in fact very efficient in the case of larger and territorially compact minorities, whereas for smaller and more scattered groups it is less adequate. Consequently, the most well-protected minorities in Italy are the larger linguistic groups living in border areas adjacent to the respective national States: German speakers along the Austrian border, French-speakers along the French and Swiss border, Slovenian-speakers near Slovenia.

Article 6 of the national constitution, the general provision for minority protection, does not specify whether minority rights should be granted by a general provision (framework law) or by different measures for every (protected) minority. For both practical (the political difficulty in drafting a general provision that satisfies the request of different minorities, numbers, political influence, etc.) and legal reasons (e.g., the international anchoring of the status of certain minorities, such as the South Tyrolean one), a general law was not passed by the Parliament until 1999, and this led to different treatment for each minority. This could even be seen as a violation of the equality principle, which imposes equal treatment for the social groups sharing the same legal nature,[30] although it is common to almost all the constitutional arrangements and is now accepted and even recognized by the Council of Europe's Charter of Regional or Minority Languages (1992)[31] and by the Framework Convention on the Protection of National Minorities of the Council of Europe.[32] It is obvious that extralegal elements have an impact in determining the legal rules (e.g., the number of the minority group members, their territorial and political cohesion, the influence of foreign national States, the economic situation, social acceptance, etc.), but it cannot be denied that in Italy the different legal treatment of the various minorities is particularly evident. For this reason, Italy is simultaneously one of the most advanced countries with respect to minority protection and one in which many small minority groups are in danger of being definitively assimilated in the near future.[33]

Because of the very asymmetrical character of Italian regionalism, of the territorial principle as the base for minority protection, and of the very nature of minority rights as cross-cutting rights, the legal instruments for minority protection in the Italian legal system also vary substantially, ranging from international and constitutional regulations to State laws to regional laws. The most relevant legal tools and minority rights will be therefore analyzed on the basis of the three different levels of protection and sources of law they are incorporated in: constitutional, national and regional laws.

Autonomous Regions and the Protection of Minorities

In the field of minority protection, national constitutional law performs two main functions. First, it states the general principle of minority recognition and protection (Article 6 of the constitution) and, in connection with other constitutional principles, "opens" the domestic legal system to the developments of international law in this field.[34] Second, it constitutes the legal guarantee of the special autonomy granted to the autonomous Regions (Article 116 of the constitution) and thus, in some cases, to the minority rights closely linked to them or even contributing to their origins.

The most powerful national constitutional instrument for minority protection is the system of legal guarantees provided for the strongest minorities. Given space limitations, we focus on the most articulated, intense, and complex system of minority protection via special territorial autonomy under Italian constitutional law, the case of South Tyrol.

South Tyrol, located in the central Alps, is a small province of about 460,000 inhabitants, 70 percent of whom speak German as their mother tongue. It was annexed by Italy after World War I and the dissolution of the Austrian empire. During the fascist regime, it underwent a strong policy of assimilation, under which mass immigration of Italians was promoted to industrialize the area and to change its ethnic composition. During World War II, the oppressive policies against the German population and culture reached their climax.[35] The postwar peace treaty recognized South Tyrol as a part of Italy, ensuring to the German-speaking community special provisions to guarantee "complete equality of rights with the Italian speaking inhabitants." In 1948 the Italian Parliament adopted an autonomy statute that transferred most of the powers to the Region (composed by South Tyrol and the neighboring Italian-speaking Province of Trento), in which Italian-speakers were the majority. After a long and sometimes even violent process of negotiations, which also included two resolutions by the U.N. General Assembly (urged by Austria), a new model of autonomy was elaborated in 1969 and put into force in 1972. This system, which was implemented through a long list of normative measures over 20 years, is still in place today. It maintains the Region as a "roof" structure above the two Provinces (Trentino, almost 100 percent Italian-speaking, and South Tyrol, where the majority is German-speaking), but all substantial legislative and administrative powers are vested with the provinces. Nowadays, the German linguistic minority in South Tyrol is the largest and best protected minority in Italy, and probably one of the most well-handled minority groups in the whole world.

The whole institutional design of the Province of Bolzano/Bozen (and of the Region Trentino-South Tyrol, where relevant) is based on the strict separation of the two main linguistic groups, the German and the Italian,[36] giving to the third, and numerically much less consistent, linguistic group (the Ladins) the right to be represented as such in the provincial Parliament (Article 48 al. 2 autonomy statute). This principle of coexistence imposed by law[37] and based on an "ethnic divided governance" provides for a large spectrum of affirmative minority rights, especially in the fields of public jobs, education, and linguistic rights.

Positions in public offices "are reserved for citizens belonging to each of the three language groups, in proportion to the size of the groups themselves, as they appear in the declarations of the official census" (Article 89). Since 1981, every 10 years the inhabitants of South Tyrol have been required to add to the standard census data a declaration of belonging to one of the three linguistic groups. Through this declaration, the size of the linguistic groups can be ascertained, and this then forms the legal foundation of the public life. In the last census (2001) the relative size of the groups was as follows: the German group, 69.15 percent; the Italian group, 26.47 percent; and the Ladin group, 4.38 percent. In addition, preference for public posts is given to citizens who have resided in South Tyrol for at least two years. This quota system, called ethnic proportional representation, is conceived of as a form of reparation for italianization during the fascist period. The intended duration of this form of affirmative action is not yet clear.[38]

The educational system in South Tyrol is based on separation and the principle that "instruction in the nursery, elementary and secondary schools is given in the Italian or German mother tongue of the pupils by instructors for whom that language is also their mother tongue."[39] The teaching of the "second language" (Italian in the German schools and vice-versa) is compulsory, from the first or second grade onward. In the Ladin valleys, lessons are conducted, in equal number of hours, in Italian and German, and Ladin is taught as well. The educational boards are also separated. The enrollment of a pupil in a school of one or the other group is based on the request of the parents, but it must "in no way influence the teaching language planned for the different schools,"[40] so that in fact it is up to the discretion of the school bodies to admit a pupil to a school of one or the other group (the decision can be challenged in the autonomous section of the regional administrative court).

Concerning language rights, in South Tyrol "the German language has parity with the Italian language, which is the official language of the State."[41] Everybody can use either Italian or German (in limited areas also the Ladin language) in their dealings "with judiciary offices and with the organs and offices of public administration located in the Province or having regional competence, as well as with concessionaires of public services in the Province itself."[42] The public employers (and the concessionaires of public services) must also be bilingual (trilingual in the Ladin valleys), which has to be proved by a public examination. Since 1993, every judicial trial can be instituted also in German (previously German could be used but the minutes had to be written in Italian). Place names must be bilingual (Article 8 al. 2 autonomy statute) and trilingual in the Ladin valleys, and the Province has also created a public media board with the duty to transmit German-speaking radio and TV programs.

As might be expected, measures such as safeguarding linguistic rights and the double/triple educational system are very expensive. For the most part, neither the Provinces nor the Region has the right to levy taxes. To cover the costs of autonomy, the majority of the taxes and duties collected in South Tyrol goes to the Province (around 90 percent), and a small part flows to the Region (5 percent). The remaining 5 percent is kept by the State for its tasks at the local level, although these costs amount to much more. The final ratio of taxes and duties paid by the inhabitants of the Province and the money spent by Province, Region, and State for public tasks within South Tyrol is around 100:110.[43]

In the end, the South Tyrolian minority protection system is very sophisticated and complex, based on territorial self-government, within which particular affirmative group rights are recognized to an extent that is not provided for other minorities.[44]

National Laws

As mentioned earlier, in November 1999 the national Parliament enacted, after many decades of failed attempts, the framework law for the protection of historic minorities (no. 482/1999), aimed to implement the general provision of Article 6 of the Constitution. Article 2 of the bill deals with the range of the law's application. It states that "according to article 6 of the Constitution and in accordance with the general principles laid down by European and international institutions,[45] Italy protects the language and culture of the Albanian, the Catalan, the German,[46] the Greek, the Slovene, and the Croat populations, as well as those speaking French, Provenzial, Friulian, Ladin, Occitan and Sardinian." The provision seems to distinguish between ethnicity (populations) and language (people speaking . . .), thus diverging from the traditional approach of Italian constitutional law, based on ethnic indifference and only recognizing linguistic diversity.[47]

As far as territorial application is concerned, the law grants to provincial assemblies the power to identify the geographic areas in which minority rights can be applied. The initiative can also be taken by citizens and municipal representatives of the concerned minorities (Article 3).[48] The law does not apply to the special Regions, and it thus does not concern the stronger and already protected minorities, although every autonomous Region can decide to enact some provision of the law as far as it contains innovative principles.

Substantively, the law provides for teaching minority languages and cultures in schools.[49] In particular, in nursery schools the minority languages will be permitted in educational activities, whereas in elementary and secondary schools the language, the culture, and the traditions of the local communities can be taught as a subject. Teaching of the minority language shall be required by the parents (Article 4 al. 5), whereas each school can decide to teach minority culture and traditions, which will be a compulsory subject for every pupil. It will then be possible to use minority languages in the municipal and provincial councils and governments (Article 7). The local authorities may also publish their official acts (and also acts of the State and of the Regions) in the minority language, but at their own expense. In addition, the minority language will be allowed in written and oral relations with the public administration located in the area, except in the relations with the army and the police (Article 9 al. 1). Italian remains in any case the only official language (Article 8). The minority languages can be used in the judiciary, too, but only in proceedings conducted by a justice of peace.[50]

In the field of media, the Ministry for Communications and public broadcasting shall jointly establish (generic) "conditions in order to grant minority protection" (Article 12 al. 1). More concretely, the Regions will also be able to sign conventions with public and private broadcasting authorities in order to ensure the transmission of news, cultural, and educational programs in the minority languages (Article 12 al. 2). Regions, Provinces, and municipalities may also grant financial aid to the media in order to implement the use of minority languages (Article 14).[51]

The approval of the framework law facilitated another law that has been discussed for decades. Finally, in February 2001, the law on the protection of the Slovene minority in Friuli-Venezia Giulia was approved by the national Parliament (law no. 38/2001). Under this law "the Republic recognizes and protects the rights of the Italian citizens belonging to the Slovene linguistic minority," basically by means of a general reference to the principles of the national framework law on historic minorities. In particular, the law grants rights that were already in force, like the right to use Slovene names (Article 7), to bilingual place names (Article 10), to bilingual schools (Article 11), and to use the Slovene language in dealing with the public administration (Article 8). Of particular interest is, on the one hand, the official recognition of inter-regional, cross-border cooperation (particularly with the kin-State) as a means for minority protection (Article 17) and, on the other, the emphasis on the territorial element as the exclusive legally relevant reference for the application of minority rights (Article 4). As with the national framework legislation, every municipality can decide to become a "minority territory," on the base of a proposal by at least 15 percent of the citizens or one third of the municipal councilors. In addition, a joint committee for the issues of the Slovene community is established that needs to be consulted in every step of the implementation of the law.[52]

Regional Laws

Since their establishment in the early 1970s, many ordinary Regions provided for protection and promotion of the minorities living in their territory. In some cases minority protection has been enshrined in the regional *statuti*, but only as a general and vague provision, in which the Region commits itself to the goal of respect for minorities. This is for instance the case of Piemonte,[53] Veneto,[54] Molise,[55] Basilicata,[56] and Calabria.[57]

More effective provisions were contained in ordinary regional laws aimed to improve the knowledge of the local languages and cultures for smaller groups running the risk of assimilation.[58] Nevertheless, regional laws have been very cautious in dealing with minority protection, because the Constitutional Court, in a first phase, denied that the Regions had any power in this regard, on the very simplistic assumption that minority protection was not mentioned in the list of competencies devolved to the Regions under the system prior to the 2001 reform.[59] It is self-evident, however, that minority protection cannot be considered a competence in the strict sense of the term, but is rather a specific use of the powers belonging to each level of government.

This was gradually recognized by the Constitutional Court, which, in the early 1980s, changed its previous jurisprudence by allowing regional legislative interventions in minority-related (and even minority-sensitive) fields.[60] It is not by chance that the reasoning of the Court for the new trend was based on the provision of Article 4 of the autonomy statute of Trentino-South Tyrol, which declares minority protection as a national interest. As a consequence, all Regions are authorized to pass legislation on the protection of their minorities, within the limits deriving from the respect of national fundamental rights and from the powers attributed to the Regions.[61]

Since then a large number of regional laws on (regional) minority protection (quite similar to each other) have been passed, providing in particular for cultural and linguistic rights of the concerned communities.[62] Moreover, several Regions used this opportunity to promote, more generally, their own regional culture, supposed to represent a minority culture within the national framework but certainly no minority at the regional level.[63] In no case were more invasive forms of protection like rights of political representation or affirmative actions enacted, because this would be considered a violation of the equality principle guaranteed by national constitutional law and would need to be enshrined in a national piece of legislation with constitutional range.[64]

It can therefore be concluded that regional laws on the protection of minorities are numerous and growing in scope. Nevertheless, they are limited to fields in which regional authorities can legitimately exercise their powers, such as culture, education, promotion and safeguard of historical, cultural, artistic heritage, and the like, and possibly many others after the complete entry into force of the constitutional reform of 2001. By no means, however, can they determine the very nature of the principle of equality, which is guaranteed only by national constitutional law: Therefore they cannot pass laws granting to minorities affirmative action programs, or specific religious rights,[65] or a more favorable political representation system, because this can only be provided for by national constitutional law.

This demonstrates why the special Regions enjoy the status of (nationally) constitutionally safeguarded autonomies. Since only in special Regions (and in particular in two of them, Trentino-South Tyrol and, to a much lesser extent, Aosta Valley) affirmative rights for minorities are established, derogating from the overarching equality principle imposed by the national constitution, only a legal source of the same range can intervene in such delicate issues. Thus, the particular range in the system of sources of law attributed to the "constitutions" of the special Regions turn out as a guarantee for their own autonomy and, in the end, for the minorities living in their respective territory.

FEDERALISM AND MULTICULTURALISM IN THE MAKING

Both the regional system and the rules on minority protection have changed radically in the last several decades in Italy. This seems to be due not only to endogenous dynamics, but also to developments in governance in Europe and worldwide. The role of the State is decreasing in terms of both the concrete exercise of powers and being the exclusive source of rights. This explains the increasing role of both subnational and supranational[66] entities in granting rights that can be considered minority rights. Three main consequences can be drawn from this development, with particular regard to the Italian situation.

First, with regard to minority rights, the national State is shifting its balance from direct intervention toward a more regulatory role, much as is happening in the economic constitution.[67] The State—and, to an increasing degree, the European Union—is less and less a direct source of concrete rights, and more and more the source of rules for determining the matter in which rights can be exercised. For our purposes, this means that the State will be the source and the controller of the equality principle, whereas other governance actors will determine the operational rules for specific rights, in the framework of the nationwide constitutional guarantee of (formal and substantial) equality. Thus, in the field of minority protection, it will also be possible to distinguish between macropolicies of the State (equality and, eventually, its integration/derogation, like positive actions) and micropolicies of the Regions, making their own choices in promoting local minorities and cultures.

Second, if this is true, asymmetry will apply not only to the scope of laws, but increasingly also to the very existence of minorities. Minorities, as such, do not exist.[68] They only become relevant in relationship to other groups having a dominant position, and in the last four centuries the criterion for determining the existence of minorities was the (nation) State.[69] If the State is no longer the unique and not even the main source of minority rights, and if the (nation) State was traditionally the only point of reference to determine what a minority is, then also the concept of minority is undergoing a process of re-elaboration. One could even argue that groups of people become minorities inasmuch as they are disadvantaged in the decision-making process at a certain level of governance.[70] Thus, the concept of minority will probably become a variable one, depending on the level of government involved.[71] Therefore, rigid, general rules will lose their appeal in favor of flexible, partial solutions, in the frame of a stronger enactment of the equality principle.

Third, the consequence of these developments seems to be a multilevel, multicultural, multirights, asymmetrical, and pluralistic society, based on the equality of all individuals, to which additional guarantees, rights, duties, and privileges can be attached. Of course, the situation of each minority is different, and in many cases (especially where smaller and endangered groups are concerned), there will be the need for a more traditional protection, based on the principle of mere nondiscrimination and (possibly) on additional, promotional rights. In general, however, it seems that simple minority protection is no longer sufficient,[72] and the trend is toward a multicultural society.[73] Thus, there is a movement from the concept of one nation recognizing linguistic diversity[74] toward a multicultural (and multinational) society,[75] with less structural minorities and more different groups claiming and exercising their rights to be different, a right that can vary on the basis of the territory involved. In this context, the further development of Italian subnational constitutional law will play a determinative role. The path will be certainly a long one and will show many contradictory elements,[76] but the tendency is already clearly identifiable.

NOTES

1. Where terminology is concerned, Italian legislation and legal doctrine make the following distinctions, which are kept in this chapter. *National* minorities are those groups that have a kin-State, live at the border with it, and have been included into Italy due to shifting borders in history (German-speakers in South Tyrol, Slovenian-speakers at the northeastern border of the State, and to some extent the French-speakers in the Aosta valley). *Historic* minorities are the

small groups living on Italian territory for centuries, who settled there for different historical reasons (trade, wars, etc.), like Croats, Albanians, Greeks, or Catalans in southern or insular Italy. In both cases, language is considered to be the distinctive element. Although there is no immediate link between the two elements, national minorities enjoy a much higher level of protection within the legal system.

The mentioned classification applies only to Italian citizens and does not include so-called *new* minorities—that is, the immigrants, who enjoy, from the legal point of view, a completely different treatment and are not considered in this chapter.

2. Further statistical data in Ministero dell'Interno, *Ufficio centrale per i problemi di confine e delle minoranze etniche, Primo rapporto sullo stato delle minoranze in Italia* (Roma, Italian Government, 1994).

3. Article 3 Italian constitution: "All citizens have equal social dignity and are equal before the law, without distinction of sex, race, language, religion, political opinion, personal and social conditions. It is the duty of the Republic to remove those obstacles . . . which constrain the freedom and equality of citizens. . . . (official translation of the Italian Parlamento, www.camera.it).

4. Article 6 Italian constitution: "The Republic safeguards linguistic minorities by means of appropriate measures."

5. This term has been developed by R. Toniatti, La rappresentanza politica delle minoranze linguistiche: i ladini fra rappresentanza "assicurata" e "garantita", in *Le Regioni*, 1995, 1271.

6. According to E. Palici di Suni Prat, *Intorno alle minoranze* (Torino, 1999), within the Italian system a distinction should be made between "super-protected minorities" (German-speakers in South Tyrol, French-speakers in Aosta Valley, and Slovene-speakers in Friuli-Venezia Giulia), "recognized minorities" (all the minorities recognized by the framework law no. 492/1999) and "not recognized minorities" (the remaining groups, including Roma and immigrants).

7. A. Pizzorusso, *Il pluralismo linguistico tra Stato nazionale e autonomie regionali* (Pisa, 1975) and A. Pizzorusso, *Le minoranze nel diritto pubblico interno* (Milano 1967).

8. According to the agreement (1946), which was attached to the Paris peace treaty between the allied powers and Italy (1947), "German speaking inhabitants of the Bolzano Province . . . will be assured a complete equality of rights with the Italian-speaking inhabitants, within the framework of special provisions to safeguard the ethnical character and the cultural and economic development of the German-speaking element."

9. A subsequent treaty regarded the particular situation of the Free territory of Trieste, which was governed by an international regime until 1954, providing special protection for the Slovenian-speaking population.

10. This was the case in Aosta Valley (a small region in the northwest of the country that had a long lasting tradition of self-government and that elaborated a plan for a strong autonomy already in 1943) and in Sicily, which elaborated its own constitution as a possible independent State in 1946, before the Italian constitution was drafted.

11. Like in the case of Sardinia, which at that time was quite isolated from the rest of the country.

12. Sicily, Sardinia, Trentino-Alto Adige/South Tyrol, Friuli-Venezia Giulia, and Aosta Valley/Vallée d'Aoste. These are the three smaller Regions of the alpine area, characterized by the presence of consistent national minorities, and the two main islands, whose special autonomy was due to different reasons:

nevertheless in both Sicily and Sardinia small minority groups are settled (Albanians in Sicily, Catalans in Sardinia), and Sardinian people is often referred to be a minority itself.

13. Moreover, the Region Friuli-Venezia Giulia (in the Northeast) was established only in 1964, after the final settlement of the Trieste situation. In 1972 the Autonomous Region of Trentino South Tyrol was redesigned, transferring almost all substantial powers to the two provinces of which it consists: Bolzano/Bozen (South Tyrol), where the majority of the population is German-speaking, and Trento, almost exclusively Italian.

14. The reasons for this delay are many. The most important ones were the lack of a genuine regional tradition and, above all, a political reason: the governing parties in Rome (especially Christian-Democrats) wanted to prevent some regional governments being "conquered" by the Communist Party, which was very strong especially in Central-Italian Regions.

15. R. Bin, Veri e falsi problemi del federalismo in Italia, in L. Mariucci et al. (eds.), *Il federalismo preso sul serio* (Bologna, 1996), 68.

16. Apart from the autonomous Province of Bolzano (South Tyrol) and the autonomous Region of Aosta Valley. In every case, special Regions were enabled to decide their own form of government, and the State rule applies only as long as the Regions do not pass their own legislation on this topic.

17. Amendments to the Italian constitution "shall be adopted by each House after two successive debates at intervals of not less than three months, and shall be approved by an absolute majority of the members of each House in the second voting." Amendments are submitted to a popular referendum when, within three months from their approval, a request is made by one fifth of the members of a House, or 500,000 voters, or five regional assemblies. A referendum shall not be held if the amendment has been approved in the second voting by each of the Houses by a majority of two thirds of the members (Article 138 constitution).

Until the reform of 2001, a conventional constitutional rule prevented use of the second amending procedure, which in practice makes it possible to modify the constitution by majority. The center-left government wanted to approve the reform before the elections held in May 2001, and so it did. The center-right parties, who opposed the change, called therefore for the confirmative referendum, and so did the center-left parties, being sure that the reform was desired by the citizens. The large majority of voters voted in favor of the reform, although less than 30 percent participated in the referendum.

18. For details on the changes introduced by the reform, see T. Groppi and M. Olivetti (eds.), *La Repubblica delle autonomie* (Torino, 2001); and B. Caravita, *La costituzione dopo la riforma del titolo V* (Torino, 2002).

19. In the 10 months following the entrance into force of the reform (November 2001–September 2002) the constitutional litigation between State and Regions increased by 400 percent compared to the previous ten months!

20. In November 2002 the process of elaboration of the new regional constitutions was progressing very slowly. Only some Regions (among them Calabria, Tuscany, Liguria, Veneto) have seriously started working on the tests. It seems that all the Regions prefer to start with the approval of their own laws on the form of government (election of the President, electoral system for the Assembly, rules on regional referenda, etc.), whereas the approval of the new constitutions will certainly take at least several years. As of August 2003, only Calabria has approved its regional constitution (August 1, 2003).

21. It is not by chance that the newly direct elected Presidents of Regions (this is now the official name) are normally referred to, in the political discourse and

in the media, as governors, underlying the (supposed) analogy with the American governors only because of popular election.

22. The right for the special Regions to be different and to enjoy a higher degree of autonomy is considered by most of the scholars one of the basic values of the constitution and thus not subject to constitutional reform. The constitutional court, in fact, has stated that the very fundamental principles of the constitutional system (like the democratic principle, the openness toward international law, etc.) cannot be changed, not even by means of a formal constitutional amendment: In such a case, the court would declare the constitutional law unconstitutional because of the breach of the fundamental principles (see judgment no. 1146/1988). See V. Onida, Le costituzioni. Principi fondamentali della costituzione italiana, in G. Amato and A. Barbera (eds.), *Manuale di diritto pubblico* (Bologna, 1997), vol. I, in particular p. 112; and S. Labriola, Il principio di specialità nel regionalismo italiano, in S. Ortino and P. Pernthaler (eds.), *La riforma costituzionale in senso federale. Il punto di vista delle autonomie speciali* (Bolzano-Trento, 1997), 84. This means that there is a constitutional privilege for the Regions to be treated differently. This opinion is shared by the Constitutional Court (see, for example, judgment no. 213/1998, in Giurisprudenza costituzionale, 1998, p. 1667). For a more detailed analysis, see L. Antonini, *Il regionalismo differenziato* (Milano, 2000).

23. Article 116 al. 3: "Additional special forms and conditions of autonomy, related to the areas specified in art. 117, paragraph three and paragraph two, letter l) [administration of justice (added by author)]—limited to the organizational requirements of the Justice of the Peace—and letters n) and s), [education, culture and environment (added by author)] may be attributed to other Regions by State Law, upon the initiative of the Region concerned, after consultation with the local authorities, in compliance with the principles set forth in art. 119. . . ."

24. The central government has recently proposed a bill in order to add to the mentioned subjects some other powers to be negotiated by the Regions with the State, like police, social and health care, and additional sectors of the educational sphere (proposal to the Senate, draft bill no. A.S. 1187). If this proposal is approved (although it does not seem that there will be the political consensus to reach the majority required for amending the constitution), the mentioned tendency toward asymmetrical devolution of powers will increase even more.

25. This structure is in the end quite similar to the solution adopted in Spain with the 1978 Constitution and its further implementation. Interestingly, the Italian regionalism, whose only (theoretical) source of inspiration was the Spanish 1931 constitution, has played an important role in influencing the present Spanish constitution of 1978 in this regard, and now again it is the Spanish model that guides the evolution of the Italian transition toward an asymmetric federalism. It is not by chance that both the Italian and the Spanish regional systems are to a large extent originated and shaped by goals of minority protection.

26. This example shows the low political importance of the regional level for a political career. See R. Bin, Veri e falsi problemi del federalismo in Italia, in L. Mariucci et al. (eds.), *Il federalismo preso sul serio* (Bologna, 1996), 70.

27. As already mentioned, the Regions are now free to determine the rules for the election of the president. They are thus theoretically free to decide that the governor shall be appointed by the assembly. Politically speaking, however, this seems highly improbable: not only was the direct election of the heads of the Regions introduced in the constitution on request of the regions, but this reform is also very popular. When a Region (Friuli-Venezia Giulia) tried to

reintroduce the indirect election of the president, the proposal was rejected by a referendum on September 29, 2002.

28. For the concepts of nation as *demos* and as *ethnos* see C. Casonato, *Minoranze etniche e rappresentanza politica: i modelli statunitense e canadese* (Trento, 1998), 22.

29. So Italian Constitutional Court, judgment no. 213/1998 (on the right to use a minority language in military trials).

30. This has been argued by one of Italy's most prominent scholars in this field, S. Bartole, Minoranze nazionali, in *Novissimo Digesto Italiano,* Appendice V (Torino, 1984), 45.

31. Signed but not yet ratified by Italy.

32. Approved on February 1, 1995, ratified by Italy with law no. 302/1997 and entered into force in 1998.

33. There are many possible explanations for this situation, not least the economic one (some affirmative rights, like the linguistic ones, are very expensive for the State budget), but the result is that this situation, by favoring the bigger minority groups, works against the survival of the smaller ones. For this very reason, several times the Constitutional Court invited the Parliament to establish at least a minimum standard for all the groups, even though it in fact accepted the different level of protection of minority groups as a basic element of the Italian minority constitution (judgments no. 28/1982, 62/1992 and 15/1996).

34. The most evident references are to Article 2 (inviolable rights of the person, as an individual and in the social groups where human personality is expressed), Article 3 (equality principle), Article 10 (automatic penetration of customary international law into the domestic legal system), Article 11 (preference for international law, especially in the field of human rights), and many others.

35. In 1939, Hitler and Mussolini decided to resolve definitively the South Tyrol problem and came to an agreement forcing the South Tyrolese, who wanted to remain culturally German, to move to the German Reich and to get German citizenship. Those who decided to stay (and not to lose their property) had to give up their language and culture, with even their names getting italianized. About 85 percent of the German-speaking population opted for the Reich. In fact, because of the war, only few of them left their homeland, and some 25 percent returned after the war. For a more detailed illustration of the history of the South Tyrolean question, see A. E. Alcock, *The History of the South Tyrol Question* (Genève, 1970) and M. Magliana, *The Autonomous Province of South Tyrol. A Model of Self-Governance?* (Bolzano/Bozen, 2000).

36. Omitting sociolinguistic remarks, legal examples of this principle include the provisions regarding the composition of the regional (Article 30, 36, 62 autonomy statute) and provincial organs (Article 49, 50, 62), as well the municipal ones (Article 61 and 62). The South Tyrol provincial Parliament can be called in some cases for votes by language groups (Article 56). Other important institutional indicators in the autonomy statute for the strict division of the groups within the public bodies are the possibility to impugn a provincial or regional law and to submit it to the constitutional Court's review (Article 56 al. 2), and the necessity of an uninterrupted residence of four years in the regional territory in order to exercise the right to an active franchise (Article 25 al. 4).

37. A. Lampis, *Autonomia e convivenza* (Bolzano/Bozen, 1999).

38. See further G. Poggeschi, La proporzionale "etnica", in J. Marko, S. Ortino, and F. Palermo (eds.), *L'ordinamento speciale della Provincia autonoma di Bolzano* (Padova, 2001), 686.

39. Article 19 al. 1 autonomy statute.

40. Presidential decree no. 89/1983. In practice it means that the school can refuse the enrollment of a pupil if the teachers consider his/her language skill not sufficient. Nevertheless, also against the refusal, a judicial remedy is provided.

41. Article 99 autonomy statute.

42. Article 100 al. 1 autonomy statute.

43. G. Pellegrini, Le finanze della Provincia autonoma di Bolzano, in J. Marko, S. Ortino, and F. Palermo (eds.), *L'ordinamento speciale della Provincia autonoma di Bolzano* (Padova, 2001), 498.

44. See recently, in English, F. Palermo, Self-Government (And Other?) Instruments for the Prevention of Ethnic Conflicts in South Tyrol, in M. Zagar, B. Jesih, and R. Bester (eds.), *The Constitutional and Political Regulation of Ethnic Relations and Conflicts* (Ljubljana, 1999), 299–312.

45. Especially the Framework Convention of the Council of Europe. See S. Bartole, La Convenzione-quadro del Consiglio d'Europa per la protezione delle minoranze nazionali, in *Rivista italiana di diritto e procedura penale* 2/1997, 567.

46. The German-speaking population of South Tyrol is not affected by the law. "German populations" are therefore only Cymbres and Mocheni (settled in the Province of Trento), the Walser (Piemonte and Aosta Valley), the Carnic people in the Province of Belluno, and the small German-speaking groups in the provinces of Vicenza and Udine.

47. It is true that the second group of minorities has been living in Italy for many centuries, but this is also true for Albanians, Catalans, Greeks, Slovenes, and Croats: Albanians and Croats came to Italy in the fourteenth century. Catalans were settled in Sardinia since the city of Alghero was taken by the Crown of Aragon in 1354. Greek populations have lived in Italy since the age of the Byzantium Empire. What is then the difference between the two groups? Do French, Provenzial, Friulian, Ladin, Occitan, and Sardinian speakers perhaps have Italian "blood," and do the others belong to different "nations"? Are not all the groups a constitutive part of the (multicultural) Italian "nation"? For further (critical) considerations, see F. Palermo, A Never-Ending Story? The Italian Draft Bill on the Protection of Linguistic Minorities, in S. Trifunovska (ed.), *Minority Rights in Europe. European Minorities and Languages* (The Hague, Asser, 2001), 55–66.

48. Initiative can be taken by 15 percent of the residents in the affected municipalities or by one third of the municipal deputies (Article 3 al. 1).

49. See also J. Woelk, Kulturelle Vielfalt und staatliche Einheit: Das italienische Rahmengesetz zum Schutz historischer Sprachminderheiten, in *Jahrbuch für italienisches Recht* (14) 2001 (Heidelberg Müller, 2002), 281; and V. Piergigli, La legge 15 dicembre 1999, n. 482: un traguardo per le minoranze linguistiche (finora) debolmente protette, in *Quaderni costituzionali,* 2000, 127.

50. In any case, the codes of civil and criminal procedure grant the right for everyone to speak his/her own language in court proceedings and to be assisted by an interpreter (Article 109 code of criminal procedure and Article 122 code of civil procedure).

51. It is important to point out that all the mentioned linguistic and cultural rights will not unduly burden the State's budget. A "national fund for the protection of linguistic minorities" (around 5 million Euros per year) is established, as well as a special fund provided by the Ministry of Education (1 million Euros per year). In addition to these costs, the State cannot spend more than 4 million Euros per year. Finally, the total costs for the State may not be more than

10 million Euros per year. The remainder of the costs will be sustained by Regions, provinces, and municipalities, in accordance with the federalist wind that has been blowing through Italy in the last decade.

52. Law no. 38/2001, Article 3. The committee is composed of an equal number of Italian-speaking and Slovenian-speaking members. Such a joint committee has been developed on the base of the very successful model provided by the autonomy statute of Trentino-South Tyrol for the approval of by-laws (Article 107 autonomy statute).

53. Article 7 statute (defense of the linguistic and cultural heritage of local communities).

54. Article 2 statute (improvement of the cultural and linguistic heritage of the local communities).

55. Article 4 statute (safeguard of the linguistic and historical heritage of the ethnic communities).

56. Article 5 statute (promotion of the original linguistic and cultural heritage of local communities).

57. Article 56 statute (promotion of traditions as well as of the historical, cultural, and artistic heritage of populations of Albanian and Greek origin; promotion of language teaching where those languages are spoken). As it might be seen, the provisions are pretty much the same. It has been pointed out that these provisions are to be intended "more as a solemn political objective than as a legal obligation" (E. Palici di Suni, *Intorno alle minoranze* (Torino, 1999), 76).

58. For example, the laws of Veneto (regional laws no. 40/1974 and 38/1979) and of Piemonte (no. 30/1979), promoting minority cultures and languages also by means of some (small) financial support.

59. In particular, Constitutional Court, judgment no. 32/1960. See on this case law, A. Pizzorusso, Tutela delle minoranze linguistiche e competenza legislativa regionale, *Rivista trimestrale di diritto pubblico,* 1974, 1093.

60. Especially from judgment no. 312/1983 onwards.

61. See judgments no. 242/1989, 290/1994, and 15/1996.

62. In Veneto, according to regional law no. 73/1994, the Region has the duty to promote ethnic and linguistic minorities living in it, especially by means of financial support of cultural activities. The law recognized the Ladins of the Dolomites area and the small German-speaking communities in two minor municipalities as ethnic and linguistic minorities.

In Basilicata, regional law no. 16/1998 states that the Region (also on the basis of Article 27 of the International Convenant on Civil and Political Rights—sic!) "promotes the protection, the safeguard and the promotion of the historical, cultural, artistic, linguistic religious and folkloristic heritage of the communities of Greek-Albanian origin settled in the territory," basically by financial support. Interestingly, a subsequent law (no. 40/1998) changed the official name of the recognized minority from "Greek-Albanian" into "Arbëreshe," because the concerned group (actually very small and settled only in two villages) has in fact no Greek origin, in spite of having preserved the Orthodox religion. Politically, however, the main reason for changing the official name of the minority was its own claim not to be confused with the recent Albanian immigrants.

Similar provisions are enshrined in the regional law no. 15/1997 of the Region of Molise in order to protect linguistic minorities (in this case the term "ethnic" is not mentioned) of Albanian and Croat origin. The same principle also inspires regional law no. 26/1998 of Sicily, which binds the Region to take measures in order to safeguard the historic, cultural, and linguistic heritage of the communities of Albanian origin.

In Piemonte the Region shall protect and promote "the original linguistic heritage of Piemonte" as well as "its knowledge," assuming this goal as "integral part of the protection and the promotion of the regional history and culture, based on the principles of equal dignity and pluralism enshrined in the national constitution" (regional laws no. 26/1990 and 37/1997). For these purposes, teaching of the "local languages" (Occitan, Franco-Provençal, and Walser—a variation of old German) is promoted and financed, and the re-establishment of original place names is encouraged. Interestingly, however, the status of "local language" (i.e., minority language) has been recognized also to Piemontese, which is actually nothing else but an Italian dialect.

For additional details on the mentioned regional laws, see E. Palici di Suni, *Intorno alle minoranze* (Torino, 1999), 82–92; E. Palici di Suni, Minoranze, in *Digesto delle discipline pubblicistiche,* vol. IX (Torino, 1994), 558; and the already mentioned report of the Ministry of the Interior on minorities: Ministero dell'Interno, *Ufficio centrale per i problemi di confine e delle minoranze etniche, Primo rapporto sullo stato delle minoranze in Italia* (Roma, 1994).

63. Friuli-Venezia Giulia (regional laws no. 11/1988 and no. 10/1998) promotes the Friulian language and culture "as essential part of the ethnic and historical identity of the regional community." It is worth noticing that in that Region a consistent Slovene minority is settled (although only in the part close to the Slovenian border), but the regional legislature never intervened with positive measures for the protection of that minority, which, as a consequence, had always to rely on national legislation (and on the Constitutional Court, which recognized the direct applicability of Article 6 of the Constitution, judgment no. 28/1982, see S. Bartole, *Gli sloveni nel processo penale a Trieste, Giurisprudenza costituzionale* 1982, 248) for seeking the legal base of its protection.

A very important—because large in scope—regional law was adopted by Sardinia to "promote culture and language of the island" (law no. 26/1997). The law mentions the existence of the "Sardinian people" (Article 1), whose cultural identity is to be promoted as "fundamental good for the growth and development" of the people. The law is designed as a framework law, on the base of which further regional legislation is to be passed in order to specifically deal with the different areas of intervention, such as language, history, arts, folklore, regional ecology, customary laws, cultural heritage, and the like. The official use of the Sardinian language is admitted within the regional and local public administration (Article 23), the original place names shall be re-introduced (Article 24), and some specific measures can even be adopted to sustain the Sardinians living "abroad" (difficult to say whether the provision means in foreign countries or also in the rest of Italy).

More "moderate" laws have been adopted by several regions like Piemonte (law no. 15/1996), Emilia-Romagna (law no. 45/1994), Lazio (law no. 44/1995), and so on, providing for the protection of local dialects.

Other Regions, especially those where most of the Italian immigrants come from, have passed legislation for the protection of the regional citizens living abroad (Abruzzo, law no. 79/1995; Veneto, law no. 25/1995; Marche, law no. 39/1997), in order to finance activities aimed at maintaining their relationships with the Region of their origin (cultural exchange, economic relations, etc.).

See, further, E. Palici di Suni, *Intorno alle minoranze* (Torino, 1999), 82–88; G. Rautz, *Die Sprachenrechte der Minderheiten* (Baden Baden, 1999), 119–84; and V. Piergigli, *Lingue minoritarie e identità culturali* (Milano, 2001), 418.

64. The Constitutional Court was clear on this in judgment no. 261/1995. The case concerned a regional law of Trentino-South Tyrol, granting political repre-

sentation to the Ladins of the Province of Trento regardless of their electoral results, the same way as it is already guaranteed to the Ladins of the Province of Bolzano/Bozen (South Tyrol). The Court affirmed that such a derogation from the principle of equality could not be prescribed by a regional law, but only by a constitutional law of the State. See, further, R. Toniatti, La rappresentanza politica delle minoranze linguistiche: i ladini fra rappresentanza "assicurata" e "garantita," *Le Regioni* 1995, 1271.

65. However, religious difference is not an issue for historic minorities in Italy, because almost all of them are Catholic like the majority of the population. The question is nevertheless of big interest in the perspective of a stronger integration of immigrant populations. See A. Guazzarotti, *Giudici e minoranze religiose* (Milano, 2001).

66. For the role of EU law in the field of minority protection, see B. de Witte, Politics versus Law in the EU's Approach to Ethnic Minorities, EUI working paper no 4/2000; and G. Toggenburg, A Rough Orientation Through a Delicate Relationship: The European Union's Endeavors for Its Minorities, in S. Trifunovska (ed.), *Minority Rights in Europe. European Minorities and Languages* (The Hague, Asser, 2001), 205–34.

67. For this development in the economic sphere, see G. Majone, *Regulating Europe* (London-New York: Routledge, 1996).

68. So R. Toniatti, Minorities and Protected Minorities. Constitutional Models Compared, in T. Bonazzi and M. Dunne (eds.), *Citizenship and Rights in Multicultural Societies* (Keele, U.K.: University Press, 1995), 205.

69. For the historical developments and the generations of minority rights, see E. Ruiz Vieytez, *The History of Legal Protection of Minorities in Europe (XVIIth-XXth Centuries),* Derby, 1999. See also S. Mancini, *Minoranze autoctone e Stato* (Milano, 1996).

In Staatsbürgerrechte und Autonomie im europäischen Kontext, in Siglinde Clementi & Jens Woelk (eds.), *1992–2002 Ende eines Streits* (Baden Baden: Nomos, 2003), Jens Woelk points out that a German-speaking inhabitant of the city of Bolzano/Bozen is an Italian and a European citizen, belongs to a linguistic minority in Italy, and is at the same time part of the majority of the population in South Tyrol and of the minority in the city. Such cases are becoming more and more frequent in today's Europe.

71. See also S. Ortino, La tutela delle minoranze nel diritto internazionale: evoluzione o mutamento di prospettiva? in *Giornata delle minoranze* (Trento, 1996), 19–34.

72. Also the terminology (protection of minorities) can be perceived as quite offensive for groups that are no longer weak and seeking somebody else's *protection,* but rather equal opportunity in a more open society.

73. See also W. Kymlicka, *Multicultural Citizenship: A Liberal Theory of Minority Rights* (Oxford, 1995); and J. Marko and G. R. Burkert-Dottolo (eds.), *Multikulturelle Gesellschaft und Demokratie* (Baden Baden, 2000).

74. C. Esposito, Lo Stato e la Nazione italiana, in *Archivio di diritto pubblico, 1937,* II, 409. See also P. Carrozza, Nazione, in *Digesto delle discipline pubblicistiche,* vol. X (Torino, 1995), 127.

75. For this trend, see R. Toniatti, Minorities and Protected Minorities. Constitutional Models Compared, in T. Bonazzi and M. Dunne (eds.), *Citizenship and Rights in Multicultural Societies* (Keele, U.K.: University Press, 1995), 195–219.

76. One interesting example is provided by the long dispute on the constitutionalization of the official status of the Italian language. Until now, the status of Italian as the official language of the whole country is stated only in the

autonomy statutes (in particular, Article 99 statute for Trentino-South Tyrol), but there is no mention of that in the national constitution. For several years a draft bill for constitutional amendment to enshrine the official status of Italian within the constitution (new Article 12) has been discussed in Parliament, and it has already been approved by the lower Chamber (March 2002). Nevertheless, there are too many conflicting interests beyond the provision, and it seems difficult that it can be definitively approved. This long lasting and finally symbolic discussion on one hand shows the emergence of a multicultural society thus making it necessary to state explicitly what used to be implicit, the official character of the Italian language; on the other hand it demonstrates how many fears there still are in recognizing the profound changes that have occurred in the society.

8

Federalism, Subnational Constitutional Arrangements, and the Protection of Minorities in Spain

Eduardo J. Ruiz Vieytez

This chapter examines the political organization of the Spanish State from a territorial approach. After a brief introduction about the Spanish Kingdom and its linguistic and national plurality, it describes the territorial model foreseen in the Constitution of 1978 and the Acts on Autonomy passed by the Central Parliament and offers some conclusions, including prospects for future development.

OVERVIEW: THE KINGDOM OF SPAIN

Linguistic, Religious, and Economic Pluralism

The Kingdom of Spain occupies most of the Iberian Peninsula and includes the Balearic Isles (Mediterranean Sea), the Canary Islands (Atlantic Ocean), and the cities of Ceuta and Melilla on the North African coast. The current population of Spain is about 39 million people. Far from being culturally homogeneous, in linguistic terms, approximately 25 percent of the Spanish population have a mother tongue that is not Spanish. Catalan, Galician, and Basque are official languages in their own communities, together with Castilian Spanish, and there are special policies to procure their normalization in the Autonomous Communities of Catalonia, Galicia, and the Basque Country, respectively. Regional varieties of the Catalan language are also official languages in the Autonomous Communities of Valencia and Balearic Isles. Linguistic policy on the Basque language in the Autonomous Community of Navarra remains, however, in conflict. In global terms, Catalan is spoken by some 6,000,000 people, Galician by some 2,500,000 people, and Basque by 600,000 people. There is also a small Occitan-speaking population in the Aragón valley in Catalonia (approximately 4,000 speakers), which is also legally protected. The linguistic minorities of Asturias (approximately 250,000 speakers) and Aragon (approximately 8,000) and the Berber-speaking minority in the city of Melilla (approximately 15,000 speakers) are also protected, although to a lesser extent.

Most Spaniards belong to the Catholic tradition. The Constitution recognizes freedom of worship, and the State has signed cooperation agreements with the Muslim, Jewish, and Protestant communities, as well as with the Catholic Church. Although non-Catholics represent very small minorities among Spanish nationals, in the cities of Ceuta and Melilla up to one third of the population is Muslim.

Foreign immigrants represent today in Spain less than 2.5 percent of the national population. Most are European citizens, but there is also an increasing number of people coming from Morocco, Latin America, China, and the Philippines.

Economically speaking, differences existing between the regions are not great. The richest areas in the State are the Basque Country, Catalonia, Madrid, Navarra, and the Balearic Isles. In contrast, the less developed areas are located in the southwest of the peninsula, principally Extremadura and parts of Andalusia and Castile. In any event, the maximum differences in average income per capita are 2 to 1. The average income of Spain as a whole is approximately 93 percent of that of the European Union.[1]

Unity and Diversity in the Constitutional History of Spain

The legal and political construction of the Spanish monarchy began during the eighteenth century. Institutional differences remained in the territories belonging to the Kingdom of Aragón (Aragón itself, Valencia, the Balearic Isles, and Catalonia), but their autonomy would be suppressed in the eighteenth century following the ascension of the French Bourbons to the Spanish throne. The differences observed in the political regime of the Basque Provinces of Biscay, Alava, Guipuzcoa, and Navarra, however, remained intact until the nineteenth century. Spanish national identity was constructed on the basis of the Catholic faith, with the expulsion of the Jews in 1492 and of the Muslims in 1609. In the linguistic sphere, the Latin inheritance evolved into different languages in the course of the medieval period. Only the Basque language remained as an exception. Castilian Spanish was progressively established as the language of the dominant kingdom and as the official language from the sixteenth century onwards, to the detriment of Latin and the other peninsular languages.

Following the French model, a Spanish nationalism began to emerge in the nineteenth century. The attempts to unify the kingdom politically came into conflict with the distinctive political regime of the Basque Provinces. Laws enacted in 1839 and 1876 were designed to suppress the most important aspects of this semi-independent political system. Romanticism and nationalism were also to develop among the national minorities in the second half of the nineteenth century, creating political and cultural movements that gained ground rapidly, especially in the Basque Country and in Catalonia.

The first constitutional attempt to reflect the plurinational nature of the State occurred during the First Republic (1873) with the drawing up of plans for a federal constitution, although it never finally came into force. In 1931, following the proclamation of the Second Republic, a system was established in the Constitution to enable some regions to gain autonomy. Catalonia (1931) and the Basque Country (1936) elected autonomous governments that were suppressed by insurgents' military victory in the Civil War (1936–1939). The Francoist period was characterized by a savage repression of national, religious, and linguistic differences. In response to this repression, new, left-leaning nationalist groupings sprang up, including in some cases the use of armed struggle to combat the dictatorship. Among these groups was the ETA (Euskadi Ta Askatasuna, meaning "Basque Country and Freedom"), founded in 1962, which still carries out violent action, mainly in the Basque Country.

THE CURRENT CONSTITUTIONAL FRAMEWORK

Under the 1978 Constitution, Spain remains structured as a single unified state, although one characterized by a high degree of political decentralization affecting the whole of the country. In fact, Spain has adopted a new model of a decentralized unified state reminiscent of the Italian regional model and the integral state envisaged in the Spanish Constitution of 1931. The post-1978 model applied in Spain may be seen as a departure in terms of the forms of decentralization of political power and is best described by what has come to be known as the complex simple State.

The Spanish model should not be confused with a federal system, given the existence of a single Constitutional Law and Sovereignty covering the whole of the country. Nevertheless, there is tacit acceptance of a degree of national plurality within the State, even though the Constitution stops short of a clear definition of the territorial model adopted. A more detailed study of the elements characterizing this model requires an examination of two levels of legislation: the Constitution and the Acts on Autonomy.

The Constitution of 1978

The Spanish Constitution was passed by referendum on December 6, 1978. Fifty-nine percent of the population voted in favor of the Constitution; there was a 5 percent negative vote. Turnout was about 67 percent. The Constitution received majority support in most regions of Spain, apart from the Basque Country, where support of the Constitution fell to 30 percent with a turnout of less than 40 percent.

The Spanish Constitution is divided into 11 titles. The Preliminary Title contains general dispositions, including those relating to the definition of the state and basic aspects of its territorial organization. The first three articles deserve extended quotation.[2]

> Article 1
> 1. Spain is hereby established as a social and democratic State, subject to the rule of law, and advocating as higher values of its legal order, liberty, justice, equality and political pluralism.
> 2. National sovereignty is vested in the Spanish people, from whom emanate the powers of the State.
> 3. The political form of the Spanish State is that of a Parliamentary Monarchy.
>
> Article 2
> The Constitution is based on the indissoluble unity of the Spanish Nation, the common and indivisible country of all Spaniards; it recognises and guarantees the right to autonomy of the nationalities and regions of which it is composed, and solidarity amongst them all.
>
> Article 3
> 1. Castilian is the official Spanish language of the State. All Spaniards have the duty to know it and the right to use it.
> 2. The other Spanish languages shall also be official in the respective Autonomous Communities in accordance with their Statutes.
> 3. The wealth of the different language variations of Spain is a cultural heritage, which shall be the object of special respect and protection.

Although Article 2 refers to the existence of "nationalities" and regions within the Spanish State, there is no concomitant legal differentiation between these terms. Moreover, neither in the Constitution nor in any other legislation is there a listing of nationalities and regions. The inclusion of these two different concepts was possibly a result of a difficult political compromise in order to satisfy both centralist forces and Catalan nationalists. On the other hand, the right of autonomy is defined as an optional principle, meaning that it is considered as a right for these regions and nationalities. The idea at that moment was neither to force all the territories to enjoy autonomy nor to draw a definitive map of the Autonomous Communities.

Title VIII of the Constitution (articles 137–158) contains the regulations dealing with the territorial organization of the State. According to Article 137, the Spanish State is organized territorially into municipalities, provinces, and any Autonomous Communities that may be constituted. All these bodies enjoy self-government for the management of their respective interests, although only Autonomous Communities enjoy actual political autonomy. The Constitution states that differences between the Statutes of the different Autonomous Communities may in no case imply economic or social privileges (Article 138.2). In this respect, all Spaniards have the same rights and obligations in any part of the State territory (Article 139.1).

Rather than establishing a closed model of national territorial organization, Title VIII confines itself to the outlining of the basic principles upon which the construction of a system of generalized political decentralization may later be based. The central element of this framework would be the establishment of Autonomous Communities, as titular entities of political territorial autonomy. As will be seen, Title VIII establishes the procedures for access to autonomy, and the powers that may be exercised by the Autonomous Communities, as well as the basic system of organization and control of such bodies. Similarly, the process of approval of the Acts on Autonomy is regulated in the same title. These Acts work as the basic institutional legislation of each Autonomous Community.

In accordance with precepts established in other parts of the Constitution, provision is made for the participation of the Autonomous Communities in a number of national constitutional bodies, notably the legislative initiative with which they are provided in Central Parliament, the constitutional reform initiative, their limited presence in the Senate, and access to several proceedings before the Constitutional Court, though they do not form part of this body.

The Statutes on Autonomy

In the exercise of the right to self-government recognized in Article 2 of the Constitution, bordering provinces with common historic, cultural, and economic characteristics, island territories, and provinces with historic regional status may accede to self-government and form Autonomous Communities in conformity with the provisions contained in Title VIII. Therefore, the Constitution does not refer to any definition of nationality or region in the sense of Article 2. The territorial basis for the constitution of Autonomous Communities would be the provinces.

To accede to autonomy, it is necessary to draft an Act on Autonomy or Statute. The draft Statute is drawn up by an assembly consisting of the members of the Provincial Council (or interisland body) of the provinces concerned and the Members of Parliament (MPs) elected in them. The Central Parliament is responsible for enacting it into an organic law.

The Statute is the basic institutional document of each Autonomous Community, but at the same time is an integral part of the constitutional legal order. According to Article 147 of the Constitution, the Statutes of Autonomy must contain

1. the name of the Community which corresponds most closely to its historic identity.
2. its territorial boundaries.
3. the name, organization, and seat of its own autonomous institutions.
4. the powers assumed within the framework established by the Constitution and the basic conditions for the transfer of the services corresponding to them.

Amendment of the Statutes must conform to the procedure established therein and requires in any case the approval of the Central Parliament through an organic law. However, if the Statute has been approved following the procedure contained in Article 151, which establishes more strict and rigorous requirements, it may only be amended by means of the procedures established therein, including a referendum of the electors of the Autonomous Community registered in the corresponding electoral rolls.

There are a number of legal differences to be found within the different Statutes of Autonomy, in terms of their process of approval and methods of reformation. The Statutes drawn up in accordance with the procedure outlined in Article 151 of the Constitution are closer to the idea of an agreement between the Central Parliament and the population of the potential Community. This emerges from the fact that a referendum among the population affected is required, for both approval of the Statute (on two occasions) and for any subsequent reform. By virtue of its special legal status, the Statute of the Region of Navarra may also be regarded as having a similar consensual nature.[3] However, the statutes drawn up in accordance with the procedure laid down in Article 143 and Article 146 more closely correspond to the model of an organic law.

The principle of contract is further emphasized in the Statute of Autonomy of the Basque Country. The Additional Provision to the Act on Autonomy of the Basque Country states:

> The acceptance of the system of autonomy established in this Statute does not imply that the Basque People waive the rights that as such may have accrued to them in virtue of their history and which may be updated in accordance with the stipulations of the legal system.

The Statute of Navarra includes a very similar Additional Provision, on the basis of the "historical rights" that belong to the "historical territories" or territories with "fueros."[4] These are the remaining consequences of the special political regime of the Basque Provinces of Biscay, Alava, Gipuzkoa (the three of them are now integrated into the Basque Autonomous Community) and Navarra (an Autonomous Community on its own).

THE AUTONOMOUS COMMUNITIES

Constituting Territorial Bodies

Title VIII of the Constitution does not establish the ultimate design of the autonomous State, but provides a set of procedures to be implemented in later years. In 1978, provision was made for the immediate implementation of autonomy in the Basque Country, Catalonia, and Galicia, without ruling out the possibility of extending autonomy to the rest of the territories at some later point. The 1981 agreements on autonomy[5] entailed the extension of the political autonomy provided for in Article 2 to all the territory of the State, and the different Autonomous Communities were set up through the various mechanisms established in Title VIII. There was a significant variation in the models finally established.

The main difference in structure depended on whether Regions and Nationalities acceded to autonomy through the procedures set forth in Article 143 (the slow-track route) or through the procedure outlined in Article 151. Article 151 provides for a fast-track process of access to autonomy based on statutes of a semicontractual nature and, above all, on the possibility of attaining a higher degree of competence from the very beginning of the autonomous system, without having to wait the term of five years to increase the scope of Community powers, as is required in Article 148.2 for Communities set up in accordance with the slow-track process envisaged in Article 143.

As a result, the different methods used to implement autonomy can be organized according to the following scheme:

1. Regions that acceded to autonomy through the process established in Article 151.
   1.1. Regions benefiting from the application of the Second Temporary Provision.
   This Provision established that those territories that had earlier approved Statutes of Autonomy by plebiscite might attain the highest degree of autonomy and competence immediately without being required to fulfil the requirements established in the first section of Article 151. This provision would apply to Catalonia, the Basque Country (excluding Navarra), and Galicia, because they had approved statutes by plebiscite during the Second Republic, between 1931 and 1936.[6]
   1.2. Other Regions.
   These were required to fulfil the requirements of Article 151 in its entirety. Only Andalusia adopted this procedure, not without serious legal and political difficulties.[7]
2. Regions acceding to autonomy through the procedure established in Article 143.
   In principle, the initial level of competence of those Communities established in accordance with the slow-track process outlined in Article 143 and Article 146 might not exceed that established in Article 148. Only after a period of five years and through reform of the statutes could these Regions increase the scope of their powers. However, among these Communities, we can distinguish some differences in the process of achieving autonomy.
   2.1. Autonomous Communities that followed the normal slow-track process: Asturias, Cantabria, La Rioja, Aragón, the Balearic Isles, Murcia, Extremadura, Castille-León and Castille-La Mancha.
   2.2. Autonomous Communities whose establishment was authorized by Parliament. In the case of Madrid, it was decided that Article 144.a would be applied in order to set up a specific autonomous community. Article 144.a foresees the possibility of creating a new autonomous community for a province that cannot be considered by itself an "historical entity." Indeed, at the same time it was considered that Madrid did not constitute a province with a historical regional identity distinguishable from Castille.
   2.3. Regions established under Article 143 and Article 146, whose competence was increased immediately through Constitu-

tional (organic) Laws of Transfer, provided for in Article 150.2. In these cases, the granting of powers to the Regions provided for in Article 151 would be effected through a law of transfer of new powers, immediately following the approval of the respective Statute. The aim of this solution was to satisfy aspirations to an intermediate level of self-government between that of nationality and region and applied to the Canary Islands and Valencia.

2.4. The Foral Community of Navarra acceded to autonomy under the procedure established in Article 143, but with a legal basis in the first Additional Provision of the Constitution, because it was considered that Navarra already constituted a statutory (foral) region, and its system was updated within the framework of the autonomous State. At the same time, the fourth Temporary Provision provides for the possible incorporation of Navarra into the Basque Autonomous Community, a provision that to date has not been adopted. In contrast, Navarra acceded to autonomy through the actualization of its political system (as did the Basque provinces of Alava, Bizkaia, and Gipuzkoa) and thus attained the highest level of competence from the very beginning of its constitution.

3. Autonomous Cities.

Finally, under Article 144.b, the Lower House of Parliament can agree on a Statute of Autonomy for territories not integrated within the provincial organization. This was the situation of the North African cities of Ceuta and Melilla, which are provided with a system of autonomy of an essentially administrative nature. These areas are not regarded as Autonomous Communities, but rather Autonomous Cities, in which the municipal and autonomous institutions are merged. These structures do not, however, include a legislative chamber and, consequently, the nature of their autonomy cannot be regarded as political. The fifth Temporary Provision refers explicitly to Ceuta and Melilla and the possibility of establishing Autonomous Cities under Article 144.

The same precept might be applied in the case of Gibraltar should Spain recover sovereignty. Under this hypothesis, the first possibility would be for the territory to be incorporated into the Autonomous Region of Andalusia. A second option would be the approval of a specific autonomous system for the territory of Gibraltar.

To date, then, 17 Autonomous Regions and 2 Autonomous Cities have been established, with their respective statutes, in accordance with the following chronological timetable and legal dispositions:

Community[a]	*Act on Autonomy*[b]	*Legal Basis*[c]
1. Basque Country	18 Dec 1979	151 + TP 2 + AP 1
2. Catalonia	18 Dec 1979	151 + TP 2
3. Galicia	6 Apr 1981	151 + TP 2
4. Andalusia	30 Dec 1981	151
5. Asturias	30 Dec 1981	143
6. Cantabria	30 Dec 1981	143
7. La Rioja	9 Jun 1982	143
8. Murcia	9 Jun 1982	143
9. Valencia	1 Jul 1982	143 + 150.2
10. Aragón	10 Aug 1982	143
11. Castille-La Mancha	10 Aug 1982	143
12. Canary Islands	10 Aug 1982	143 + 150.2
13. Navarra	10 Aug 1982	143 + AP 1[d]
14. Extremadura	25 Feb 1983	143
15. Balearic Isles	25 Feb 1983	143
16. Madrid	25 Feb 1983	143 + 144.a
17. Castille-León	25 Feb 1983	143
18. Ceuta	13 Mar 1995	144.b + TP 5
19. Melilla	13 Mar 1995	144.b + TP 5

a. The order of the Communities is chronological; it must be respected for all purposes, including protocol.
b. Date of the Organic Law enacting the Statute. It is not the date of the referendum for the Statutes elaborated under Article 151.
c. Articles of the Constitution: TP = Temporary Provision; AP = Additional Provision.
d. Temporary Provision 4 relates also to Navarra and its possible incorporation into the Basque Autonomous Community; it has not been applied so far.

Institutional Organization

As of 1978, the ruling political forces did not fully foresee the future application of the right to autonomy. Thus, following the approval of the Statutes of the Basque Country, Catalonia, and Galicia, in 1981 the two main political parties agreed on the basic aspects of the ordering process of the plan for autonomy. Essentially, these agreements included the following:

a. The territory of the State would in its entirety be organized into Autonomous Communities, with the exception of the special status of the cities of Ceuta and Melilla. As a result, all the provinces of the State would in the future form part of a particular autonomous Region. Both parties agreed on a definitive map of autonomies.

b. With the exception of the constitution of the Communities of Basque Country, Catalonia, Galicia, and Andalusia, the remaining Communities would be formed on the basis of the procedure outlined in Article 143.
c. All the Communities would have their own parliament, elected by universal suffrage, and government. The president of the government would be elected by the respective parliament, in accordance with the customary political process of a parliamentary system.
d. Thirteen Communities would be established under Article 143 (7 being composed of a single province).
e. The 13 slow-track Communities would hold their respective elections concurrently to coincide with municipal elections. Therefore, in the majority of the Autonomous Communities, the possibility of an early dissolution of parliament was excluded. However, the Regions of Aragón, Madrid, and Castille-León do provide for this eventuality, but the duration of the parliament elected following dissolution does not extend beyond the remaining term of the dissolved legislature.
f. The cities of Ceuta and Melilla would have a special administrative autonomy.

As for the institutional organization of Autonomous Communities, Article 152 of the Constitution stated that in the cases of Statutes passed by means of the procedure contained in Article 151, the organization should be based on a Legislative Assembly elected by universal suffrage in accordance with a system of proportional representation that should assure, moreover, the representation of the various areas of the territory; a Governing Council with executive and administrative functions; and a President elected by the Assembly from among its members and appointed by the King. This President and the members of the Governing Council, nominated by him, would be politically accountable to the Assembly. The President would also be the supreme representative of the Autonomous Community as well as the ordinary representative of the State within the Community. This institutional organization, initially compulsory only for those Autonomous Communities set up through the procedure of Article 151, was later extended to all the rest of communities established on the basis of Article 143 of the Constitution.

The only peculiarity of any particular importance relates to the Autonomous Community of the Basque Country, within which the Historical Territories (Provinces) function in turn as territorial entities with political, legislative, and executive powers, in a kind of internal federal system. Thus, the Basque Historical Territories have parliaments elected by universal suffrage, which designate a member as president of an executive answerable to the chamber. As in the case of the Communities established under Article 143, the territorial parliaments cannot be dissolved in advance, and elections are held every four years to coincide with municipal elections.

Finally, it is interesting to note that the Constitution prohibits the federation of two or more Autonomous Communities.[8] Even more, cooperation agreements between Autonomous Communities require in most cases the authorization of the Central Parliament.[9]

Legal and Political Powers

The Autonomous Communities enjoy executive and legislative powers within the framework provided by Title VIII of the Constitution and the Statutes. In spite of the fact that initially the Autonomous Communities constituted under Article 151 held, in principle, more powers than those established under Article 143 (except in the cases of the Canary Islands, Valencia, and Navarra), there is currently a trend toward harmonization of the competences of the various Communities.

In this regard, the autonomous parliaments can pass laws, with the same degree of force as State (national) laws, with which they are related by virtue of the principle of competence. Thus, there are areas in which the Autonomous Communities have full executive and legislative powers; areas in which legislative powers are shared between the State and the Communities, which hold executive powers; and finally, areas in which legislation is in the hands of the State and only execution powers are the responsibility of the Autonomous Community.

The Autonomous Communities may assume, through their respective Statutes (or additional legislation) sole jurisdiction in respect of matters such as these:

- Organization of their institutions of self-government
- Town and country planning and housing
- Public works of benefit to the Autonomous Community, within its own territory
- Railways, roads, and transports whose routes lie exclusively within the territory of the Autonomous Community
- Agriculture, woodlands, and forestry
- Environmental protection management
- Monuments, museums, libraries, and music centers
- Promotion of tourism and sports
- Social assistance

In other matters, the Autonomous Communities are required to provide further legislative development of the basic legislation of the State or to execute State legislation. This is the case in matters such as these:

Labor legislation

Prison legislation

Public health

Education

Mass media

However, under Article 149.1, the State holds exclusive jurisdiction over the following relevant matters:

Nationality, immigration, status of aliens, and asylum

International relations

Defense and armed forces

Administration of Justice

Commercial Law

Criminal Law

Monetary system and exchange

General planning of economic activity

Public safety

Authorization for popular consultations through the holding of referendums

As international relations is the exclusive competence of the State, a problem emerges with regard to the representation of the Autonomous Communities in the European Union, particularly when the latter intervenes in areas of autonomous competence. The participation of the Autonomous Bodies in the ambit of the European community is yet to be resolved. The Autonomous Communities governed by political parties different from the one in power in the central government are particularly affected by this situation.

In practice, most of the Acts of Autonomy show a very similar scheme. Nowadays, after the reformation of the Statutes approved in respect of Article 143 and Article 146, most of them include almost the same number of powers. It may be concluded that the Autonomous Communities will ultimately hold a similar level of autonomy, with the exception of the Basque Country and Navarra, which, as a result of their historical rights, have specific powers, notably an independent treasury and tax system.[10]

THE POLITICAL DEBATE ON THE TERRITORIAL STRUCTURE

Although the territorial organization of the State in Spain is not a subject of widespread political debate, it nonetheless raises important issues that remain unresolved. Logically, the debate swings back and forth according to the position of the different parties and the support that each receives at the ballot box.

The political map of Spain is structured around three predominant political forces at the state level (two big parties with possibilities of acceding to the control of the government) and a large number of political groupings within more limited territorial areas, showing important political differences. A systematization of the current differences in political approach to the territorial question is outlined next. Taking account of the main parties represented in the Central Parliament, we find three main positions at the state level.

1. Parties defending the current model
   - The Popular Party/Partido Popular (PP): This party has a conservative ideology and was the governing force in the State from 1996–2004. It is also the governing force in seven Autonomous Communities.[11] Current electoral support ranges between 35 and 45 percent nationwide, differing widely among the regions.
   - The Spanish Socialist Workers Party/Partido Socialista Obrero Español (PSOE): This party, which has a social-democratic ideology, has been in the government since the general election in March, 2004. It also is represented in the government of 6 Autonomous Communities.[12] Its share of the vote ranges between 35 and 45 percent, with a relatively homogeneous presence in the various regions.
   - In a number of Communities there are regional parties, generally center-right, which defend the current model of autonomy, on occasion in opposition to nationalist parties in neighboring regions. These parties pursue increased scope of powers for their Autonomous Bodies, without calling into question the unity of the State or the Constitution. Parties of this type govern in Navarra (UPN)[13] and the Canary Islands (CC)[14] with strong electoral support; others participate in government coalitions in Aragón (PAR) and the Balearic Isles (UM and PSM). At the state level, only the Canary Islands Coalition, with four members of parliament, has its own parliamentary group within the Parliament in Madrid.
2. Parties calling for modifications in the current model
   - United Left/Izquierda Unida (IU): This is a left-wing coalition, which supports a federal model for Spain[15] that would also

recognize the right to self-determination of the nationalities of which it was comprised. Nationwide, its share of the vote is between 5 and 10 percent, and it is only represented in three autonomous governments.[16]

- Democratic Convergence and Union of Catalonia/Convergencia i Unió (CDC and UDC): This is a coalition of liberal Christian-Democratic Catalan nationalist parties. CiU defends the right to self-determination of Catalonia but has no declared aims beyond the ambit of Spain. It supports the rereading or possible gradual reform of the current Constitution in order to increase Catalonian self-government. CiU was in sole control of the autonomous government of Catalonia from 1980–2003, with popular support of about 40 percent in Catalonia, but it is now in opposition. The party has its own parliamentary group of 10 MPs in the Spanish Parliament in Madrid.

3. Parties that strongly question the current model
   - The Basque National Party/Partido Nacionalista Vasco (EAJ/PNV): Historically the party that has defended Basque nationalism, it has an essentially Social-Christian ideology. Electoral support in the Basque Country is between 30 and 40 percent, and it has its own parliamentary grouping in Madrid with seven seats. The party has been in power in the Basque Country since the establishment of the autonomy system. The PNV does not support the Spanish Constitution and claims the right of the Basque People to self-determination, without committing itself on the final political status. Within the party, there are factions in favor of independence and those supporting a weak relationship with the Spanish State.
   - Other left-wing nationalist parties of the Basque Country (Unity/Batasuna—EH[17]), Basque Solidarity/Eusko Alkartasuna—EA[18]) or Catalonia (Republican Left of Catalonia/Esquerra Republicana de Catalunya—ERC) that are represented in the central parliament (two and seven MPs, respectively) call for outright independence. These parties have electoral support of between 15 and 25 percent in Euskadi and between 10 and 20 percent in Catalonia. A more ideologically ambiguous stance is that of the Galician Nationalist Block/Bloque nacionalista Galego (BNG), which has a 20 to 30 percent share of the vote in Galicia, and two MPs in the central parliament. The same position could be claimed for Aragón/Chunta Aragonesista, with a share of 10 to 15 percent in Aragón and one representative in Madrid.

Generally speaking, it may be said that there is a high degree of consensus at the State level with regard to the expediency of maintaining the autonomic model as a solution to the territorial diversity of the State. At the same time, there is also a widely held conviction that the Senate should be reformed in order for it to become a chamber for genuine territorial representation. However, the fear of opening up a process of constitutional reform and the conflict of electoral interests of parties in the majority is a serious impediment to this. Moreover, even though the suitability of an asymmetrical system that acknowledges the specific differentials has been alluded to on numerous occasions, there are significant political sectors that are opposed to the idea of the existence of different levels of Autonomous Territories. Proposals for the development of the system toward a federal model meet with similar and even greater resistance. In fact, the territorial question does not normally take very much space on the political agenda of the major parties during election campaigns.

However, the questioning of the sovereignty of the State by a number of political sectors, particularly in Euskadi and Catalonia, provokes strong political reaction at the State level and conditions the debate on the territorial model. In the case of Catalonia, the desire for independence appears to be clearly limited to a minority, and the role played by the ruling party (CiU) in alliance with the party in government in Madrid has helped to ease political tensions.

Although in Catalonia the possibility of an open rupture with the State does not appear likely, the antagonism between centralist Spanish parties and Basque parties favoring sovereignty does not bode well for a solution to the political conflict in the Basque Country. The two main Spanish parties share support for the existing constitutional model, and the Basque question remains the most sensitive subject in Spanish politics.

In fact, in the Basque Country, the political situation is extraordinarily tense. The campaign of violence carried out by ETA distorts political debate on territorial structuring, while the Basque nationalist political stance (and even that of IU) is readically opposed by the two main Spanish parties. A majority of the Basque electorate favors the idea of Basque sovereignty,[19] which means that the Basque question has yet to be resolved. The Basque question dominates the domestic political agenda in Spain, and in the medium term there appears to be no possibility of political agreement between the Spanish parties and those defending the right to self-determination. The current system of autonomy does not seem to satisfy the demands for self-government of the majority of the Basque population. This situation is aggravated by the existence of a significant Basque minority in Navarra desiring unification of the two Autonomous Communities. In the Parliament of the Basque autonomous Community, Basque National Parties control 40 of the 75 seats (with 32 held by Spanish National Parties and 3 by the

United Left), whereas in the Parliament of Navarra Spanish National Parties control 38 of the 50 seats (with 8 held by Basque National Parties and 4 by the United Left).

In February 1990, the Basque national parties approved a political resolution in the Basque Parliament proclaiming the right of the Basque People to self-determination (including the possibility of independence). The resolution was then passed with 39 votes in favor and 23 against.

CONCLUSIONS AND FUTURE PROSPECTS

Spain is organized politically as a single State, with the 1978 Constitution emphasizing national unity as a basic principle. Nevertheless, the Constitution does acknowledge the existence of nationalities and regions within the State and envisages the possibility of territorial self-government for them, without defining a map or a definitive model. Constitutional development has given rise to the division of Spanish territory into 17 Autonomous Communities, each endowed with broad legislative and executive powers, with the legal status of each Autonomous Community defined by its Statute of Autonomy. The territorial map may be regarded as closed and unquestioned, except in the case of Navarra and its relationship with the Basque Country. Minor problems exist with regard to the status of some enclaves, and there is a very remote chance of changes in the legal status of Ceuta, Melilla, or Gibraltar.

In practice, there is an increasing degree of harmonization of the level of competence of the different Autonomous Communities, with the exception of a number of special powers for the Basque Country and Navarra. In this regard, a situation of ongoing tension exists resulting from the conflict between the desire of some Communities for recognition of their specific differences and the trend toward system uniformity.

The Senate does not adequately fulfill its role as a chamber for territorial representation as it does not provide the Autonomous Communities with sufficient channels of participation. Although there is a general consensus on the need for the reform of the Senate, the prospects for reform appear remote, given the differences among political parties and the fear of wider constitutional reform.

The model of the autonomous State is perceived politically and socially as an important advance in the democratic consolidation of the State. Proposals exist for the transformation of the system into a federal model, although there are many obstacles arising from the difficulties in creating an asymmetrical federalism in Spain. Only in the case of the

Basque Country does the political trend toward independence or the right to self-determination provoke a serious questioning of the system.

The structuring of the Basque Country within the Spanish State remains a source of conflict, and consensus among parties representing different political tendencies does not appear likely. Even in the most moderate nationalist sectors, the prevailing view is that the powers conferred by the Statute are increasingly devalued and their potential undercut by the central institutions. In any event, there is a majority calling for increased powers of self-government. Nevertheless, the two main Spanish parties strongly oppose demands for self-government in Euskadi or the Basque Country.

The autonomous State has succeeded in dealing with a number of the problems related to the protection of national minorities. In particular, policies have been developed within the framework of the Autonomous Communities for the protection of autochthonous languages and cultures. However, these policies have been developed by the governments of Autonomous Communities and not by the central authorities of the State. In fact, the Spanish State does not recognize the existence of national minorities within its territory, other than the ethnic Roma population. In this regard, the official position of Spain resembles that of France in the sense of considering that the formal principle of equality precludes the recognition of national minorities. Such is the conclusion to be drawn from the Spanish State's interpretation of Article 27 of the International Covenant on Civil and Political Rights or of the Framework Convention for the Protection of National Minorities from the Council of Europe.[20]

The foreseeable future development of the system points to a consolidation of the Autonomous Communities, with a relatively homogeneous and coordinated level of autonomy in which there may be some particular exceptions in the cases of the Basque Country, Navarra, and Catalonia, which will probably continue to be governed by nationalist parties. In the mid-term, a reform of the Constitution to restructure the Senate should not be ruled out, although it does not appear that the territorial and institutional organization of the State will undergo significant alteration. It is also likely that the national conflict in Euskadi will continue. The political situation there remains uncertain. Although the continuing armed violence lacks popular support, it strongly affects the debate on the political future of the Basque Country.

NOTES

1. Source: www.mineco.es.
2. English version from H. Hannum, *Documents on Autonomy and Minority Rights* (Dordrecht: 1993), Martinus Nijhoff, Dordrecht.

3. See Article 71 of the Act on Autonomy for Navarra. The case of Navarra is rather peculiar, because it formally followed the system foreseen in Articles 143 and 146, but in consideration of its "historical rights" recognized in the first Additional Provision for the Basque Provinces, it got the maximum level of autonomy from the beginning.

4. This word has no clear traslation into English. In terms of Public Law it refers to the special regime enjoyed till the nineteenth century by the provinces or territories of Biscay, Alava, Gipuzkoa and Navarra.

5. They were agreements adopted by the two main parties of the moment: the party in government (Unión de Centro Democrático—UCD, Union of Centrist Democrats) and the main opposition party (Partido Socialista Obrero Español—PSOE, Spanish Socialist Workers Party).

6. Catalonia had voted in favor of the Statute in 1931, the Basque Country in 1933, and Galicia in 1936. Only the Statutes of Catalonia and the Basque Country came into force, although the latter under the very special circumstances of the civil war.

7. The first referendum was not fully successful in the eight Andalusian provinces. The Law asked for positive support of more than 50 percent of the population in each of the provinces affected. However, in Almeria the percentage of support did not reach 50 percent of the population. A change in the Referendum Act was made to avoid the locking out of the Andalusian access to autonomy, by which 50 percent of support was only necessary for the whole territory of the future Community (eight provinces in the case of Andalusia) and not in each of the provinces involved.

8. Article 145.1 of the Constitution.

9. Article 145.2 of the Constitution.

10. We could add at this point that Catalonia also enjoys a higher level of autonomy in some matters, as having its own police forces (as the Basque Country and Navarra have), but Catalonia does not have historical rights or tax powers.

11. Galicia, Cantabria, Castile-Leon, Madrid, Murcia, Valencia, and La Rioja.

12. It holds by itself the governments of Andalusia, Extremadura, Castile-La Mancha, and Asturias. The PSOE takes part also in coalition governments in Aragon and Balearic Isles.

13. Unión del Pueblo Navarro (Union of the Navarrese People)—UPN governs in minority in Navarra. The Party has a permanent agreement with the Popular Party for general and European elections.

14. Coalición Canaria (Canary Coalition).

15. The federal model is also supported by some sector of the Socialist Party, especially in Catalonia.

16. The current government of the Balearic Isles can be considered as a Rainbow government. The dominant force is the Socialist Party, but some other parties take part in it. These parties are Union of Majorca/Unión Mallorquina-UM (center-right regionalists), Nationalist Block of Balearic Isles/Entesa nacionalista—PSM-EN (left wing nationalists), United Left and The Greens. The Popular Party is the only one in the opposition. United Left is also present in the Basque Government.

17. In 2003 Batasuna—EH was banned as a political force.

18. EA makes part of the coalition government of the Basque Country together with the PNV and United Left.

19. According to the result of the polls of 13 May 2001, 60 percent of the voters supported parties defending the right to self-determination (PNV-EA, EH or IU), whereas 40 percent voted in favor of the PP and PSOE.

20. See the report submitted by Spain to the Council of Europe in relation to this Convention. On the other hand, the State report on the application in Spain of the European Charter for Regional or Minority Languages shows the same idea of no responsibility of the state authorities in respect to the linguistic pluraliuty of the kingdom.

BIBLIOGRAPHY

Agranoff, R. (ed.). *Accommodating Diversity: Asymmetry in Federal States.* Baden-Baden: Nomos Verlagsgesellschaft, 1999.

Aguado Renedo, C. *El Estatuto de Autonomía y su posición en el ordenamiento jurídico,* Madrid: Centro de Estudios Constitucionales, 1996.

Alvarado Perez, E., and Paniagua Soto, J. L. *Introducción al estudio de las Comunidades Autónomas.* Madrid: Editorial Universitas, 1997.

Aparicio, M. A. *La descentralización y el Federalismo. Nuevos modelos de Autonomía Política (España, Bélgica, Canadá, Italia y Reino Unido).* Barcelona: Cedecs editorial, 1999.

Fossas, E. *Asymmetry and Plurinationality in Spain.* Barcelona: Institut de Ciències Polítiques i Socials, 1999.

Genieys, W. "Autonomous Communities and the State in Spain. The Role of Intermediary Elites," in P. Le Gales and C. Lequesne (eds.), *Regions in Europe.* London: Routledge, 1998.

Gonzalez-Trevijano, P., and Núñez, C. *El Estado Autonómico. Principios, organización y competencias.* Madrid: Editorial Universitas, 1998.

Hannum, H. *Documents on Autonomy and Minority Rights.* Dordrecht: Martinus Nijhoff, 1993.

Iglesia Ferreiros, A. (ed.). *Autonomía y Soberanía.* Madrid: Marcial Pons, 1996.

Ministerio de Administraciones Públicas. *El funcionamiento del Estado autonómico.* Madrid: Ministerio de Administraciones Públicas, 1996.

Monreal, A. "The New Spanish State Structure." In M. Burgess (ed.), *Federalism and Federation in Western Europe.* London: Croom Helm, 1986.

Serra, N., et al. *Organización territorial del Estado.* Salamanca: Ediciones Universidad de Salamanca, 1993.

Souviron Morenilla, J. M. *Realidad y Perspectivas de la Organización Territorial del Estado. Balance y Futuro del Estado Autonómico.* Granada: Comares, 2000.

Williams, A. "Regionalism in Iberia," in P. Wagstaff (ed.), *Regionalism in Europe.* Oxford: Intellect, 1994.

APPENDIX: LIST OF RELEVANT CASES

List of relevant cases on the construction of the Autonomous Communities and the definition of their powers. All the cases refer to decisions of the Constitutional Court.

Year	*No.*	*Date*	*Subject*
1981	4	February 2	Difference between sovereignty and autonomy
1982	18	May 4	Relation between Constitution and Acts on Autonomy
1862	35	June 14	On distribution of powers State-Autonomous Communities

Year	*No.*	*Date*	*Subject*
1983	56	May 13	On distribution of powers State-Autonomous Communities
1983	76	August 5	On "Organic Law for autonomous process" Theory on acts on autonomy
1985	94	July 29	Definition of symbols of the Autonomous Communities
1986	82	June 26	Officiality of regional and minority languages
1986	99	July 11	Territorial changes among Autonomous Communities
1988	69	April 19	On distribution of powers State-Autonomous Communities
1989	103	June 8	On distribution of powers State-Autonomous Communities
1989	147	July 4	On distribution of powers State-Autonomous Communities

IV

Multinational Federations

9

A Dynamic Federalism Built on Static Principles: The Case of Belgium

Wouter Pas

LINGUISTIC DIVERSITY AND SOCIAL DIVISION

The kingdom of Belgium is a small but densely populated Western European State, with about 10 million inhabitants in a territory of not more than 30,000,000 square kilometres. It is one of the wealthiest states of Europe and one of the founding member-states of the European Communities as well as of the Council of Europe. The official languages are Dutch (or Netherlandic), French, and German. The Dutch-speaking region, commonly referred to as Flanders, forms the northern part of Belgium and has approximately 5.9 million Dutch-speaking inhabitants, called the Flemings or the Flemish. The southern part of Belgium, commonly referred to as Wallonia, has approximately 3.2 million French-speaking inhabitants, called the Walloons.[1] In a small group of eastern municipalities, the German-speaking linguistic region, there are about 70,000 German-speaking inhabitants. In the bilingual region of Brussels—the capital of Belgium and the 18 surrounding municipalities—about 1 million inhabitants reside. On these four linguistic regions, three communities, and three regions are based the component autonomous entities of the Belgian state.

The Belgian State was created in 1830, after a secession from the United Kingdom of the Netherlands. This Belgian revolution was based on a French-speaking liberal bourgeoisie and on the Catholic Church, united in resistance against the enlightened despotism of King Willem I of the Netherlands. The support of the European superpowers consolidated the young and small state in 1839 and made its survival possible. With this new state, an end was made to a multicultural[2] and plurireligious[3] state—ruled, however, by a King who did not have an eye for the necessary liberalization of society. This new state was the product of a French-speaking bourgeoisie that based its power on an electoral system with a "property assessment franchise." They created a liberal *Rechtsstaat,* in the form of a parliamentary monarchy and unitary state.

Although the language of a minority of the population, the official language of this state was French on every level—in the legislation, the administration, the courts, the army, the church, and in secondary and high schools, as well as the universities. The French-speaking elite controlled political, cultural, and economic life.[4] The freedom of language, enshrined in the constitution, was nothing more than a safe-conduct provision for French domination. As in the French republic, the aim was to absorb the cultural and linguistic differences and particularities in one neutral central state that guaranteed the equality of each citizen. However, this aim failed, and the central state evolved, rather, into a federal state, with extended autonomy for the communities and the regions. In the nineteenth century, a Flemish movement emerged, demanding in the first instance equal treatment of Dutch and French as official languages. At the end of the nineteenth century and in the first half of the twentieth century, several bills were passed that gradually created equality in the status of the two national languages within the Belgian State, at least as legally spoken.[5] The legislation on the use of languages was organized mostly on a territorial basis.[6] The language legislation therefore did not create a bilingual state, but a state with two languages. The reasons, therefore, are twofold: the refusal of Walloon civil servants to learn and to use Dutch, and the fear of the Flemings of domination by French.

On the basis of the territoriality principle, in 1970 the Belgian State was divided into four territorial linguistic regions:[7] the Dutch-speaking region, the French-speaking region, the bilingual region of Brussels-Capital, and the German-speaking region.[8] The boundaries of these regions can only be changed with a special majority in the federal Parliament. It is important to note that, apart from the bilingual region of Brussels-Capital, all linguistic regions are in principle monolingual.

The authorities in each region may, in principle, only use the official language of that region in their dealings with citizens. In some municipalities, where a significant number of the inhabitants speak another language, special provisions were enacted to give individuals the right to continue to use their own language in their relations with the local authorities. In the bilingual region of Brussels-Capital, Dutch and French are both official languages.

The ethnic diversity, therefore, is essentially a linguistic one, reinforced and combined with a social division. The struggle for recognition of the Dutch language and the Flemish culture has also been the struggle for social development and liberation of the lower classes. For the Flemish movement, language became the ethnic marker for mobilization because of the link between the relative backward social position of the Flemish middle class with a mother tongue that was held to be inferior. Even if they adopted French as a means of communication, they remained outsiders, stuck in a disadvantaged position.[9] Nowadays the linguistic separation is grafted onto broader cultural differences and important economic and political differences.

In this picture, Brussels takes a moderate but central position. It is linguistically and politically divided, but economically mainly orientated to Flanders. A majority of the population of Brussels-Capital (further on we speak about Brussels, as referring to the 19 municipalities) is nowadays French-speaking. In order to understand Belgian federalism, it is crucial to note that, at the Belgian level, the Dutch-speaking population constitutes a demographic majority, whereas in Brussels, the Dutch-speaking population is a demographic minority.[10]

INSTITUTIONALIZING DIVERSITY: THE CREATION OF THE FEDERAL STATE

The struggle for equal treatment of Dutch led to the creation of the language legislation and the linguistic regions. The language legislation culminated in the 1960s in statutes that, at least in theory, established equality between the two languages. It also made clear that the French political and social dominance would come to an end. The Flemings gradually claimed the political representation to which they were entitled, having regard to their demographic majority. This development provoked a Walloon fear of being soon politically outnumbered by the Flemings. The French-speaking politicians felt that their political majority, supported only on a demographic minority, was slipping away, and they felt hostile toward a unitary state in which they had to cope with a Flemish majority.[11]

In fact, the described linguistic differences went and go hand-in-hand with important economic and ideological differences. Wallonia was in the nineteenth century a rich and very industrialized area; Flanders was mostly a rural area. After World War II, the Walloon mines and industry experienced an economic crisis, while at the same time Flanders saw enormous growth. Ideologically the Flemish society was strongly influenced by the Catholic Church, whereas in Wallonia the workers movement produced a secularization of society much earlier. Speaking in terms of political parties, the Christian Democrats dominated in Flanders,[12] the Socialists in Wallonia.

All this provoked a profound division. This division only grew with the democratization of the country, enhancing the power of the numerically dominant group, weakening the powers of the French-speaking elite, and increasing the sense of threat of the Walloon minority.

In order to maintain the balance of powers that was considered necessary, the Belgian State was (in a first stage not at all as a federal state) in the 1960s reformed into a paritarian and bipolar state. The bipolarity of the Belgian State was and is essential and very profound. The country functions (and exists) only insofar as the two main "ethnic" groups want it to. This is shown within the institutions, but also in the political and sociological reality. There are no federal Belgian political parties: There are only Flemish and Francophone parties, representing their regions and populations. The media and the press are organized by community; almost every cultural or sport institution is organized by community.

This bipolar and essentially confederal structure, however, contributes to a deadlock on the Belgian level. The presence of two groups that have the same powers (as a result of elevating the minority to the same position as the majority) as well as the deep mistrust between them have made a profound decentralization necessary. This decentralization took the form of the creation of the communities and the regions. The creation of the linguistic regions and the language legislation did not in itself provide an answer to the increasing demands for autonomy. On the contrary, the territorial basis of the language legislation enforced this search for autonomy.

The Flemish movement urged cultural autonomy, as they understood that this was the only way for a real protection and development of their culture and language. To meet this demand for cultural autonomy, the notion of "communities"[13] was created. The Francophones endorsed the idea of cultural communities, as they hoped to create a community, uniting all the Belgian Francophones, wherever they lived within Belgium. A kind of personal, nonterritorial federalism was striven for, which should make possible the protection (or the preservation of the privileged position) of Francophones living in Flanders. This idea of a personal federalism was never realized, as was clearly confirmed by the case law of the Court of Arbitration,[14] the Council of State, and the European Court of Human Rights (ECHR).[15]

In 1970, three constitutionally based Communities were created: the Flemish Community, the French Community, and the German-speaking Community.[16] The communities have legislative powers in matters such as education, culture, health, and social policy.[17] The Flemish Community has authority in the Dutch linguistic Region and partly in the Brussels-Capital Region; the French Community in the French linguistic Region and partly in the Brussels-Capital Region; and the German-speaking Community in the German linguistic Region.

The Communities are autonomous political entities within the Belgian State. They have directly elected legislative assemblies, as well as proper governments.[18] It is important to note that the Communities have legislative powers: They can enact decrees[19] that have the same legal authority as federal statutes.[20] Unlike in many federal systems, the legislative measures of the federal authority do not prevail over the decrees of the communities.

Wallonia has experienced, since the 1950s, a profound economic crisis. The sense of crisis was reinforced by a growing fear of being marginalized within the Belgian State. A Walloon movement urged, therefore, economic autonomy, which would allow it to deal in a proper way with its economic problems and to stop the favoring of the Flemish economy.

To meet these demands, the regions[21] were created in 1970 (and made effective in 1980 through 1988). Flanders hoped by creating the regions not only to increase its autonomy but also to strengthen the territoriality principle. In 1992 the regions effectively became the territorial basis for the elections of the autonomous parliaments of both the communities and the regions.

There are three regions: the Flemish Region, the Walloon Region, and the Brussels-Capital Region.[22] These regions should not be confused with the linguistic regions.[23] Just as is the case for the communities, the linguistic regions constitute the territorial foundations for the three regions. However, the territories of the communities and of the regions do not coincide. The Flemish Region overlaps with the Dutch linguistic region; the Brussels-Capital Region overlaps with the bilingual region of Brussels-Capital; and, finally, the Walloon Region overlaps with both the French and the German linguistic regions.[24]

Just like the communities, the regions have their own political bodies: a directly elected council and a proper government.[25] Their legislative norms (decrees) have the same legal authority as federal statutes.[26] They have substantial powers with regard to economic and employment policy, environmental and energy policy, local authorities (municipalities and provinces), roads and transport, and so on.

MAIN CHARACTERISTICS OF BELGIAN FEDERALISM

A Bipolar Federal Structure

Although Belgium has three communities and three regions, two groups emerge as the most important: the Dutch-speaking population and the French-speaking population. These two main communities are the core of the Belgian State and her functioning.

In many ways Belgian federal institutions are structured according to this bipolarity.[27] Examples of this are legion.

- The so-called parity in the federal government, which means that it has an equal number of Dutch-speaking and of French-speaking ministers (with exception of the prime minister who is linguistically "asexual."[28] From this standpoint, Belgium forms a confederal state, with a complete equalization of the two main groups, despite the demographic differences.
- The federal administration is based on linguistic frames. A fixed number of civil servants of each language have to be appointed. At the higher levels, an equal number of its language group is imposed.
- Practically all members[29] of the federal Parliament[30] belong to one of both linguistic groups that exist in each of both Chambers.[31] These linguistic groups play a decisive role in fundamental legislation, and with regard to the so-called alarm-bell procedure.
- The alarm-bell procedure gives to each linguistic group the right to block the normal parliamentary procedure. If at least three quarters of the members of one of the linguistic groups sign a motion, the parliamentary procedure is suspended. The motion is then referred to the federal (paritarian) government, which—within a period of 30 days—makes known its findings on the motion and invites the Chamber concerned to reach a decision.[32]

The subnational entities do not participate as such in a revision of the constitution or in the amending of the Special Acts, except through the presence of the 21 Community Members of the Senate.[33] The linguistic groups, though, being the representation of the two major ethnic and cultural groups that form the basis of Belgian federalism, represent the two important communities in both federal chambers. A majority in each of these communities is practically and politically necessary for constitutional reform.[34] Moreover, the constitution often imposes, for fundamental legislation, a special and double majority. These special majority acts can be considered as semiconstitutional texts. A Special

Majority act requires, besides an overall two-thirds majority in each Chamber, a majority in each linguistic group.[35]

- The directly elected members of the Senate are elected on the basis of two electoral constituencies: a Flemish one and a French one, sharing the zone of Brussels-Halle-Vilvoorde, in the center of the country. Moreover, according to a major political agreement in the spring of 2002, the Senate will be reformed into a paritarian House. It would exist of 35 members of each linguistic group, nominated by their respective community parliaments.
- The Court of Arbitration, as the constitutional court with still formally limited powers, is composed of equal numbers of Dutch-speaking and French-speaking judges.
- All the important political parties are organized on a community basis. There are no federal political parties.
- The constitutive autonomy or very limited constitutional powers are only awarded to the Flemish Community, the Walloon Region, and the French Community.

These two ethnic groups meet (or confront) each other in the capital, Brussels, which is also organized on a bipolar basis.

A CENTRIFUGAL OR DEVOLUTIONARY FEDERAL STRUCTURE

The Belgian federal state was created out of a centralized state and not out of several independent states that decided to gradually unify in a centripetal federal structure. This explains several typical traits of Belgian federalism—for instance, why the federal authority is vested with the residuary powers,[36] why no supremacy clause for federal legislation exists, and why neither the communities nor the regions have subnational constitutions.

A Dual-Layered Federal Structure

The fact that the Belgian federal state features two types of component units makes it rather unique. The communities and regions have distinct, sometimes overlapping, territories, but in each instance the three of them cover the whole of Belgium. The communities and regions are vested with different powers, which are in principle strictly separated.[37] The importance and the consequences for the Belgian type of federalism is still crucial, although due to some of the asymmetries in the federal structure, the difference between the two types of federal entities is slowly blurring the political reality. From a legal and constitutional point of view, the distinction can still be sharply drawn.

The dual-layered character is especially relevant and noticeable in Brussels. Brussels-Capital is a region with its own government and own council (parliament). It is, however, not a region just like the Flemish or the Walloon regions. Therefore, the official name is the Region of Brussels Capital, indicating the special status of the city as the capital of the country and its communities. Within these institutions, important protection mechanisms are foreseen for the Flemish minority (that was created as a result of creating the Brussels region). These protection mechanisms can be considered as the mirror of the protection existing on the federal level for the French-speaking minority.

As there is no cultural and linguistic unity or maybe even identity, Brussels is not a Community. In this bilingual territory both the French and the Flemish Community exercise their powers in matters of education, culture, and social policy. The recognition of the presence and the authority of the two Communities did not lead to the introduction of a so-called subnationality.

This combination of the regional and community identity is probably the most remarkable and positive achievement of the Brussels and Belgian system. In fact the region gives protection to the French-speaking Brussels population, with a built-in protection for the Dutch-speaking population. The presence of the Communities (directly and through the community commissions) guarantees the cultural and social rights of each group. It does this in a positive way, by offering choice to the population.

An Asymmetrical Federalism

The existence of this double structure itself makes Belgian federalism asymmetric. On the original basis of the division of the territory into four linguistic regions, two types of substates are established. The bilingual region of Brussels-Capital constitutes the pivot of this institutional separation between the communities and the regions.

The *prima facie* conclusion that Belgium is composed of two times three substates, each with their distinguished powers and institutions, is not quite right. In actuality, the reality is somewhat more complex. The clear division between communities and regions is partly offset by a North-South asymmetry. In fact, on the Flemish side there exists a fusion between the Flemish Community and the Flemish Region.[38] On the other hand, in the south of the country, an inverse process took place. A merger of the institutions appeared to be impossible due to the fact that the Walloon Region embraces two linguistic regions and the sociological and political independence of the Brussels francophones with regard to Wallonia. This means that some regional powers are exercised by the organs of the German-speaking Community.[39] It also means the dismantling of the French Community. Powers of the French Community can be exercised by the organs of the Walloon Region and the French Community Commission in Brussels.[40] The decrees of the Walloon Region with regard to these transferred community matters are applicable in the territory of the Walloon Region, with the exception of the territory of the German-speaking Community.[41] For the territory of Brussels-Capital, the French Community Commission thus gets the power to enact decrees.

A second important asymmetry exists between the big and small communities and regions. This difference exists between the Flemish Community (the Flemish region), the French Community, and the Walloon Region on one hand and the Brussels-Capital Region and the German-speaking Community on the other hand. Only the first group has so-called constitutive autonomy. At the same time the legal norms of the Brussels-Capital Region have in a certain way a subordinated position.

A third important asymmetry is between the directly elected parliaments or councils and the legislative assemblies that are composed in an indirect manner. Apart from the federal Parliament, there are seven organs with legislative power: the Flemish Parliament, the Walloon Regional Parliament, the Council of the German-speaking Community, the Council of the Brussels-Capital Region, the French Community Council, the Assembly of the Joint Community Commission, and the Assembly of the French Community Commission. The first four of these Councils are elected directly. Indeed, the elections of the Councils are organized on a territorial basis within the limits of their respective linguistic regions. The other councils or assemblies are derived from the first four.

Finally, the asymmetry within the bilingual region of Brussels-Capital can be mentioned. It is expressed in the different status and composition of the French and the Flemish Community Commissions, one being a legislative body, the second only an administrative organ, as well as in the election of the members of the community parliaments.

When summarizing all these asymmetries, we find that there are indeed six entities within the Belgian State. However, the political importance of one of these entities, the French Community, is decreasing considerably.[42] The five principal entities are Flanders (i.e., the Flemish Community), Wallonia (i.e., the territory of the French linguistic region and the competencies of the Walloon region), the German-speaking Community, Brussels-Capital (i.e., the Brussels-Capital Region and the Joint Community Commission), and the

Francophones in the territory of Brussels-Capital (the French Community Commission).

Flanders is exercising all the responsibilities of the community and the region. Wallonia uses all the powers of the region and some powers of the community. The German-speaking Community exercises all community powers and some regional powers. Brussels-Capital disposes of all regional competencies. It also exercises in a personal union[43] the jurisdiction over some bilingual community institutions and for some bicommunitarian matters. The Brussels French-speaking population exercises certain community responsibilities through the French Community Commission. If we bear in mind that the Brussels Francophones form the main part of Brussels-Capital, we recognize the four linguistic regions as the base of the Belgian federal structure.

Dynamic and Pragmatic Character

The creation and the development of this structure are clearly not finished. The federal state, which is already very weak, is still undermined by its bipolar structure. This bipolar structure constantly runs the risk of mutual vetoes and political deadlock. In fact, even in the regular federal decision-making process, the practical and political necessity for a majority in each linguistic group is evident. One could even assess that there is no real federal representation and federal decision-making process, but that there exists only the representation of the two major ethnic communities, negotiating a rather confederal process in order to find agreements that are acceptable to both groups.

Parity in the federal government and the nonexistence of federal political parties imply that every government will be a coalition government of at least one party of each linguistic group. Due to the system of proportional representation, a majority in a linguistic group requires already a coalition of various political parties. Federal governments are therefore fragile constructions of at least four political parties. This requires a strong party discipline within the governing political parties. Consequently, in practice, every act of parliament, every statute, requires a majority in each linguistic group. Although the Dutch-speaking group holds more than 60 percent of the seats in the House of Representatives and more than 57 percent of the seats in the Senate, it is never able to pass a bill that has no majority in the French-speaking group.

This de facto confederal character of the federal decision-making process bears in itself a permanent risk of deadlock and frustration. It makes a permanent and devolutionary evolution of Belgium federalism unavoidable. The static character of the Belgian (national) institutions is one of the main reasons for the dynamic character of Belgian federalism.

This dynamic process is reinforced by the positive energy that emerges from Belgian regionalism and moderated nationalism. The dynamics of the regions and the communities have proven to be fruitful and productive for the country as a whole. Especially in Flanders the process of decentralization has contributed to cultural and economic development. The economic recovery of Wallonia will doubtless depend on the capacity to develop a proper regional project, not dependent on federal financial means. The creation of the Brussels institutions made an end to a period of political lethargy and anarchy in the capital and encouraged the emergence of a real urban policy.

The dynamics of Belgian federalism are, for the same reasons, very pragmatic. When a problem arises, until now usually at the federal level, but more and more also in the relations between the regions and the communities, an *ad hoc* solution is created. This *ad hoc* solution is often based on an agreement to disagree. The *ad hoc* character is also showed by the whole list of asymmetries and by the sometimes overwhelming complexity of the system.

FUTURE PROSPECTS

The form that the further decentralization of the state will take is not perceived in the same way in the north as in the south. Generally it is stated that on the Flemish side a communitarian development is taking place; on the French-speaking side there is a clear tendency toward the regions.

Bearing in mind the existing complexity, some argue for the abrogation of the communities, thereby reducing the substates to four regions. Proponents of this position insist, inter alia, that every successful form of federalism has to be organized on a territorial basis and that only the regions provide a clear, exclusive division of the Belgian territory. Recent developments—especially the state reform of 2001—seem to confirm this regional approach. New powers were especially given to the regions, in particular with regard to the municipalities and tax-policy. The Brussels institutions were adapted in a way that diminished the influence and the role of the Flemish minority (even in the bicommunitarian issues that until now were based on a paritarian logic).

However, the idea of the Communities remains essential to the Belgian federal system. The two main ethnic groups (the Dutch-speaking and the French-speaking populations) are the essence for the functioning of the Belgian State. Proof of this is abundant, as mentioned before. These two groups meet (or confront) each other in the capital, Brussels. Brussels cannot be organized as a region like the others. Moreover, for the Flemings an institutional and political link between the Flemings in Brussels and the rest of Flanders is indispensable and vital. The Flemish Community ensures this link. Thus, in the whole of this complex federal system, Brussels takes a central position. As Brussels was the heart of unitarian Belgium, it can now be considered as the rivet of a highly disintegrated state.

The So-called Constitutive Autonomy or Institutional Autonomy

Contrary to the general rule in almost every federal state, the Belgian federated entities have no proper constitutions of their own. The institutions of the communities and regions are laid down in the federal constitution and statutes. The Flemish Community, the Walloon Region, and the French Community only have so-called constitutive autonomy. This autonomy is very limited. The federal legislature has given some regulating powers in matters relating to the election of the parliaments and to the composition and functioning of the parliaments and their government.

Following the devolutionary logic of Belgian federalism, these constitutional powers are granted by the federal legislature. Commanded by the federal Constitution[44] to specify these matters, a special majority act[45] recognized their constitutive autonomy in such areas as the fixing of electoral constituencies, defining conflicts of interest between the offices of members of parliament and government members, and the various rules relating to the functioning of parliaments and governments. These powers must be exercised through special majority decrees passed by a two-thirds majority vote in the council concerned.

It must be acknowledged that some of the areas that fall within the scope of constitutive autonomy are of minor importance. Others—like the relations between the council and its government—appertain to the balance of powers, which can thus be adjusted by a more flexible procedure than is required at federal level.

The constitutive autonomy thus conferred, however, seems very modest when compared with what is found in the main federal states and would not seem to provide a legal base for the communities and the regions to adopt a proper constitution.

Constitutive autonomy is not granted to the Brussels-Capital Region nor to the German-speaking community. The special position of Brussels explains why its institutions remain entirely regulated by a federal special-majority law. For the German-speaking community, the explanation probably has to be found in the fact that Belgian federalism is essentially bipolar, determined by only the two dominant linguistic, ethnic groups.

Thus, constitutive autonomy is very limited—it has been called an embryo of constitutional power. This also means that the subnational governmental structure is very similar to the federal governmental structures. However, the federal (special) legislature itself introduced some differences. For example, the subnational parliaments are elected for a five-year term. A previous dissolution, contrary to the federal parliament, is excluded. The mechanism of electing the members of government are well determined, contrary to the federal level where the King still plays a vague but important role.

Very little use is made of the little consitutive autonomy that was granted by the three main subnational entities. However, taking into account the dynamic character of Belgian federalism, the introduction of subnational constitutions can be expected in the future. The growing autonomy of the substates and their increasing sociological and political differences seem to make necessary a translation of their fundamental options and concepts into a proper constitution. A constitution is indeed the legal translation of the essential principles on which a community wants to organize itself.

These principles are expressed in the institutions that are created, and in the way the relation between citizens and these institutions is conceived. Therefore a constitution is in the first place a dedication to certain values. A constitution must express the fundamental choices of a society. This is why constitutions are necessary, as well as for the subnational entities as for the federation. The values that are expressed in such constitutions must and will coincide with the universally recognized values, as laid down in international treaties or in the federal constitution. The subnational constitution, however, allows also particular accents: special attention, special protection.

This possibility of subnational constitution-making today does not exist for the two constitutive peoples of Belgium. It seems, however, that there is a growing need and a growing awareness of the necessity of such constitutions. The Flemish Parliament in particular is striving for a Flemish constitution.[46] This need and awareness are illustrated by two academic projects and especially by the political reactions to these projects. In fact, there are two (academic) drafts: "Proeve van Grondwet voor Vlaanderen"[47] and "Projet pour lancer un débat sur un projet de Constitution wallonne."[48] The academic interest for such projects probably can also be explained by the fact that the Belgian constitution, although since 1970 frequently amended, still is a constitution dating from 1831. By European standards, this means that this constitution is old. There seems to be a clear need for a new, modern constitution. Possibly subnational constitutions will be more able to provide such modern ideas. This expectation goes hand-in-hand with the observation that the social, economic, and political dynamics in Belgian society have almost completely shifted to the regions and communities, as a consequence of the deadlock on the federal level.

The Concept of Minorities Within the Belgian Federal State

As we have described, the Belgian response to the country's linguistic, cultural, and social diversity was, after a long period of denial, the creation of a highly decentralized federal state. The bipolar national structures, as well as the creation of the federated subnational entities (the communities and the regions) do themselves appear as the first and most important form of minority protection. The constitutional system grants a very large degree of participation in the decision-making process to all groups, together with a very wide cultural, social, and economic autonomy. Added to this is a developed and sophisticated language legislation that regulates the use of languages in the public sphere. This legislation is based on the linguistic borderline that was accepted with a large majority in the Belgian Parliament, supported by members from all parts of the country. Of course, a linguistic borderline is, by its very nature, always something arbitrary.[49] Therefore, the language legislation contains exceptions to the use of a single language. In the bilingual region of Brussels, the Dutch-speaking minority is protected by the bilingual status of the institutions. In the unilingual zones, in 27 municipalities bordering on a different linguistic region, so-called facilities have been installed. These facilities give the citizens the right to demand that the municipal authority use another language than the one that is compulsory in the linguistic region to which the municipality belongs. Facilities also imply that parents have the right to have their children educated in kindergarten and primary schools of their language.

The linguistic legislation is in principle a power of the Communities, but precisely excepted are those aspects that touch the protection of minorities, namely the determination of the linguistic regions, the so-called facilities, or the use of languages in the bilingual area of Brussels Capital. The power of the Communities is therefore rather limited. All the mentioned matters fall under the powers of federal special legislation and require a majority in each linguistic group.

For all these reasons, it seems that a specific approach toward minorities is no longer relevant within the Belgian context. The same goes for international legal instruments that pay little or no attention to the institutional protection of minorities by means of participation in the decision-making process or by means of substantial autonomy (e.g., federalism that is essentially based on a territorial division).[50] However, the question whether or not there are minorities in Belgium remains at the center of an important political and legal debate. The discussion is linked to the anticipated ratification by Belgium of the European Framework Convention for the Protection of National Minorities.

Belgium signed the Framework Convention for the Protection of National Minorities on 31 July 2001. It made the reservation that "the notion of national minority will be defined by the Belgian inter-ministerial conference on foreign policy."[51] This reservation is the expression of a highly sensitive political debate about the question of what groups can be considered national minorities in the sense of this Convention and whether the Convention would imply changes in the existing constitutional and legal treatment of minorities. Once again, a wide gap exists between Flemish and Francophone lawyers and politicians. Both groups fit more or less in a definition of minority. They agree that a minority is a group of nationals in number inferior to the majority that finds itself in a nondominant position. This element of nondomination is correctly considered essential. The general concept in Flanders is that only the German-speaking community can be considered a minority in the sense of the Convention. It is evident that the Francophones are not in a position in which they can fear Flemish domination. As we pointed out before, the institutions on the national level have in fact a confederal character. The two groups are in all on an equal footing. On the Francophone side, emphasis is placed on the fact that even if a minority is strongly protected, that does not in itself deprive it of the status of minority. According to this view, there is no dominating group, which means that all the groups can be considered minorities, the Flemish demographic majority included. It seems that in this view, the concept of minority is deprived of any meaning. Considering the Francophones a national minority seems also to deprive the Framework Convention of its real meaning. The position of power given to or kept by the Francophones, on an equal basis, is no longer the protection of a minority. It involves a qualitative leap. However, the question on national minorities seems less important, due to the existing protection. The Framework Convention would not imply any extra rights. The main issue is that of the possible existence of so-called regional minorities.

In fact, by creating the communities and the regions, some groups became minorities within a particular region or community. This is the case for the Flemish living in Brussels, who became regionally outnumbered. The protection of the francophone minority situated in Brussels by the creation of regional autonomy creates a new minority. Also the Francophones living in the outskirts of Brussels—belonging to the Flemish region and community—no longer have the dominating role they once had in the unitary state. The importance of the division into linguistic regions grows with the increasing autonomy and power of the Communities and Regions that are based on these linguistic regions.

Traditionally, the existence of regional minorities (in a legal sense) has not been accepted. In this context, one can refer to the decision of the United Nations' Human Rights Committee of March 31, 1993, in the case of *McIntyre v. Canada*.[52] This case concerned the interpretation of Article 27 of the International Covenant on Civil and Political Rights. The committee judged that minorities are groups of people that represent a minority at the State level and not at the substate level. There seems, however, to be an evolution in this matter on the level of the Council of Europe. In a resolution of September 26, 2002, the Parliamentary Assembly of the Council of Europe considered the existence of subnational, regional minorities.[53] The resolution was based on an opinion, adopted by the Venice Commission, that argued that applying the strict interpretation of the MacIntyre-case on the Framework Convention would be manifestly incompatible with the object and aim of the Convention.[54] With regard to Belgium, the opinion states that, at the state level, the French-speakers do not constitute a minority within the meaning of the Framework Convention. However, in the Commission's opinion, French-speakers may be considered as a minority in the Dutch-language Region and in the German-language Region, as may Dutch-speakers and German-speakers in the French-language Region.[55]

A thorough analysis of this opinion and of the mentioned resolution would fall outside the scope of this chapter. However, some remarks should be made regarding crucial characteristics of Belgian federalism to which the Venice Commission paid no attention.

If one should accept their existence, minority groups can only be considered minorities with regard to the powers of the region or the community. In this regard what is especially relevant are the community powers in the domains of culture, education, language, and social aid.

However, as we have noted, the communities and regions have very limited powers with regard to minorities. Indeed, the main principles are laid down in the constitution, determining the linguistic regions and the liberty of language in private relations.[56] The power of the communities and the regions is also limited by the constitutional principle of equality and nondiscrimination. In the field of language legislation, the communities are not competent for precisely those sensitive areas where groups of different languages are present: Brussels Capital, the German linguistic region, and all the municipalities with facilities. As the regions in 2002 became competent to deal with local institutions, the existing minority protection was specifically excluded and reserved to the federal legislature. As we speak of federal and constitutional legislation, once again we have to return to the strong institutional guarantees existing on the federal level. For example, the federal language legislation with regard to the facilities municipalities is laid down in special majority acts.[57] Moreover, all this legislation and its application are supervised by the Court of Arbitration, the Council of State, or other paritarian institutions with an equal number of Francophones and Dutch speakers. Did the experts of the Venice Commission really consider the whole balance of powers (factual and legal) existing within the Belgian state? And is the Venice Commission prepared to apply the criteria used in the Belgian case in the situation of major Western European countries?

In any event, the debate on regional minorities is open, and the outcome is difficult to predict. The discussion touches the heart of the Belgian balance that enables peaceful and constitutional conflict-solving mechanisms. The territorial linguistic regions were created to protect both major linguistic groups and especially to create a security area for the socially and culturally weaker group. It provides protection against the proved and normal expansion of a greater European culture and language. Exceptions to this territoriality principle exist, without questioning the principle itself. This principle remains the fragile and therefore static basis on which the actual Belgian state rests. The concept of regional minorities could imply the possible risk of undermining this principle. Can Belgium afford to do away with this founding principle, and risk abandoning its tradition of pacification?

NOTES

1. Flanders and Wallonia are not legal or constitutional terms. We use them only for didactic purposes.
2. The languages used in public life were French and Dutch.
3. The north was predominantly Protestant, the south Catholic. The borders between both zones do not coincide with the actual (dating from 1839) State borders between Belgium and the Netherlands.
4. Already in 1830 the majority of the Belgian population spoke Dutch (Nederlands) or a Dutch-Flemish dialect. The Flemish lived especially in the northern provinces. The upper class of Flanders—2 to 3 percent of the population—was French-speaking. The same was true for the elites in the capital of Brussels and Wallonia. The Walloons lived in the southern provinces. This population spoke French or a Walloon dialect.
5. These bills regulate the use of languages in legislation, in administrative matters, in judicial matters, in education matters, and in the armed forces. See E. Witte and H. Van Velthoven, *Language and Politics* (VUBPress, 2000).
6. See also A. Alen, "Nationalism—Federalism—Democracy. The Example of Belgium," *Revue européenne de droit public* (1993): 54–58.
7. *Taalgebieden—régions linguistiques*
8. This principle was eventually laid down in the constitution (Article 4) in 1970.
9. See R. Van Dyck, "Divided We Stand. Regionalism, Federalism and Minority Rights in Belgium," *Res Publica* (1996): 431.

10. The relation of majority-minority on the Belgian level is quite unchanged since the creation of the state. The demographic situation in Brussels, however, has changed radically in the last century. As a result of a complex social evolution, in the capital of Brussels, a switch in language use took place. Unil 1794 (French annexation) 90 to 95 percent of the population of the city of Brussels was considered to be Dutch-speaking. Nowadays this proportion is estimated at 15 percent. This proportion is an estimation, because there is no official language count. The number is based on the result of the Flemish political parties at various elections in Brussels.

11. See also A. Alen, "Nationalism—Federalism—Democracy." 50–51.

12. After the general elections of 1999, for the first time since 1954 a federal government, and for the first time ever, a Flemish government was formed, without the Christian Democrats.

13. *Gemeenschappen—communautés.*

14. The Court has emphasized the system of exclusive territorial allocation of powers: the powers of the Communities and Regions are exclusive and always restricted to their territory, so that every situation is and can only be regulated by one legislature. See A. Alen and P. Peeters, "The Competences of the Communities in the Belgian Federal State: The Principle of Exclusivity Revisited," *European Public Law*, no. 2 (1997): 165–73.

15. See ECHR, July 23, 1968, *Belgian Linguistic Case*, and March 2, 1987, *Mathieu-Mohin and Clerfayt*.

16. Article 2 of the Constitution.

17. Articles 127 to 130 of the Constitution and Articles 4 and 5 of the special majority act of August 8, 1980.

18. Article 115, § 1 and Article 121, § 1 of the Constitution.

19. *Decreten—décrets.*

20. Article 127, § 2, Article 128, § 2, Article 129, § 2 and Article 130, § 2 of the Constitution.

21. *Gewesten—régions.*

22. Article 3 of the Constitution.

23. The very small German linguistic region has a proper community (the German-speaking Community), but no proper region.

24. Article 2 of the special majority act of August 8, 1980, and Article 2, § 1 of the special majority act of January 12, 1989.

25. Article 115, § 2 and Article 121, § 2 of the Constitution.

26. The legislative norms of the Brussels-Capital Region are called ordinances (ordonnanties—ordonnances) and do not have entirely the same legal force.

27. See, for example, A. Alen, *Treatise on Belgian Constitutional Law* (Deventer, Kluwer, 1992), 288.

28. See Article 99 of the Constitution.

29. The only exception is the one German-speaking senator, designated by the German-speaking community council (Article 67 of the Constitution).

30. The composition of the federal Parliament is laid down in Articles 61–65 (House of Representatives) and 67–70 (Senate) of the Constitution.

31. Article 43 of the Constitution.

32. Article 54 of the Constitution.

33. Article 67 of the Constitution.

34. The amending of the constitution requires a complicated procedure, culminating in a two-thirds majority of the total votes cast in both houses of the Federal Parliament (see Article 131 of the Constitution).

35. Article 4 of the Constitution.

36. Article 35 of the Constitution transfers the residual powers to the communities and/or regions.
37. Article 39 of the Constitution.
38. Article 137 of the Constitution, implemented by Article 1, § 1 of the special majority act of August 8, 1980.
39. Article 139 of the Constitution.
40. Article 138 of the Constitution.
41. Or, in other words, in the French linguistic region.
42. This is illustrated by the fact that this Community calls itself today "Community of Wallonia and Brussels."
43. The Joint Community Commission, which is composed of the same members as the council of the Brussels-Capital Region.
44. Article 118, § 2 and Article 123, § 2 of the Constitution.
45. The precise matters are listed in Article 35, § 3 of the special majority law of August 8, 1980.
46. See the resolution of the Flemish Parliament of March 3, 1999, or the official address of its president on July 11, 2002 (both to be found at www.vlaamsparlement.be).
47. J. Clement, W. Pas, B. Seutin, G. van Haegendoren, and J. Van Nieuwenhove, *Proeve van Grondwet voor Vlaanderen* (Brugge, die Keure, 1996): 353. The drafted constitution is, with some comments, translated into French: J. Brassinne, *"La Constitution flamande". Essai de constitution pour la Flandre* (Courrier hebdomadaire, Brussel, Crisp, 1997).
48. Project dated on 2 July 1997. It can be found at http://www.wallonie-enligne.net/donnees/walevent/constw1.htm.
49. See, for example, A. Alen, and P. Peeters, "The Columberg Report on the Belgian Linguistic Legislation: A Storm in a Teacup," *European Public Law* (1999): 155–66.
50. See as an illustration the inaccurate assertion that places Belgium in a series of countries that "have significant minorities, which ought to be protected, and whose rights are not officially recognised." Recommendation 1492 (2001) on the rights of national minorities of the parliamentary assembly of the Council of Europe.
51. This conference will consist of representatives of the seven authorities that will have to agree with the Convention.
52. Revue universelle des droits de l'homme, 1993, vol. 5, 156–64.
53. Resolution 1301 (2002) on the Protection of Minorities in Belgium.
54. Opinion, adopted by the Venice Commission on 8–9 March 2002, on possible groups of persons to which the Framework convention for the protection of national minorities could be applied in Belgium (CDL-AD (2002)1). This opinion was based on the comments of four experts (F. Matscher, G. Malinverni, P. van Dijk, and S. Bartole). See www.venice.coe.int.
55. It is astonishing that the opinion and the resolution consider these groups to be regional minorities on the whole territory of the respective linguistic regions, without any territorial delimitation. This does not correspond with any social or demographic reality.
56. Article 30 of the Constitution.
57. The electoral system allows French-speaking inhabitants of Flanders (in the district of Halle-Vilvoorde) to vote for or to be elected in the French linguistic groups in Parliament.

10

Federalism and Consociationalism as Tools for State Reconstruction? The Case of Bosnia and Herzegovina

Jens Woelk

THE DAYTON PEACE AGREEMENT: ENDING A WAR AND RECONSTRUCTING A MULTIETHNIC SOCIETY?

From 1945 to 1991/1992 Yugoslavia was a multinational state with a federal constitution, and Bosnia and Herzegovina was one of its constituent units. Indeed, Bosnia and Herzegovina was rightly described as a "Yugoslavia in miniature" on account of its demographic structure: in 1991, Muslims comprised 43.7 percent, Serbs 31.45 percent, and Croats 17.3 percent of the population, while 5.5 percent considered themselves "Yugoslavs." In addition to the three largest ethnic groups members of other nations and nationalities (according to the terminology of communist constitutional law) lived in the country and were entitled to equality under the Constitution.[1] None of these groups was settled in a separate, territorially defined or closed area.

The independence of the Republic of Bosnia and Herzegovina and its recognition in accordance with international law at the beginning of January 1992, after the dissolution of Yugoslavia, resulted in a worst-case scenario of ethnic conflict.[2] Before it was ended by the Dayton

Peace Agreement in Paris in December 1995, the war left more than 250,000 people dead or registered as missing and led to the displacement of an estimated 1.2 million persons and to extensive physical and economic destruction.[3] The Dayton Agreement laid the institutional basis for the political and economic reconstruction of Bosnia and Herzegovina and for the continuation of its legal existence under international law as a multiethnic state.

However, despite the designation of "Bosniaks" (i.e., Muslims),[4] Croats, and Serbs as "Constituent Peoples" of the State in the Constitution of Bosnia and Herzegovina (annex IV of the Dayton Peace Agreement, preamble), it is rather the subdivision of the country into two "Entities" that is fundamental for the new political system. The Muslim-Croat "Federation of Bosnia and Herzegovina" and the "Republika Srpska" are the *de facto* recognition of a territorial and ethnographical division that was created by war and operations of ethnic cleansing. The ceasefire line between the armies, dividing the country with 51 percent held by the Federation and 49 percent held by the Republika Srpska,[5] became the so-called interentity boundary line. The fact that the new system introduced by the Dayton Peace Agreement depends to a certain degree on this ethnic homogenization of the territories (through the war) conflicts with the right to return for refugees (so-called minority returns, annex VII, Agreement on Refugees and Displaced Persons) into the areas from which they had fled or were expelled, a right that if implemented would transform Bosnia and Herzegovina back into the multiethnic society it was before the war.

The first years of implementation have revealed the fundamental dilemma inherent in this peace settlement. After the atrocities of ethnic cleansing, should the ensuing ethnic and national structures and segregative institutional mechanisms[6] be accepted as a sign of political realism? Or should an attempt be made to restore the multiethnic structures of 1991 for the sake of justice and under varying amounts of pressure from the international community? This in turn requires that the important question of who can be considered a minority in Bosnia and Herzegovina has to be reframed: There are only very small autochthonous groups that are minorities in the common and traditional sense of the term.[7] However, the refugees and displaced persons who lost their homes during the war can also be considered a minority (as underlined by the term "minority-return" in the Constitution). As a result, the underlying fundamental question is whether the members of the three larger groups—Bosniaks/Muslims, Serbs, and Croats—really are "constituent peoples" as the Constitution refers to them, with equal status throughout the whole country, or whether they are subject to different legal treatment at different territorial levels (State—Entity—local).

To some extent, the situation is similar to that in Switzerland and Belgium, where the term "minorities" cannot be applied, in a technical sense, to the main constituent groups.[8] In these paritarian multinational states,[9] the constitutional order aims at integration and reflection of the multinational society based on the principles of parity and equal representation of the groups or nations that is realized by means of territorial organization as well as through substantive legislation. Consequently, from a legal perspective, there are neither national majorities nor national minorities. Paradoxically there are hardly any promotional and affirmative legislative actions toward its own multinational components, differentiation is the general law, the exception is the rule. In this sense and for the purpose of this chapter, given the present situation in Bosnia and Herzegovina, it seems justified to refer to the constituent peoples as (*de facto*) minorities at the subnational level. Although there is a clear conceptual difference between minorities and constituent peoples, both at the State and at the subnational level, the instruments adopted to guarantee groups' status as "constituent peoples" in those parts of the country, where they are not in a dominant position, are the same as those typically used to enhance minority-protection.

This chapter illustrates the complex federal/confederal and consociational arrangements of the present tripartite federal structure of the State of Bosnia and Herzegovina—two Entities and the State—that have been designed for the reconstruction of an ethnically plural society (though by means of an initial separation of the three groups) after the traumatic experience of civil war and human rights violations on a massive scale. Emphasis is put on the question whether federalism and consociationalism are useful tools for reconstruction of a multiethnic society after violent conflict and whether they are compatible with one another. At the end, the special role of the international community is examined, as it has acted not only as a mediator and guarantor, but as the motor of reform, when the authorities in Bosnia and Herzegovina were unwilling to work together to rebuild the country.

CONSOCIATIONAL DEMOCRACY IN A TRIPARTITE FEDERAL FRAMEWORK

The Entities: The Federation of Bosnia and Herzegovina and Republika Srpska

The Entities constitute the level of primary political power in Bosnia and Herzegovina. All governmental functions and powers that are not expressly assigned in the constitution fall within the preserve of the Entities (Article III.3a). The Entities are also responsible for civilian law enforcement, health care, agriculture, and local affairs. Although foreign policy is in the purview of the central government (and the Entities are constitutionally obliged to provide "all necessary assistance" to the central government in order to enable it to honor its international obligations [Article III.2b]), the Entities can establish relationships with neighboring states, and enter agreements with foreign states and international organizations (with the consent of the federal Parliamentary Assembly [Article III.2d]). Certainly very important is the power of taxation that is exercised by the Entities in the framework of general guidelines regarding their financial responsibilities vis-à-vis the federal institutions.[10]

Even though the term "Entities" was deliberately chosen in order to underline their nonstate nature, both Entities have a fully developed statelike structure, including a president, a government, a legislature, and a judiciary. Although their relations to the federal level are symmetrical, the Republika Srpska is a unitary state with a highly centralized structure, whereas the Federation is organized as a federal system comprising 10 cantons, 8 of which are more or less ethnically homogeneous and 2 are mixed cantons. The legislature in the Republika Srpska consists of the National Assembly as a single chamber with its members elected by simple proportional representation. The Republika Srpska government—as cantons or other structures do not exist—directly oversees the municipalities. In the Federation, the presidency, the vice presidency, and the office of the prime minister rotate between the two ethnic groups—Bosniaks and Croats. A bicameral system has been instituted with a directly elected House of Representatives (140 members) and a House of Peoples (or Nations), the latter representing the 10 cantonal assemblies. Its 74 members are elected from members of the cantonal legislatures in the proportions of 30 Bosniaks, 30 Croats, and 14 Others.

Neither the Federation nor the Republika Srpska has been able to exercise effective control over its respective territory. The cantonal, decentralized structure of the Federation of Bosnia and Herzegonia has contributed to the fact that Croat cantons and army units have maintained separate and parallel institutional structures as well as direct political, institutional, and financial relations with the Republic of Croatia.[11] In the Republika Srpska, political centralization and geographic disintegration have led to a similar degree of political dysfunctionality. The Dayton Peace Agreement did not create a contiguous territory that, in the future, might join Serbia proper, but instead two territories, linked only by the city of Brčko in northern Bosnia, which by decision of international arbiters in March 1999 has been transformed into a *condominium*,[12] thus removing the only link between the already politically divided parts of the Republika Srpska.[13] Other factors promoting dysfunctionality have been Slobodan Miloševič's detrimental role, the continued economic and social decline of Serbia, and the division within the Republika Srpska over whether to cooperate with the international community.[14] Furthermore, in order to encourage the return to a multiethnic society by actively promoting minority-returns, refugees and displaced persons are allowed to vote in their prewar residence independently from their effective return.[15] By adding a virtual community to the inhabitants (and consequently changing—virtually—the ethnic composition of the population), this makes political representation more diverse than its actual population distribution. However, power sharing is neither explicitly foreseen in the Republika Srpska institutions nor favored at lower levels due to the lack of effective decentralized structures.[16]

Common Institutions of the State of Bosnia and Herzegovina

The powers of the State are relatively modest and basically comprise only foreign affairs, foreign trade relations, customs, monetary and refugee policies, parts of financial policy, issues of criminal law enforcement, air traffic control, and communication facilities (Article III.1). All further powers have to be negotiated with the Entities. Interestingly, the Entities also provide for the budget of the common State institutions, thus creating a situation of almost total dependence: The Federation is to provide two thirds of the revenues required for the central budget and the Republika Srpska one third.

Given the modest competencies, it is no wonder that the set of state institutions is relatively underdeveloped: The head of the State is not a single person, but in the Yugoslav tradition, a presidency consisting of three directly elected representatives, one from each constituent people in the respective entities. The chair in the presidency is determined by rotation (Article V.2b). Each member of the presidency is to have "civilian command authority over armed forces" (Article V.5a), which are still separated, but the Constitution does not provide for unified civilian command over the military.[17]

The chair of the Council of Ministers is nominated by the presidency following approval by the House of Representatives, which also approves the nomination by the chair of all other ministers and of deputy ministers, who must not be of the same ethnic group as their ministers (Article V.4). The Constitution, though indicating a Minister for Foreign Affairs and a Minister for Foreign Trade Relations, and leaving the nomination of further ministers to later decision, prescribes that no more than two thirds of the government's components can be from the federation, thus introducing the principle of parity among the three constituent peoples.[18] The Council of Ministers is constitutionally weak (its powers are not described separately, but in the article on the presidency!) and it must resign, if the Parliamentary Assembly passes a vote of no confidence (Article V.4c). In order to strengthen the State government, in December 2002, the High Representative imposed a reform law on the Council of Ministers, ending the rotation principle for its chair and introducing a four-year mandate coinciding with parliament's mandate. It also leaves the chair without any additional portfolio and creates two new ministries—justice and security.[19]

On the State level, the bicameral Parliamentary Assembly comprises, as in the Federation, a House of Representatives and a House of Peoples. The 42 representatives are elected in separate caucuses: one third by the population of the Republika Srpska, two thirds in the Federation. This scheme is repeated for the House of Peoples, with 5 members delegated by the National Assembly of the Republika Srpska and 10 members by the Federation. The representation of all three constituent peoples is extended to the chair of the two parliamentary chambers with a rotating system of one chair and two vice chairs.

Both chambers must approve all legislative decisions. A quorum is required for action: In the House of Peoples at least nine members (three of each constituent people); in the House of Representatives a majority has to be present. Decisions are generally taken by a simple majority vote. However, there is a kind of suspensory veto for the representatives of each entity: If a cross-community minimum approval of at least one third of deputies from each entity cannot be achieved, the chairs of each House are obliged to present a re-elaborated draft within three days. If this fails, to win approval, a simple majority is sufficient for the adoption of the decision. But an absolute veto is possible, if in the second voting procedure two thirds of the members representing one entity vote against the decision (Article IV.3d).

A "vital interest-mechanism" available to each of the constituent peoples for blocking any decision adds to these veto powers. In case of a declaration that an issue touches upon a "vital interest," a majority within the three groups of present members is required (Article IV.3e).[20] If a majority of another group expresses doubt on the vital-interest statement, a Joint Commission is established to work out a compromise within five days (one member selected by the Delegates of each ethnic group). If no compromise can be achieved, the Constitutional Court determines whether a vital interest has been affected (Article IV.3f). Of course, this leaves a high number of unresolved political controversies to the Constitutional Court.

This complex institutional design for legislation, budgetary issues, ratification of international treaties, and coordination with the entities is complicated by extensive *de facto* veto powers in the presidency as well as in the legislative organs. Article V.2c requires the presidency to decide unanimously, which is often not possible as the organ is composed of three representatives elected independently from any intention to act as a coalition. In the event of disagreement, majority decisions are possible, but at the risk of an appeal to the Parliament of the respective Entity by the outvoted member of the presidency. The majority-decision by the presidency can be blocked by the support of a two-thirds majority of either the National Assembly of the Republika Srpska or the Federation's House of Peoples. This becomes in effect a veto right for each member of the presidency.

The parity-pattern is also reflected in the composition of the Constitutional Court (two judges are to be appointed by the Republika Srpska and four of them by the Federation) while adding three international judges nominated by the President of the European Court of Human Rights (Article VI.1a). This unusual appointment of foreigners reflects international concerns about the fragility of the Dayton scheme and its implementation.[21] By majority vote, the Court decides on all controversies between the State and the Entities, as well as on issues referred to it by each member of the presidency, the president of the Council of Ministers, the chair or deputy chair of each chamber of Parliament, or a quarter of all members of each chamber, at either the State or entity level (Article VI 3a).[22]

Constitutional amendments require approval by the Parliamentary Assembly, including a two-thirds majority in the House of Representatives (Article X). However, no amendment may eliminate or diminish any of the rights and freedoms listed in Article II of the constitution. These rights, as contained by the European Convention for the Protection of Human Rights and Fundamental Freedoms and its Protocols, have priority over all other law (Article II.2). Specific emphasis is placed on the rights of refugees and displaced persons to return to their places of origin as well as on the related right of restoration of property lost because of the war (Article II.5). To guarantee these rights, a Human Rights Commission is set up comprising an ombudsperson (appointed by the chairperson of the OSCE) and 14 members, 6 of them from Bosnia and 8 noncitizens of Bosnia and Herzegovina (Article II.1).[23]

In sum, the main features of the Bosnian model of consociational democracy are the direct (and separate) election of the presidency, the division of the electorate in two groups corresponding to the population of the entities, the far-reaching autonomy of these Entities, as well as various articulated veto rights.[24]

Power-Sharing Arrangements and Five Levels of Government

The federal structures reflect the complexity of the ethno-territorial arrangement reached at Dayton. The main ingredient of the system established for both levels in Bosnia and Herzegovina is power sharing, or consociationalism between the different groups or peoples. This includes the diffusion of power from the center to the periphery, resulting in the weakness of the Common Institutions and their limited powers, and comprises four main elements:[25]

1. Participation of the representatives of all significant groups in the government, through joint exercise of governmental and particularly executive power.[26]
2. Proportionality as the basic standard of political representation, public service, appointments, and allocation of public funds. In theory, proportional representation should not exclude minority representation and participation. But such exclusion does occur in the House of Peoples and the presidency, which are based on the idea of representing the constituent peoples on the principle of parity. Neither the Constitution nor the General Framework Agreement for Peace defines roles for citizens not belonging to one of the three peoples or of mixed ethnic heritage. Thus, members of other ethnic groups and people refusing to declare their affiliation with one of the three peoples cannot stand as candidates for the post of delegate or member of the presidency, a clear violation of minority protection standards.

   Moreover, at the level of the Entities, the Constitution of the Republika Srpska declares that entity a "national state" (of Serbs), whereas the formula in the Constitution of the Federation—Bosniaks and Croats as "constituent peoples (along with Others) and citizens"—merged two opposing concepts, namely those of the national state and the state-nation, thus excluding Serbs and other citizens. These arrangements therefore express a fundamentally nondemocratic construct: Minorities do not have the same democratic rights as the majority, that is, the "constituent people(s)." On the symbolic level and in the specific situation of postwar Bosnia, such a constitutional construct can only be read as a disincentive for the minority return of refugees thus constituting an obstacle for the re-creation of a multiethnic state.
3. A high degree of autonomy for the groups, especially for issues that are not of common concern. In the case of Bosnia and Herzegovina, most of the responsibilities traditionally related to statehood (such as the military, police, etc.) are assigned to the so-called "Entities." "Negotiations with a view to including in the responsibilities of the institutions of Bosnia and Herzegovina other matters" (as provided for by Article IV.5b) have not begun yet, because there is a clear lack of will to do anything that could

strengthen the Common Institutions of the State. The constitution even acknowledges citizenship on both levels, without defining their meaning and relationship (article I.7)

Furthermore, despite the exclusive State power on foreign policy, Article III.2a allows for "special parallel relationships" between the Entities and neighboring states—that is, Croatia and Serbia and Montenegro. This invitation for a *de facto Anschluss* has already been used by both Entities to conclude treaties with Croatia and Yugoslavia, respectively. It is a general trend in the era of globalization that subnational entities increasingly behave as actors on the international stage as well as engage in cross-border activities. However, as in all federal (and regional) systems, the question is how to draw a clear line between constitutionally valid special parallel relationships and those that unconstitutionally affect the sovereignty of the State. In the specific situation of Bosnia and Herzegovina, this question is of particular importance, because the political influence of its neighbors can hardly be overestimated. This became evident in a positive way, after the nationalists lost political power in 2000 in Croatia and in Serbia, leading to an immediate increase of moderate and multiethnic parties in elections in Bosnia and Herzegovina.

4. The minority veto as the ultimate weapon for the protection of vital interests. These veto rights complement the other main characteristics of consociational arrangements, serving as emergency mechanisms in case the normal consultation procedures fail. Though probably necessary for ending a war, they do not contribute to building up peace and reconstructing a country. They have been (ab)used by those groups, especially Croat and Serb nationalists, who had no interest in strengthening the State, to block each step toward integration.[27] Often the primary loyalty of political representatives in State-level institutions lies with the Entities, where the real power is exercised, with the national groups they represent, and—most importantly—with the nationalist political party they represent.[28] Thus, numerous efforts to block State action between 1995 and 2000 further weakened an already structurally weak central government, contributing to the continuous disintegration of the State, while both entities operated nearly independently from each other.

Finally, one has to take the institutional complexity into consideration. Thirteen governments (cantons, Entities, State) can rightly be defined as "institutional overkill" in the face of the scarce financial resources and of the limited capacities and staff at each level. Human rights protection may serve as an instructive example. On the one hand, there is certainly a lack of an appropriately differentiated administrative and judicial system for the State of Bosnia and Herzegovina, for instance a regular State Court besides the Constitutional Court.[29] On the other hand, however, numerous bodies deal with the protection of human rights in general or in specific cases, such as property rights, on the State level, and the same is true at the level of the Entities. There are 10 different organs expressly charged in the three Constitutions for dealing with human rights violations: in Bosnia and Herzegovina the Constitutional Court, the Ombudsperson, the Chamber of Human Rights, and the commission established by Annex VII; in the Federation the Constitutional Court, the Supreme Court, the Human Rights Court, the Federation Ombudsmen, and the Federation Implementation Council; and in the Republika Srpska the Constitutional Court and the Supreme Court.

But what does this mean for the effective protection of the individual in concrete terms? It not only creates confusion as to which route to pursue but also drags out getting a final and binding decision (not to mention the difficulties of enforcing such decisions in an often hostile environment). And, which institution has the final say, the Human Rights Chamber or the Constitutional Court of Bosnia and Herzegovina? This is by no means clear from the text of the Constitution, and had to be decided by the Constitutional Court in connection with an appeal against a decision of the Chamber brought before the Court.[30]

Hence, the overcomplex legal framework of the Dayton Agreement left (and continues to leave) important constitutional questions unanswered. As a result of the tension between the two fundamental but conflicting principles underlying the Dayton Peace Agreement—(partial) recognition of the situation created through the war in order to end it versus re-establishing multiethnic Bosnia—the legal framework often did not provide the necessary rules for the proper functioning of the political process. Moreover, some of the institutional arrangements have, in practice, even undermined the declared goal of maintaining Bosnia and Herzegovina as a multiethnic state, by practically entrenching and strengthening division along ethnic lines. This has necessitated a number of corrections. Due to the prevailing negative elite-consensus (following the *divide et impera* principle), "local ownership" in this process could hardly be expected. This has made the role of two institutions, the High Representative and the Constitutional Court, fundamental. Their emphasis on the rule of law as the superior principle vis-à-vis the democratic principle is an instructive example of how complex consociational arrangements can be implemented and enforced despite obstruction by nationalist forces that have come to power or been confirmed through elections.[31]

IMPLEMENTATION BY THE INTERNATIONAL COMMUNITY VERSUS "LOCAL OWNERSHIP"

The massive engagement of the International Community is a distinctive feature of the situation in Bosnia and Herzegovina. Most important is the institution of the High Representative of the International Community who is responsible for the implementation of the civil aspects of the Dayton Peace Agreement (annex 10). He is authorized to moderate the peace process and support the conflicting parties in power-sharing; in addition, he has the last say on the interpretation of the Agreement's text. The unwillingness of some of the parties to comply with the Dayton Agreement, as can be seen from the obstructionist politics in the common institutions or on the level of the Entities, has had to be overcome by direct intervention from the side of the High Representative, thus transforming the institution from a mere facilitator to an integral part of the current system of government.[32] At the Conference of the supervisory Peace Implementation Council in Bonn in December 1997, the High Representative was given executive and legislative powers. In particular he can remove officials violating the Dayton Peace Agreement from office and impose laws, thus substituting for the legislative bodies that are unable or unwilling to meet their responsibilities.[33] Thus, an impressive number of laws and other decisions has been imposed by decree by the High Representative, including necessary legislation such as property laws, passport regulations, state symbols and license plates, and the like, as well as the recent constitutional amendments in the Entities. Over 60 public officials have also been removed from office (including a president of the Republika Srpska and a Croat member of the Bosnian [i.e., State] presidency).[34]

Despite its tangible success in passing necessary legislation and dismissing obstructive officials, this protectorate has not significantly reduced the role of nationalist parties.[35] It has rather further weakened the institutional structures based on power sharing: the probability of the imposition of decisions relieves the institutional representatives from negotiation and compromise.[36] However, given the political situation and the continued strength of nationalist political parties, less international intervention would probably leave legitimate national and minority rights unprotected in the face of unacceptable nationalist demands.

One way to avoid bypassing domestic institutions is to include international participation, without representing the international community as such. The Governor of the Central Bank (appointed by the International Monetary Funds) and the three international judges of the Constitutional Court (appointed by the High Representative) do not belong to one of the constituent peoples and can thus act as neutral mediators within the institutions, thus becoming Bosnian actors facilitating the interethnic dialogue and power sharing.[37]

"CONSTITUENT PEOPLES" AND "MINORITIES": IMPROVING POWER SHARING

The federal Constitutional Court has issued a number of landmark decisions improving power sharing. At the federal level, the Court declared a consociational arrangement in the Law on the Council of Ministers (1996) to be unconstitutional. The Court ruled that a provision stating that the chair of the Council of Ministers consists of two cochairs and a vice chair and providing for a rotation between these positions, conflicted with Article IV of the constitution, according to which the chair has to be a single individual. The decision left the country without a government for some time.[38]

Judgment U 5/98-III of the Constitutional Court

Probably the most important milestone so far for improving power-sharing at the Entity level, with obvious consequences for the multiethnic character of the whole country, was the Constitutional Court's decision of July 2000.[39] The essential question the Court had to resolve was whether the list of Bosnia's constituent peoples in the preamble of the State constitution—"Bosniaks, Croats and Serbs, as constituent peoples (along with Others), and citizens of Bosnia and Herzegovina"—gave these three peoples equal status throughout Bosnia and Herzegovina, or whether they were equal only at the State level. In effect, the Court had to decide on nearly all basic questions of a multinational democracy, such as the normative meaning of the constitution, the concepts of "constituent people" and of "minority group," the right to self-determination, the federal structure of the State, and—last but not least—the political representation of the groups.

With regard to the last issue, the Court first drew a clear distinction between constituent peoples and minorities, thus indicating the constitutional mandate to treat differently what ought to be different. For the Court "the adopters of the Dayton Constitution would not have designated Bosniaks, Croats, and Serbs as constituent peoples, in marked contrast to the constitutional category of a national minority, if they wanted to leave them in such a minority position in the respective Entities as they had, in fact, obviously been placed in at the time of the conclusion of the Dayton Agreement" (at 63). The Entities thus have a constitutional obligation not to discriminate against those constituent peoples of the state who are as a matter of fact a numerical minority within their territory (i.e., Serbs in the Federation, Bosniaks and Croats in the Republika Srpska). The principle of nondiscrimination thus applies not only to individuals,[40] but also to groups as such, prohibiting special adverse treatment. For the Court, a principle of "collective equality" of the constituent peoples exists that "prohibits any special privilege for one or two of these peoples, any domination in governmental structures or any ethnic homogenization through segregation based on territorial separation" (at 59 and 60).[41]

The judgment focused on the violation of human rights, as a common practice in the Entities, and in particular on the right of refugees and displaced persons to "voluntary return and harmonious reintegration, without preference for any particular group" as provided for in Annex 7 of the General Framework Agreement for Peace (Article II.1, the so-called minority returns). The Court cited the domination of institutions in the Entities (especially courts and police)[42] by privileged peoples to illustrate the discriminatory effect of the contested provisions in the Entities' constitutions. It pointed to population figures in order to demonstrate that these constitutions established discriminatory frameworks aimed at discouraging return.[43] As a result, the provisions of the Entities' constitutions that declare only one or two peoples as constituent in the respective entity and ensure a more favorable treatment of those peoples in the governmental structure of the Entities violate the constitutional principle of collective equality as well as Article 5 of the U.N. Covenant of 1966 against racial discrimination (right to equal access to governmental posts) and are thus unconstitutional.

The Court then indicated how the decision would be implemented. In addition to the necessary amendments, further measures would be required to guarantee the protection of equal rights and to promote minority returns. Fair representation would need to be assured in the constitutional institutions and in particular in the judiciary and the police. Special attention would have to be paid at the subentity level to avoid ethnic homogenization in cantons or municipalities.

The ruling offered "a probably unrepeatable chance to push the Dayton Peace Agreement to their limits and to permit Bosnia and Herzegovina to become a functional multinational state" by reforming the existing Entities within the Dayton architecture.[44] The Court's decision was condemned by most Serb parties, but welcomed by the Bosniak and Croat parties as well as by the international community. The ruling would not have been possible if a minority veto existed within the Court. The decision was taken with a narrow majority: The three international and the two Bosniak judges voted for it, four judges (Croat and Serb) against. Furthermore, addressing not only the constitutionality of the institutionalization of ethnic dominance but also its impact on the quality of democracy, the ruling has raised fundamental questions at the State level. Apart from the overinstitutionalization of ethnic identities, a whole segment of the population, the "Others" (i.e., minorities, persons from ethnically mixed marriages, or persons simply unwilling to affiliate with one of the three peoples), remains generally excluded from the power-sharing structures.[45]

Implementation through Constitutional Amendments by Decree

In the aftermath of the Constitutional Court's decision, constitutional commissions for each entity were created in January 2001 and charged with drafting amendments complying with the Court's ruling. But there was virtually no progress, and a series of deadlines set by the High Representative were missed by both Entities—the commission in the Republika Srpska could not agree on an amendment, and in the Federation a draft of the commission had been blocked by the major parties.[46] The High Representative—under time pressure because by April 19 the elections were to be called for October 2002, and thus the amendments should have been passed by that date—called all parties for negotiations. On March 27 an agreement, outlining the principles of the Court decision that the parties would comply with, was reached, although it was not signed by all parties. In the end, on April 19, the High Representative, Wolfgang Petritsch in his last days in office, imposed three decisions in order to bring the two Constitutions fully in line with the Court ruling.[47]

In essence, the agreement (as well as the imposed constitutional amendments) recognized Bosniaks, Croats, and Serbs as constituent peoples in both entities. An upper house was created in the Republika Srpska, as well as two vice presidential posts in each Entity, for the representation of all three constituent peoples (requiring the holders of the three offices to come from different constituent peoples). The agreement defined "vital interest" (examples include education, religion, language, culture, promotion of tradition, and equal representation in government institutions) and the procedures to protect such interests. This detailed elaboration of the vital-interest clauses was intended to limit their abuse for the sole purpose of obstruction. Finally, the "constitutional principle" of proportional representation for all ethnic groups in the "public institutions"—ministries at the Entity, cantonal, and municipal levels as well as the courts within both Entities—has been introduced. The mentioning of "time lines" to be established for the development of the principle in line with the regional ethnic structure might be a useful indication for following a gradual approach in the implementation through the legislation in the Entities.

According to the High Representative, the main principle of agreement and amendments can be described as "symmetry in substance": Most important is the identical level of protection throughout the country, which is not necessarily to be achieved by identical mechanisms (a reasonable approach in the face of a political elite in both Entities in profound disagreement over the issue of mechanisms).[48]

FUTURE PERSPECTIVES

Bosnia can only be understood by taking into account the interrelations and mutual influence of three levels: the local level within Bosnia, the regional level (i.e., the neighboring states), and the international community. Though the international community can rightly be referred to as the "fourth constituent part" of Bosnia and Herzegovina,[49] due to its direct involvement in the implementation process, it has its own distinct set of actors and interest(s), and it influences and is also itself influenced by the other two levels.

The postwar period in Bosnia has been characterized by extensive reconstruction financed and directed by the international community. Although Bosnia and Herzegovina has recorded high levels of growth since the end of the war, its GDP is still well below prewar levels and is the second lowest in the region. Furthermore, assistance will decrease in the coming years, and this will reduce growth levels. Reforms have not proceeded at the desired pace, in part due to the reluctance of the local political elites to take ownership. Currently, power is exercised primarily by the High Representative or by the Entities, both of which have no, or only inadequate, power-sharing mechanisms.[50] In addition, federal structures and the related autonomy of the entities may have certainly been a precondition for stabilization, but they also put too much stress on territorial organization (in a context of *de facto* segregation). However, as in any federal system, autonomy of the entities is only one element; the other is the integration of the parts into the whole. Thus, the main challenges for the country's future remain the strengthening of the State of Bosnia and Herzegovina, creating the conditions for a sustainable return, reinforcing the administration, achieving self-sustained economic development, and establishing an effective and accountable legal system.[51]

Until these conditions have been created, implementation cannot be left to the parties alone. Therefore, direct involvement of external actors will be required, preferably less as the motor of the process and more—as initially intended—in the role of a guarantor. However, the Bosnian experience shows that functioning institutions and the rule of law are more important than individual officeholders: The insistence on frequent elections as a means for changing the political elites did not and cannot solve the problems of divided societies. On the contrary, they often contribute to keep in power nationalist elites that do not have any interest in progress because their source of power is the status quo. Nevertheless, there is a tension between active intervention of the international community (sometimes criticized as "protectorate")[52] and the promotion of power sharing and cooperation among local actors. This is complicated by the fact that there often is no international community in a unitary sense with uniform positions.

In the final analysis, the long-term stability of the institutions of a democratic Bosnia and Herzegovina requires a political concept for the whole region within the framework of European integration. The regional context seems to offer new opportunities, especially after the political and constitutional changes in the important neighboring countries of Croatia and Serbia/Yugoslavia. Furthermore, recently, the perspective of EU integration has begun to emerge "as the *Archimedian point* of the entire process of stabilization and development of the region," providing a real prospect for a breakthrough that would lead the region toward stability, cooperation, and prosperity.[53] The way, however, will differ from the one that has led Central and Eastern European countries to Eastern enlargement, as a higher degree of regional cooperation will be required already before, due to considerations of stabilization and scale. Consequently, international cooperation was the underlying idea of the Stability Pact, the first principal strategic instrument for reconstruction and stability in the Region.[54] The Stabilization and Association Process between the European Union and five countries (Albania, Bosnia and Herzegovina, Croatia, Serbia and Montenegro, and the Former Yugoslav Republic of Macedonia) offers the prospect of EU integration, based on a progressive approach adapted to the individual situation of each country. However, by emphasizing bilateral conditionality (i.e., contractual relationship with the EU in return for compliance with the relevant conditions), it may—at least—potentially cause new fragmentation or division: "some countries can progress faster than others."[55] These contradictions and the importance of a viable perspective for the whole region call for comprehensive rearrangement of the current structures and for a single strategic framework: an "Agenda for Southeastern Enlargement."[56]

Although they created the conditions for stabilization of postwar Bosnia, the Dayton Peace Agreement and the Constitution with their complex institutional structures are certainly no blueprints for a functional and equitable state. Their fundamental contradiction is the attempt to accommodate the highest level of individual rights and the demands of nationalists to "preserve collective rights in 'cleansed' enclaves. The constituent peoples decision is important, because it attempts to square this particular circle and to use Dayton to improve Dayton."[57] Despite its limits and problems, a system of consociational democracy associated with federal and confederal structures for the time being seems to be the "most viable institutional option" for Bosnia and Herzegovina "short of formal partition, redrawing of boundaries and exchange of populations."[58]

"Therefore, the elements of a democratic state and society and the underlying assumptions—pluralism, fair procedures, peaceful relations following from the text of the Constitution—must serve as a guideline to further elaborate the question of how Bosnia and Herzegovina is construed as a democratic multi-national state."[59] This is a useful reminder for the continuous task of balancing individual rights, collective rights of the constituent peoples, and the right to minority return. Though this responsibility is currently mostly borne by the international community, the way into European integration ultimately requires the population of Bosnia and Herzegovina to embrace and respect this guideline.

NOTES

1. Whereas the other (former) Yugoslavian republics could and can be regarded without exception as nation-states—that is, with a majority population conceived in ethnic terms as the nation—different social, demographic, and structural factors conditioning the protection of minorities prevailed and prevail in Bosnia and Herzegovina. Joseph Marko, "Bosnia and Herzegovina—multi-ethnic or multinational?" in Zelim Skurbaty (ed.), *Beyond the One-Dimensional State* (Den Haag, Kluwer Law International, in print). For a short historic overview, see Marie-Joelle Zahar, Bosnia and Herzegovina, in Ann L. Griffiths (ed.), *Handbook on Federal Countries* (Montreal: Forum of Federations, McGill-Queen's University Press, 2002), 75–89.

2. This is to be understood in a purely temporal sense and does not imply any cause-and-effect relationship. Joseph Marko, "Bosnia," p. 1. Cf. Marie-Janine Calic, *Der Krieg in Bosnien-Hercegovina. Ursachen—Konfliktstrukturen—internationale* (Frankfurt/Main: Lösungsversuche, 1995).

3. It had been initiated in Dayton on 21 November 1995; see www.ohr.int.

4. For the evolution of these concepts in history, see Joseph Marko, "Bosnia," p. 2; W. Libal, Bosnier-Bosniaken-Muslime: Versuche einer Entwirrung, in *Europäische Rundschau* (1998): 79, and ICG, Implementing Equality: The 'Constituent Peoples' Decision in Bosnia & Herzegovina, *ICG Balkans Report N. 128* (Sarajevo/Brussels, 16 April 2002), p. 2, http://www.crisisweb.org.

5. For the precise implementation of that formula as basis for the Dayton Peace Agreement, see Richard Holbrooke, *To End a War* (New York: Random House 1999), 294–92. It is evident that *de facto* recognition and incorporation of both war-created Entities were the price for the continuity of Bosnia and Herzegovina.

6. What is probably the most comprehensive analysis of the whole nexus of problems was supplied by Edin Sarcevic, *Ustav i politika. Kritika etniãkih ustava i postrepubliãkog ustavotvorstva u Bosni i Herzegovini* (Constitution and Politics.

Criticism of the ethnic constitutions and the postrepublican constituent in Bosnia and Herzegovina) (Sarajevo, 1997).

7. These groups are dispersed over the whole territory and small in numbers: In the last census (1991), the members of all other ethnic groups (besides Muslims/Bosniaks, Croats, Serbs, and "Yugoslavs") accounted for only 0.74 percent.

8. See the chapters by Giovanni Biaggini (Switzerland) and Wouter Pas (Belgium) in this volume.

9. Roberto Toniatti, "Minorities and Protected Minorities: Constitutional Models Compared," in Tiziano Bonazzi and Michael Dunne (eds.), *Citizenship and Rights in Multicultural Societies* (Keele, U.K.: Keele University Press 1995), 206–10.

10. See especially Article VIII ("The Federation shall provide two-thirds, and the Republika Srpska one-third, of the revenues required by the budget [of the State]) and Article III.2.b ("provide necessary assistance to the government of Bosnia and Herzegovina"). According to Article IV.4, the Parliamentary Assembly (of the State) shall "decide on sources [*sic*] and amounts of revenues of the institutions of Bosnia and Herzegovina."

11. Florian Bieber, "Governing Post-War Bosnia and Herzegovina," in Kingal Gál (ed.), *Minority Governance in Europe* (Budapest: LGI Books, 2002), 328f. Areas in Herzegovina, controlled by the Croat nationalist party HDZ were never effectively integrated into the structures of the FBH: Until the end of HDZ-rule in Croatia in January 2000, which led to the cessation of funding from Croatia, Herzegovina could virtually be considered a part of Croatia. See also Florian Bieber, "Croat Self-Government in Bosnia—A Challenge for Dayton?" *ECMI Brief*, No. 5, May 2001 (http://www.ecmi.de/doc/download/brief_5.pdf).

12. Brčko Arbitration Tribunal for Dispute over Inter-Entity Boundary in Brčko Area, Final Award (5 March 1999), para. 1 & 11, granting Brčko a similar status to the one of the District of Columbia within the United States of America.

13. F. Bieber, *Governing*, 329. The arbitration decision occurred at the same time as the removal from office of the Republika Srpska president, Nikola Poplašen, and shortly before NATO's air strikes in Kosovo and Yugoslavia. It increased the considerable opposition of the political elite in the Republika Srpska.

14. These factors made effective governance of and in the Republika Srpska difficult. For more details, see F. Bieber, *Governing*, 329.

15. See the provisional and the permanent electoral laws (Article 20 para. 8).

16. Decentralization seems to be the only way to empower administrations not dominated by Serbs—for example, in areas of minority-return.

17. The Constitution provides for a Standing Committee on Military Matters, selected by and including the three prsidency members, which is to "coordinate the activities of the armed forces" in Bosnia and Herzegovina. However, neither the precise nature of the presidential authority over the military nor the relationship between individual members of the presidency and distinct armed forces is specified. See, however, the dissenting opinion of judge Joseph Marko in Partial Decision IV of case 5/98, in *Sluzbeni glasnik Bosne i Hercegovine* (Official Gazette of Bosnia and Herzegovina) Nr. 36/2000, pp. 959–61.

18. This is extended by Article V.3b to the ambassadors in the diplomatic representations of Bosnia and Herzegovina.

19. Article 5 and Article 9 of the new Law on the Council of Ministers (HR Decision, 3rd December 2002). In addition, the law introduced changes to the decision-making process in the ministries: Only decisions that fall into the

competencies of the Council of Ministers still necessitate consensus, whereas those that subsequently subject to a vote in parliament are now taken by majority (Article 18). Under the new law, the three leading positions in the single ministries (minister and two deputy ministers) do no longer rotate between the three ethnic groups, but are fixed, although all three groups still must be represented (Article 7). The same principle applies to the two Deputy Chairs of the Council of Ministers (Article 6). See East European Constitutional Review, Fall 2002/Winter 2003, p. 9, and http://www.ohr.int/decisions/archive.asp.

20. This means that for a veto on legislation, an ethnic group of Delegates constituting only 20 percent of the House of Peoples is sufficient.

21. M. J. Zahar, *Bosnia and Herzegovina*, 79.

22. Decisions of the Court are to be final and binding, but the Constitution did not specify how decisions are to be taken or whether they are subject to an ethnic or other veto. The Court, however, when determining its rules of procedure by majority vote, decided that decisions are taken by a simple majority without any further requirement: see Constitutional Court, Rules of Procedure, Article 35 (http://www.ustavnisud.ba/en/rp/default.asp).

23. Four of the Bosnian citizens have to be from the Federation, two of them from Republika Srpska; the foreigners are appointed by the Committee of Ministers of the Council of Europe after consultations with the parties.

24. Ulrich Schneckener, *Auswege aus dem Bürgerkrieg* (Frankfurt a.M.: Suhrkamp 2002), 295.

25. According to Arend Lijphart, *Democracy in Plural Societies* (New Haven: Yale University Press, 1977). Arend Lijphart, "The Power Sharing Approach," in Joseph V. Montville (ed.), *Conflict and Peacemaking in Multiethnic Societies* (New York: Lexington Books, 1991), 492–94. See also Florian Bieber, "Recent Trends in Complex Power-Sharing in Bosnia and Herzegovina," in Eurac/ECMI (eds.), *European Yearbook of Minority Issues*, vol. 1, 2001/2 (The Hague: Kluwer Law International, 2003), 269–82.

26. For a comparative analysis, see Florian Bieber, "Institutionalizing Ethnicity in Former Yugoslavia: Domestic vs. Internationally Driven Processes of Institutional (Re-)Design," *The Global Review of Ethnopolitics* 2 (January 2003): 3–16.

27. M. J. Calic, *Der Krieg*, 259.

28. F. Bieber, *Governing*, 328.

29. Such a State Court has been established in the meantime, by decree of the Office of the High Representative (official gazette of Bosnia and Herzegovina, Nr. 29/2000). It is, however, not a Supreme Court, because his competencies do not comprise appeals against decisions of the Entities' courts, but refer only to civil and criminal proceedings arising from federal laws.

30. The Constitutional Court declared appeals against decisions of the Human Rights Chamber inadmissible in cases U 7/98 through U 11/98 in Official gazette of Bosnia and Herzegovina, Nr. 9/1999.

31. Richard Holbrooke, the Clinton administration's special envoy to the Balkans before the 1998 elections in Bosnia and Herzegovina: "Suppose the election was declared free and fair [and those elected] were racists, fascists and separatists who are publicly opposed to [peace and reintegration]? That is the dilemma." *The Economist*, April 12, 2003, p. 28.

32. F. Bieber, *Governing*, 330; and F. Bieber, *Recent Trends*, 276 ff. See also various discussion papers published by ESI—European Stability Initiative (e.g., Reshaping International Priorities in Bosnia and Herzegovina. Part Two. International Power in Bosnia, 30 March 2000, and In search of politics: the evolving

international role in Bosnia and Herzegovina, 1 November 2001) available at http://esiweb.org.

33. Bonn Peace Implementation Conference, 10th December 1997 (http://www.ohr.int/docu/d971210a.htm). The Peace Implementation Council acts as a supervisory institution taking the guideline decisions for the work of the OHR.

34. Decisions in numbers: 1997: 1; 1998: 31; 1999: 92; 2000: 86; 2001: 54; and 2002: 153. See full list of all decisions at http://www.ohr.int/decisions.htm.

35. Despite an intermezzo of a coalition of moderate and interethnic parties, the Alliance for Change, governing at the State level between February 2001 and October 2002. However, the latest State elections, on 5 October 2002, again strengthened above all nationalist parties. See election results at the OSCE Web site: http://www.oscebih.org.

36. Marcus Cox, "State-Building and Post-War Reconstruction: Lessons from Bosnia," *The Rehabilitation of War-Torn Societies* (Geneva: CASIN, January 2001), 12–15. See also the recent—and very critical—analysis of continuous and increasing "international rule" by Gerald Knaus and Felix Martin, "Travails of the European Raj, Lessons from Bosnia and Herzegovina," *Journal of Democracy* 14, No. 3 (July 2003): 60–74 (http://www.journalofdemocracy.org/KnausandMartin.pdf); and for the following debate, provoked by the authors' main thesis that "you can't create a stable democracy by these authoritarian methods," see http://www.esiweb.org/europeanraj/reactions.php.

37. F. Bieber, *Governing*, 331. In this context, also other bodies with international participation have to be mentioned: the OSCE-Election-Commission, the UNCHR-led Refugees Commission, and the Human Rights Chambers (with 8 out of 14 members appointed by the Council of Europe).

38. Constitutional Court Bosnia and Herzegovina, Judgment, Case No. U 1/99, in *Službeni glasnik* (official gazette) no. 16/1999, 28 September 1999 (http://www.ustavnisud.ba/en/decisions/case.asp?u1=1&u2=99) and M. J. Zahar, *Bosnia and Herzegovina*, 82. After the judgment, Parliament adopted a law that provided for the rotation of the chair between the three constituent peoples every eight months; on 3 December 2002, the High Representative enacted a Law on the Council of Ministers by decision.

39. Constitutional Court Bosnia and Herzegovina, Judgment, Case No. U 5/98-III (1 July 2000), in *Službeni glasnik* (official gazette) no. 23/2000, 14 September 2000 (http://www.ustavnisud.ba/en/decisions/case.asp?u1=5&u2=98). The case had been brought before the Court in 1998 by Alija Izetbegovic, the then Bosniak chair of the Presidency, arguing that 14 provisions of the Republika Srpska constitution and 5 provisions of the FBH constitution violated the Bosnia and Herzegovina constitution. See further Joseph Marko, "The Ethno-National Effects of Territorial Delimitation in Bosnia and Herzegovina," in Institut suisse de droit comparé, Commission européenne pour la démocratie par le droit du Conseil de l'Europe (eds.), *Autonomies locales, intégrité territoriale et protection des minorités* (Zürich: Schulthess, 1996), 121; Francesco Palermo, "Bosnia-Erzegovina: la Corte costituzionale fissa i confini della (nuova) società multietnica," *Diritto Pubblico Comparato ed Europeo* IV (2000): 1479–89; Carsten Stahn, Die verfassungsrechtliche Pflicht zur Gleichstellung der drei ethnischen Volksgruppen in den bosnischen Teilrepubliken—Neue Hoffnung für das Friedensmodell von Dayton? Zugleich eine Anmerkung zur dritten Teilentscheidung des bosnischen Verfassungsgerichts vom 1. Juli 2000 im Izetbegovic-Fall, *ZaöRV—Zeitschrift für ausländischen öffentliches Recht und Völkerrecht* 60/3–4 (2000), 661–701.

40. As established in Article II.3 and 4 of the Bosnia and Herzegovina constitution (annex IV to the Dayton Peace Agreement).

41. The Court ruled that "despite the territorial delimitation of Bosnia and Herzegovina by the establishment of the two Entities, this territorial delimitation cannot serve as a constitutional legitimation for ethnic domination, national homogenisation or a right to uphold the effects of ethnic cleansing" (at 61).

42. For instance, the government of the Republika Srpska was composed only by Serbs (21 members out of 21), and the same was true for police forces (93.7 percent) and the judges (97.6 percent). Analogous figures were in place in the Federation.

43. See at 92 (Republika Srpska) and at 137 (Federation). Since the Court's ruling, the rates of refugee return have improved markedly: More refugees went back to their prewar homes in the Republika Srpska in 2001 than in the five years before, even though these numbers are doubled by those returning to the FBH, see ICG, *Balkans Report No. 128*, p. 4 (http://www.crisisweb.org).

44. ICG, *Balkans Report No. 128*, p. 1 (http://www.crisisweb.org).

45. F. Bieber, *Governing*, 332.

46. For information on the discussion and options for implementation of the U 5/98 judgment, see the reports by Valery Perry, Constitutional Reform and the 'Spirit' of Bosnia and Herzegovina, ECMI Brief 7, February 2002 (http://www.ecmi.de/doc/download/brief_7.pdf), and ESI, Imposing constitutional reform? The case for ownership, 20 March 2002 (http://esiweb.org).

47. The first decision imposed all the amendments of the Constitution of the Federation; the second decision corrected perceived shortcomings of that of the Republika Srpska; the third decision amended the election law according to the previous constitutional amendments.

48. Go to www.ohr.int for further information as well as for the content of the Sarajevo agreement (27/03/2002); for a detailed and critical analysis, see ICG, *Balkans Report No. 128*, esp. pp. 12–14 (http://www.crisisweb.org).

49. Besides host-state, kin-state, and minority; Sumantra Bose, *Bosnia after Dayton: Nationalist Partition and International Intervention* (London: Hurst and Company, 2002), 267.

50. F. Bieber, *Governing*, 331.

51. European Commission, Bosnia and Herzegovina, Country Strategy Paper 2002–2006. For the state of the judiciary, see ICG, "Courting Disaster: The Misrule of Law in Bosnia & Herzegovina," *Balkans Report No. 127*, 25 March 2002 (http://www.crisisweb.org).

52. See in particular G. Knaus and F. Martin, *Travails of the European Raj*, 60–74, who, above all, criticize the international regime in Bosnia for the absence of checks and balances on the High Representative's powers and the lack of accountability whether locally or internationally.

53. Wim van Meurs and Alessandros Yannis, *The European Union and the Balkans. From Stabilisation Process to Southeastern Enlargement* (CAP—Center for Applied Policy Research, September 2002), 8–12. (http://www.cap.uni-muenchen.de/publikationen/cap/analyse_soe.htm)

54. The Stability Pact for South Eastern Europe, established in Cologne, 10 June 1999, is a political declaration of commitment and a framework agreement on international cooperation to develop a shared strategy among all its partners for stability and growth in South Eastern Europe. The Stability Pact is not a new international organization nor does it have any independent financial resources or implementing structures; see http://www.stabilitypact.org.

55. For further information, see EU Commission, DG External Relations, From Regional Approach to the Stabilisation & Association Process, *The EU's Relations with South Eastern Europe* (http://europa.eu.int/comm/external_relations/see/actions/sap.htm).

56. W. van Meurs and A. Yannis, *The European Union and the Balkans,* 18–20.

57. ICG, *Balkans Report No. 128*, p. 25 (http://www.crisisweb.org).

58. S. Bose, *Bosnia after Dayton*, 247.

59. Constitutional Court Bosnia and Herzegovina, Judgment U 5/98-III (para. 54).

11

Federalism and Nonterritorial Minorities in India

Arshi Khan

Mechanisms such as federalism and subnational constitutions were developed to promote participatory governance and power sharing in modern liberal democracies, in which individualism had replaced or was dominant over history-bound communities or groups. The success of these mechanisms in the West has led some commentators to view them as effectual for protecting the rights of minorities and of other vulnerable groups in countries throughout the world.[1] This is not to say that these mechanisms have completely remedied the problem of oppression of cultural and ethnic minorities, which persists as a serious concern even in developed federal societies such as the United States. Nevertheless, the difficulties in securing multicultural coexistence, integration, and peace seem even greater in other parts of the world, where ethnic tensions and ethnicization of the political establishment are common. Indeed, conflicts among different ethnic, language, religious, and cultural groups remain a primary cause of the failure of social modernization in the Third World, as well as of war in the Middle East, the Balkans, and in various nations where different ethnic groups coexist.[2] A crucial question, therefore, is whether the mechanisms of federalism and subnational constitutions can be equally effective in protecting minority rights and defusing ethnic conflict in nonliberal societies. The experience of India, a federal system with diverse minorities, sheds some light on this issue.

THE RELEVANCE OF FEDERALISM

On its face, federalism seems appropriate for both traditional and modern societies, and federal arrangements exist in both. However, the federal idea developed as part of liberal political discourse, and it is therefore not surprising that federal principles and arrangements particularly suit the modern temper. As basically covenantal arrangements, they fit a civilization governed by contractual relationships.[3] The whole edifice of federalism is based on the liberal premise of modern society, in which individuality and civic community form the basis of compromise and relationship among persons and groups for achieving political integration. Federalism does not involve traditional kinds of group-rights-based pluralism but instead encourages a post-traditional pluralism. Federal principles grow out of the idea that free people can voluntarily enter into lasting yet limited political associations to achieve common ends and to protect certain rights without sacrificing their respective integrities. In sum, the federal idea rests on the belief that political and social institutions and relationships are best established through covenants, compacts, or other contractual arrangements rather than, or in addition to, simply growing organically.[4]

Federalism achieves its purposes by dividing power territorially. Groups that are geographically concentrated and share ethnic, linguistic, and/or religious ties are recognized through the creation of subnational constituent units that share powers with the federal government under the principles of self-rule and shared rule. This has occurred in Europe, in the United States, in Canada, and in other countries. But scholars have thus far not broadened the concept of federalism to address the concerns of dispersed minorities or to encompass illiberal societies.

This does not mean that federal principles are meaningless for nonmodern societies or for situations in which a consensus is lacking for state-building and constitution-building. Even if not fully applicable, federal principles remain suggestive in illustrating patterns of relationships for power sharing and promoting justice. In addition, federalism recognizes the existence of essentially permanent religious, ethnic, cultural, or social groups around which political life must be organized. Whether or not the polity is formally structured around those groups, they serve as its pillars.[5] So the federal principles of governance also provide an opportunity to consider both citizenship rights and differential rights. Finally, as Daniel Elazar, a leading student of federalism, has observed, the territorial division of power under federalism can be used to protect minorities and minority communities by allowing them greater autonomy within their own political jurisdictions. This makes clear that federal territoriality is not designed to deprive minorities within the territorial units of their rights.

INDIAN CONSTITUTIONALISM AND THE PROBLEM OF DIVERSITY

With a population of more than 1 billion exhibiting differences based on religion, sect, language, dialect, region, culture, caste, race, and class, it is fair to say that India's diversities are continental in their manifestation. Perhaps the most important distinction in India is religion, because religious consciousness is strong among the various communities in India, and modernization projects have failed to impact this community/communal consciousness.

India has eight major religious communities—Hindus (82 percent), Muslims (more than 12 percent), Christians (2 percent), Sikhs (2 percent), and Buddhists, Jains, Zoroastrians, and Jews, each with less than 1 percent of the population. The Muslim community, India's largest minority community, is found in all the States and Union Territories, with concentrations varying from more than 94 percent in Lakshadweep Island and 62 percent in Jammu and Kashmir to less than 1 percent in Mizoram. Christians are likewise dispersed throughout the country varying from over 80 percent in Nagaland and Mizoram and 30 percent in Goa and Manipur to less than 1 percent in Himachal Pradesh. The territorial dispersion of these religious groups means that they are minorities in most constituent units within India. This raises the question of how adequately a federal polity based on territorial divisions can protect their rights and avoid majoritarian oppression.

The Structure of Indian Federalism

After independence, India opted for a federal polity, and the Indian federation includes 28 States and 7 Union Territories. The Indian Constitution contains special provisions dealing with several of these constituent units. For example, Article 370 of the Indian Constitution authorizes the state of Kashmir to have its own constitution, making it the only state with that authority. Articles 371 and 371A—371I contain special provisions with respect to the states of Maharashtra, Gujarat,

Nagaland, Assam, Manipur, Andhra Pradesh, Sikkim, Mizoram, Arunachal Pradesh, and Goa.

The federal arrangements that divide powers and responsibilities between the Union and the state governments are based on the principle of territoriality. Nevertheless, the Indian federation is not the result of an agreement among the states that comprise it, nor are those states free to secede from it. It appears that the Indian Constitution places an excessive emphasis on unity and on territorial integrity. One Indian scholar has described the constitutional system as basically federal with striking unitary features.[6] A leading foreign scholar has suggested that the Constitution creates a highly centralized federalism.[7] Indians do not enjoy dual citizenship, state and national. There is a single integrated public service, a single judiciary, and a single governmental apparatus for elections and for fiscal matters. The Parliament of the Union is not obliged to seek the consent of affected states in order to alter their boundaries, and the states are in most cases not consulted by the Union on constitutional amendments or in the framing of foreign policy. The states are not equally represented in the Upper House of Parliament, and that house has not been assertive in protecting the interests of the states. The Union appoints the State Governor, who works as the Union's representative.

The distribution of powers in India favors the Union. It retains residual powers, and it is paramount in dealing exclusively with the 97 matters on the Union List. The Union also dominates in the 47 matters listed in the Concurrent List. Article 249 of the Constitution further empowers the Union Parliament to legislate with respect to matters in the State List when that would serve the national interest, and the Parliament can legislate with respect to any matter in the State List if a state of emergency is proclaimed in the respective state.

As the states in India exist under the shadow of the Union, the rights of minorities are very much limited within the premises of liberal democracy and common citizenship. Although the Objectives Resolution of 1946 and the Preamble of the Constitution commit the country to safeguard the interests and rights of minorities and to seek social, economic and political justice and equality of status and opportunity, the provisions of the Constitution do not envisage any safety valve for protecting minority rights in case of exclusion.

Legal Protections

As noted, religious consciousness remains strong among all communities in India. The Constitution and laws of India include numerous provisions that reflect and affect this religious character of the population. The government first of all recognizes the caste system, a hierarchical and segmental division of the Hindu society that accounts for more than 84 percent of the total population.[8] This includes more than 16 percent Scheduled Castes, 8 percent Scheduled Tribes, 44 percent Backward Castes, and 16 percent Upper Castes. Among the legal provisions guaranteeing the interests of the castes and tribes are the Constitution Order of 1950 and various Articles of the Indian Constitution (e.g., Articles 15(4), 16(4), 46, 244, 330, 332, 335, and 338–342).

Articles 14–29 of the Indian Constitution guarantee to majority and minority alike fundamental rights such as equality before law, equality of opportunity, freedom from discrimination, freedom of speech and expression, the right to life, freedom of conscience, and the freedom to manage religious affairs. Article 30 deals exclusively with the rights of religious and linguistic minorities, permitting them to establish and administer educational institutions of their choice. But this right is not absolute, and the government retains the power to regulate the administration of religious institutions. Article 29, which recognizes the right of all citizens having a distinct language, script, or culture to conserve their cultural heritage, is generally associated with minorities, but in fact it extends to the majority as well.

Supplementing these constitutional guarantees are other legal protections. In 1982 Prime Minister Indira Ghandi announced a Fifteen Point Program for minorities, and government ministries have instructed law-and-order agencies not to practice discrimination. In 1992 the National Commission on Minorities was established in order to look into matters affecting minorities. Both the Criminal Procedure Code and the Indian Penal Code contain measures outlawing communal prejudices and activities reflecting such prejudices. If minority rights are inadequately protected in India, the problem lies not in the legal tools available but rather in their implementation.

RELIGION AND OPPRESSION OF MINORITIES IN INDIA

The Indian Constitution is premised upon the liberal principle of common citizenship and a first-past-the-post electoral system that is successful in a social environment free from communal consciousness. But India's liberal democratic order has failed to create a civic community free from religious conflict and from discrimination directed particularly against Muslims, the country's largest ethnic minority. In such circumstances, where community consciousness prevails over individualism, the liberal democratic system fails to prevent domination by the majority group and the exclusion and oppression of nondominant and vulnerable ethnic groups.

The Politics of Exclusion

When the Constituent Assembly of India met in 1947, it initially planned to safeguard minority rights by guaranteeing minorities representation in elected bodies, in public employment, and in other areas of public life. Provisions to that effect were included in the 1948 Draft of the Constitution. But these provisions were removed from the Draft a year later, on the pretext that such a move would strengthen liberal democracy, unity, and secularism. The framers of the Indian Constitution asked minority groups—and particularly Indian Muslims—to trust the good will of the majority to secure them justice and equality. Minority group members, particularly the Muslims belonging to the Congress Party, were crucial in eliminating the approved package of political safeguards for minority rights, believing that this compromise would benefit them more than would the assurance of inclusion created by the minority guarantees. However, Muslim members of other parties remained skeptical and demanded the reservation of 30 percent of legislative seats and a separate electorate for the Muslim community. Ultimately, the system of reserving seats for minorities was abolished altogether, and no safeguards were included in the Constitution or established later by the judiciary to ensure the representation of minority interests in case the majority violated its promise of good will.

The result of eliminating these safeguards was, not surprisingly, a marginalized representation of the Muslim community in elected bodies and in many enforcement agencies. The empowered majority community never took seriously the Muslim community's demands for protection of the rights of its members and for proportional participation in politics and in governmental agencies through affirmative action programs or other mechanisms. This exclusion in turn has encouraged a consolidation of communal prejudices. It also stands in marked contrast to the special recognition accorded to elements of the Hindu community. For example, the Scheduled Castes and the Scheduled Tribes have reserved positions in elected bodies, in employment, and in other realms, as do other "backward classes" belonging to the majority. Moreover, government practices have served to strengthen religious identity and to favor the majority religion. Most formal and informal activities of governmental and nongovernmental agencies begin with religious symbols and gestures. Most cultural programs have religious themes. Most government offices, including banks and other entities dealing with the public both at the federal and state levels, display religious stickers and calendars. Public television stations give wide coverage to the festivals and cultural programs associated with the majority faith. Political parties distribute constituency tickets on the basis of caste and communal considerations. In practice, issues related to religion/community have increasingly shaped the agendas of parties in national and state elections. Therefore, religion has become the fundamental basis of identification for the individual and group in the Indian polity and society.

Communal Violence

Official sources document 8,175 riots and incidents of communal violence, as well as 8,730 ethnically based killings, from 1950 to 1992.[9] Since 1992, there have been major communal upheavals in Indian politics (causing thousands of deaths and destruction) when the twin issues of religion and ethnicity were taken as an agenda for consolidating the votes of the majority community.

The growing vulnerability of minorities to violence by organized militant groups stems in part from the inaction and/or complicity of governmental agencies, particularly those responsible for internal order and security. Vigilant action by the police can protect members of minority groups, and strong action by the judiciary can control communal violence. Instead, the tragic violence in Gujarat in 2002 exposed a nexus between the state administration and the groups engaged in genocidal activities against the Muslims. In fact, a succession of national inquiry commissions have documented police complicity in communal violence against the Muslim minority. The report of the Justice B. N. Srikrishna Commission on the Bombay riots (1992–1993) stated that "the response of police to appeals from desperate victims, particularly Muslims, was cynical and utterly indifferent on occasions, the attitude was that one Muslim killed was one Muslim less. . . . Police officers and men, particularly at the junior level appeared to have in built bias against Muslim."[10] The report of the Justice Jaganmohan Reddy Commission on the Ahmedabad riots (1969) identified "half a dozen instances where Muslim religious places adjoining police lines or police stations were attacked or damaged. The argument advanced by the police . . . did not impress the commission . . . because not a single case of damage to a Hindu place of worship near the police station was reported to the commission."[11] The report of the Justice Madon Commission on the Bhiwandi, Jalgaon, and Mahad riots (1970) said that "the working of the special Investigation Squad is a study in communal discrimination. The officers of the Squad systematically set about implicating as many Muslims and exculpating as many Hindus as possible irrespective of whether they were innocent or guilty."[12] The report concluded that "the police practiced discrimination in making arrests and concentrated upon Muslim rioters turning a blind eye to what Hindu rioters were doing."[13] Members of the Muslim minority have been particularly likely to suffer injuries or death when the police have used force in attempting to quell communal violence.

The indifference of the police to violence against the Muslim minority is also reflected in the verbal abuse directed by police personnel against Muslims, which tracks the language used by members of Hindu militant groups. Resorting to force against the members of the minority that had organized action in Katipalla (Karnataka State) in 2001 in response to the killing of a group member, the police were reported as saying:

> "You Muslims deserve to be displaced to Pakistan. You have no place in India."
>
> "Right now we need only men. We will come at night to pick your women."
>
> "You Muslims have been spoiled by eating too much of cow meat."
>
> "You beardys [alluding to the Muslim community in the District] are anti-nationals."[14]

Legislatures at both the national and state levels have criticized the pattern of police misconduct but have failed to address the source of these problems. The judiciary that has been active on so many fronts has not been so regarding violations of the rights of minorities. For example, the public interest litigation to prosecute the Hindu militant leader of *Shiv*, for venomous writings in the *Marathi* daily *Samna* during riots, was dismissed by both the Bombay High Court and the Supreme Court of India. Moreover, many members of the Hindu majority accused of involvement in riots have been acquitted by the courts and escaped punishment for their actions. A lower court in Bhagalpur, for example, acquitted 39 persons accused in one of the cases related to the killing of 24 Muslims in the Bhagalpur riots of 1989.[15]

In 1993, the People's Union for Civil Liberties concluded that the polarization in Indian civil society was mirrored in the agencies and institutions of government.[16] Certainly, the actions of the police and the courts have raised serious questions about the impartiality of the Indian political establishment.[17] A recent seminar report by the chairman of the Minorities Council noted the ineffectiveness of sections of the Indian Penal Code dealing with hate speech and disturbing communal harmony. The report also documented prejudice in media reporting, bias in the intelligence service, communal discrimination by police and administration, marginalization of Muslims in the police force, and nonimplementation of the recommendations of the National Police Commission, the National Commission of Minorities, and the National Human Rights Commission.[18] The report recommended fundamental reform of the agencies responsible for internal order and security, so that the rule of law could become a reality and so that all vulnerable groups could enjoy reliable protection of life, limb, dignity, property, and places of worship.[19]

INDIAN FEDERALISM AND THE PROTECTION OF MINORITY RIGHTS

Why have Muslims in India been subjected to exclusion and violation of their rights despite an abundance of legal protections? Why has the government failed to implement those rights and ensure the rule of law? It is sometimes said that the public is the keeper of the Constitution, but problems arise when a self-interested and oppressive majority can pursue its majoritarian agenda over and above the Constitution. This has happened in India, as it has in many other traditional societies. There is nothing in the Constitution that obliges the majority community to share power with minorities that are excluded from a place in the government, and it has not.

This raises the question of how to deal with minority rights and concerns, particularly in multicultural societies in the nonliberal or illiberal world, in order to achieve the broader objectives of federal governance. It appears that federal polities must directly address the issues of ethnic conflicts, exclusion of minorities, and ethnicization of the state. The Indian situation illustrates what can happen when a federal polity fails to do so. The federal arrangements in India failed to institutionalize nonmajoritarianism and a power-sharing role for minorities in the subnational units of the Union.

Some scholars take a more positive view of Indian federalism. For example, Daniel Elazar has described India as largely successful in managing ethnic and intercommunal conflicts, which he attributes to the creation of linguistically based states in India.[20] However, in actuality these linguistic states have failed to prevent violence, discrimination, and exclusion directed at the Muslim minority. Similarly, many Indian scholars have offered an unduly positive interpretation of Indian federalism. They tend to envision India as a civic community rather than as a society of communities, and they view the Indian Constitution as an unproblematic part of the Indian political system, particularly in its treatment of minorities. The country's ills are blamed on leftists, rightists, or fanatics rather than on structural problems in the nation's political arrangements. For example, in the case of massive violence against the Muslims in the state of Gujarat, commentators attributed the problem to a particular party and its organization, while ignoring the factors that encouraged the party to indulge in these crimes.[21] When India's political ills are discussed, many Indian scholars place all the blame on Britain's colonial rule, ignoring the fact that the basis of India's nation-building, its nationalist ideology, and its sources of political mobilization have all been majoritarian-centric. What the Indian Constitution prescribed for post-British India was a polity that could have succeeded in a society of individuals. This constitutional vision was always vulnerable in a country in which the nationalist discourse, governing responsibilities, and patriotism were bracketed with the majoritarian consciousness, and in which Muslims were depicted as an undesirable and unreliable sociopolitical element. Put differently, majoritarian nationalist discourse and the glorification of identity and ideology have influenced and indoctrinated leadership at both the national and subnational levels. As a result, minority-group members have not only been excluded from power but also have been subject to ethnic violence, discrimination, and other deprivations. This suggests that the federal features of the Indian polity need to be considered in light of these realities and redesigned to address the needs of those victimized under existing arrangements.

The key question appears to be whether federalism can serve not only to allocate power among governing institutions but also to encourage a commitment to the interests and well-being of all segments of society. On the one hand, federalism empowers subnational units within their specified area of influence. On the other, it may be reasonable to limit the powers and autonomy of these units in order to safeguard the well-being of all the people, and in fact the Indian Constitution empowers the Union Government to supervise and direct state governments in the case of a constitutional breakdown or a threat to the people. Moreover, the governor of a state, appointed by the Union, takes an oath to ensure the "well-being of the people." What do these obligations mean in a multicultural society? More specifically, what should the responsibilities of the Union government be when, as has happened in several states of India, a subnational unit itself engages in oppression of a minority or minorities?[22]

One gets a sense of what should be done from the Government of India Act, adopted in 1935 under British rule, which gave the provincial governors special responsibilities such as preventing grave menace to the peace or tranquility of the province and safeguarding the legitimate interests of minorities. As the issue of minority rights has become a more pressing concern for the Indian federal polity, more attention must be paid in how federal principles of governance, with their emphasis on diffusion of power and a combination of self-rule and shared rule, can guide the different layers of Indian federal polity and the Hindu majority in their dealing with minorities.

FEDERALISM AND NONMODERN SOCIETIES

Federal principles grow out of the idea that a people can voluntarily enter into a lasting yet limited political association, in order to achieve common ends and protect certain rights, while simultaneously preserving a degree of differentiation. It therefore assumes the existence of a civic community, territorial divisions, and a modern society, none of which may exist in societies comprised of conscious communities. Thus, one may ask what safeguards federalism can provide in a country in which consciousness of territorialism is overshadowed by communitarian or ethnic consciousness. Scholars of federalism, such as Daniel Elazar, find an opportunity for liberty and citizen participation in governance even within the limited and traditional understanding of federalism. After all, federalism promotes a recognition that one may be governing people that have different political identities. It also encompasses an implicit commitment to justice that holds, among other things, that a distribution of power among groups in a society is both necessary and desirable.[23] Thus, since the 1950s, scholars of federalism have been attracted to consociationalism and have sought to integrate the two principles of governance.[24]

In most nonmodern societies, federalism has not developed in the same way that it took root in modern societies. Rather, in nonmodern societies people typically surrendered their power and submitted to the administration of a single government, and that government subsequently divided power among distinct governments. Nonetheless, the introduction of federalism in any society, modern or nonmodern, can encourage a realization of the need for power sharing among all elements of society in order to create a compound majority and appropriate autonomy for regional minorities. It can thus serve as the impetus for considering all viable mechanisms, be they minority rights, regionalism, consociationalism, proportional representation, or other steps, that can ensure power sharing. Without such a concern, federalism would only serve the cosmetic purpose of division of powers and not sharing of powers. In the case of India, a full commitment to this understanding of federalism would mean that both the Union and state governments would create mechanisms to protect minorities not only from threats of violence but also from majoritarianism. Otherwise, the federal arrangements would be merely a constitutional mask for the majoritarian leadership in the Union and the states to violate the rights of minorities.

It is, therefore, important to look into some constructive elements provided by federalism. According to Elazar, federalism has to do with the need of people and polities to unite for common purposes yet remain separate to preserve their respective identities.[25] He writes,

> One of the major recurring principles of political import which informs and encompasses all three themes (the pursuit of political justice to achieve political order; the search for understanding of the empirical reality of political power and its exercise; and the creation of an appropriate civic environment through civil society and civil community capable of integrating the first two themes) is federalism—an idea that defines political justice, shapes political behavior, and directs humans towards an appropriately civic synthesis of the two.[26]

In a changing world, federalism must also change so that it can become a means of "accommodating the spreading desire of people to preserve or revive the advantages of small societies with the growing necessity for larger combinations to employ common resources or to maintain or strengthen their cultural distinctiveness within more extensive polities."[27] There is more than one way to apply federal principles. Issues in multiethnic societies will be addressed peacefully only through the application of federal principles that will combine kinship (the basis of ethnicity) and consent (the basis of democratic government) into politically viable, constitutionally protected arrangements involving territorial and nonterritorial polities.[28]

In sum, federalism needs to be adapted to serve as a practical response to real situations, in which problems stem from conflicting national, ethnic, linguistic, or racial claims arising out of particular historical experiences. This adaptability means that the term federalism will lack a clear-cut definition. Its conceptual ambiguity makes it similar to democracy and republicanism. The essence of federalism is not to be found in a particular set of institutions but in the institutionalization of particular relationships among the participants in political life. Thus, as long as the proper relations are created, a wide variety of political structures can be developed that are consistent with federal principles.[29] Federalism offers the possibility of creating publics that transcend the divisions among peoples and thereby makes possible the establishment of civil society and political order, even as it acknowledges the ethnic revival in various parts of the nonliberal world and the need to address this reemergence of primordial ties. Federalism thus stands as an alternative to secession and partition, while promoting meaningful popular sovereignty. In this sense, federalism can be described as one of the best means of democratic governance. Nicholas Haysom has rightly pointed out that individual pluralism, the solution offered by liberal democracy, is not always an answer to the resolution of identity conflicts.[30] One can also add that Haysom's idea can be extended to include other areas where liberal democracy has been disastrous for minorities.

How to make contemporary democracies inclusive and nonmajoritarian remains the key issue for historical societies. Federalism's emphasis on power sharing provides one way of increasing a minority's sense that it has a stake in the polity. It encourages a rethinking of how one balances nation-building and the consideration of subnational identities in order to create a healthy pattern of political integration. Suitably adapted to the realities of nonliberal societies, it can make a vital contribution to the creation of a durable and just political order.

NOTES

1. See, for example, Ellis Katz and G. Alan Tarr, eds., *Federalism and Rights* (Lanham, MD: Rowman & Littlefield, 1996).
2. Wolf Linder, *Swiss Democracy: Possible Solutions to Conflict in Multicultural Societies* (New York: St. Martin's Press, 1994), xv.
3. Daniel J. Elazar, *Exploring Federalism* (Tuscaloosa: The Univesity of Alabama Press, 1987), 83.
4. Ibid., 33.
5. Ibid., 70.
6. D. D. Basu, *Introduction to the Constitution of India* (New Delhi: Prentice-Hall of India, 1995), 50; Nine-Judge Bench Supreme Court of India decision in *S.R. Bommai v. Union of India*, A. 1994 S.C. 198, para. 211.
7. Granville Austin, *Working a Democratic Constitution: The India Experience* (New Delhi: Oxford University Press, 1999), 7.
8. *India 2002* (New Delhi: Research, Reference and Training Division of the Ministry of Information and Broadcasting, Government of India, 2002), 15–20.
9. Information based on Indian Parliament—*Answers to Starred and Unstarred Questions and Annual Reports of the Ministry of Home Affairs*, mentioned in Rasheeduddin Khan, *Bewildered India: Identity, Pluralism, Discord* (New Delhi: Har-Anand Publications and the Center for Federal Studies, 1995), p. 223.
10. Akshaya Mukul, *The Times of India* (New Delhi), 3 March 2002, p. 5.
11. Ibid.
12. Ibid.
13. *Report of the Commission of Enquiry* into the communal disturbances at Bhiwandi, Jalgaon, and Mahad in May 1970 by Justice D. P. Madon, Vol. III, Part III (Bombay, n.d), p. 13.
14. P. B. D'sa, "Police Atrocities at Katipalla: Muslims Treated as Anti-national Enemies," *Human Rights Today* (New Delhi) 4, no. 1 (January-March, 2002): 13.
15. News Report—"39 acquitted in Bhagalpur riot case," *The Hindu* (New Delhi).
16. Excerpts from the Editorial—"Reform the Law and Order Machinery to Save the Republic," *PUCL Bulletin* (February 1993).
17. *Sixth Report of the National Police Commission* (1981), paras 47.11, 47.12, 45.57, 47.58.
18. Report of Iqbal A. Ansari, Chairman of the Minorities Council, India, prepared for a seminar on Recurring Gujarat Malady Focus on Law and Enforcement Agency, Indian Law Institute, New Delhi, October 4, 2002.
19. *IOS Bulletin Human Rights Today* 4 (July–September 2002): 5.
20. Elazar, *Exploring Federalism*, 224.

21. See M. L. Sondhi, "The BJP's Responsibility for the Gujarat Tragedy," in M. L. Sondhi and Apratim Mukarji, eds., *The Black Book of Gujarat* (New Delhi: Manak Publications, 2002), 3–11; Shamsul Islam, "RSS: Marketing Fascism as Hindutva," in John Dayal, ed., *Gujarat 2002 Untold and Re-Told Stories of the Hindutva Lab* (Delhi: Media House, 2002), 62–83.

22. Arshi Khan, "Beyond Federalism and Constitutionalism: Painful Politics and Implications of Communal Consciousness in Gujarat," *Mainstream* (New Delhi) 40, 7 September 2002, pp. 27–29.

23. Elazar, *Exploring Federalism*, 84.

24. Arend Lijphart, "Consociation and Federation: Conceptual and Empirical Links," *Canadian Journal of Political Science* 12 (September 1979): 499–515.

25. Elazar, *Exploring Federalism*, 33.

26. Ibid., 1.

27. Ibid., 6.

28. Ibid., 9.

29. Ibid., 12.

30. Speech at the International Conference on Federalism in a Changing World—Learning from Each Other, St. Gallen, Switzerland, 27–30 August 2002.

12

Federalism, Subnational Constitutional Arrangements, and the Protection of Minorities in Switzerland

Giovanni Biaggini

THE HISTORICAL AND GEOGRAPHICAL CONTEXT

For many people Switzerland is just a small, beautiful, rich, and expensive country in the heart of Europe, a land of chocolate, cheese, watches, and numbered bank accounts. But Switzerland is also multicultural, multilingual, and multiconfessional, a political nation shaped by the will of its people. The cliché used in Switzerland is "*Willensnation*"—"nation by will." Switzerland can also be seen as an historically built—in some way even archaic—entity that happened to have escaped from the process of centralization in the modern era.

The Swiss Confederation[1] is composed of 26 cantons. It became a federal state in 1848 after a short civil war, the so-called *Sonderbundskrieg*, in November 1847. Seven conservative Catholic cantons, which formed the Sonderbund, fought against the rest of the Confederation.[2] Before 1848 the cantons had founded a confederation of more or less sovereign states (*Staatenbund*) that was based on a treaty (*Bundesvertrag*). The first Federal Constitution entered into force in 1848. It was completely revised in 1874. On 18 April 1999, the Swiss people and cantons adopted a new federal constitution, which entered into force on 1 January 2000. The aim of this revision was to set down on paper constitutional case law and to texture the constitution in a systematic way.

Geography

As of 1999, Switzerland (41,285 sq km) had 7.164 million inhabitants, 19.6 percent of whom were of foreign nationality.[3] The 26 cantons differ considerably with regard to size and population. The two most highly populated are the canton of Zurich, with 1.2 million inhabitants and covering 1,729 sq km, and the canton of Berne, with 943,000 inhabitants (6,000 sq km). Fewer than 100,000 inhabitants live in nine cantons.[4] The smallest one, the canton of Basel-City, with 188,500 inhabitants, has a territory of only 37 sq km. The largest one, the Grisons, with 186,000 inhabitants, is 7,100 sq km, or 192 times larger than Basel-City.

Languages

Article 4 of the Swiss Federal Constitution recognizes four national languages[5]: German, French, Italian, and—since 1938—Romansch.[6] These four national languages correspond to the four old, traditional cultures (*Kulturen*).[7] According to the 1990 census,[8]

- 63.7 percent of the population (about 4.4 million persons) speak German, which is more than 70 percent, if only persons of Swiss nationality are counted.[9]
- 19.2 percent are French-speaking (1.3 million).
- 7.6 percent speak Italian (525,000).
- 0.6 percent or about 40,000 use (Raeto-) Romansch as their mother-tongue (as compared to 1.1 percent in 1941).[10]

The linguistic boundaries do not coincide with the boundaries of the cantons. This fact results from the historically heterogeneous demographics of the concerned cantons. Berne, Fribourg, and Valais are bilingual (German-French), and the Grisons are trilingual (German-Italian-Romansch). The majority of people living in the canton of Berne mostly use German, namely 84 percent (French: 8 percent; others: 8 percent). About 60 percent are French-speaking in the cantons of Fribourg and Valais, and a minority of about 30 percent speaks German. In the Grisons 65 percent of the population are German-speaking, 17 percent (30,000) speak Romansch (1941: 31.3 percent) and 11 percent speak Italian. In the Italian-speaking canton of Ticino, one commune called Bosco Gurin is traditionally German-speaking.

Confessions

Two principal confessions or religions exist in Switzerland. In 1990, 46.1 percent of the population belonged to the Roman Catholic church, and about 40 percent were Protestants. Due to immigration, the Muslim confession ranks third with 2.2 percent.[11]

Most of the cantons are either traditionally Catholic or Protestant. On the other hand, bi- or multiconfessionalism characterizes some cantons, for example, Argovia or St. Gall, and an old confessional minority lives in several cantons (e.g., Fribourg). Nowadays, the confessions have mingled due to the migration within Switzerland. Two examples may illustrate the developments of the last centuries. About 49 percent of the population in Geneva, where the religious reformer John Calvin was active in the sixteenth century, belong to the Roman Catholic church today in comparison with only 18 percent of the inhabitants who believe in Protestantism. In Zurich, another stronghold of the Reformation, namely Ulrich Zwingli's town, Roman Catholics account for 34.5 percent of the population and Protestants for only 31.2 percent. In conclusion, the geographical distribution of religious groups, like the distribution of language groups, does not correspond with the cantonal boundaries.

Describing the situation of minorities in Switzerland, we also must take into account the three levels of the federal state. A German-speaking Protestant living in Murten, a town in the canton of Fribourg, is a member of the linguistic majority there. At the cantonal level, however, he belongs to a double—religious and linguistic—minority. Nevertheless, at the federal level, this German-speaking Protestant is part of the linguistic majority and belongs to the second largest confession. Almost everybody in Switzerland belongs at the same time to a majority and to a minority depending on the level of government. Thus, we tend to say that Switzerland is a land of minorities, especially if we take into account that there are other kinds of minorities, too, like aged persons, disabled persons, children, the working-poor, foreigners, homosexuals, and so on.

I should add (and emphasize) that Switzerland has no homogeneous majority. Of course, one may speak about the *Deutschschweiz*, for example, but it is largely a statistical majority, the sum of all German-speaking people or cantons. In fact, each of the German-speaking cantons has its cultural peculiarities and its own identity due to historical factors and cantonal autonomy. The differences between the canton of Basel-City and, say, Appenzell Inner Rhodes are enormous. The German-speaking Basel is in many aspects much more similar to the French-speaking Geneva than to the cantons of Grisons or the German-speaking Obwald. The *Suisse Romande* or *Romandie* (or *Welsche Schweiz*), the French-speaking part of Switzerland is likewise not an entity as such but rather an artificial entity. Like the German-speaking cantons, the French-speaking cantons are divided by culture, education, religion, and social customs. Therefore, the Suisse Romande has no real national identity.

THE SWISS FEDERAL SYSTEM

The Swiss federal system combines federalism, fundamental rights, and direct democracy in a unique way that encourages a minority-friendly political culture. The Federal Parliament or Federal Assembly (*Bundesversammlung*) consists of two chambers with equal powers. The National Council (*Nationalrat*) has 200 members (representatives of the people), and the Council of States or Senate (*Ständerat*) has 46 members who are delegates of the cantons. The cantons elect two senators due to the fundamental federalist principle that all cantons are treated equally. The six so-called "half-cantons" (*Halbkantone*) elect only one senator each.[12]

Under the system of proportional representation, the members of the National Council are elected directly by the people, whereas the members of the Council of States are chosen in accordance with provisions differing from canton to canton. Today, all senators are elected directly by the people. In both cases, the cantons form the constituencies.[13]

The Federal Parliament in Berne is the highest authority of the Confederation (Article 148 Federal Constitution), but it is subject to the rights of the people and the cantons. In order to encourage understanding between the regions and the linguistic communities, the Federal Parliament held sessions in the cities of Geneva in 1993 and in Lugano (Ticino) in March 2001.

The federal government (or executive branch), called the Federal Council (*Bundesrat*), consists of seven members (*Bundesräte*, Federal Councillors) who are elected by the Parliament for a fixed term of four years. Article 175 Federal Constitution provides that the national languages (*Sprachregionen*) and the regions (*Landesgegenden*) must be represented in an appropriate way. Usually, there are two, if not three Federal Councillors of French and/or Italian mother-tongue, which means that the linguistic minorities are regularly over-represented. (This over-representation is also the case by the composition of the Federal Supreme Court.[14]) Therefore, the Swiss political system has typically converted the vague constitutional mandate of Article 175 into clear and minority-friendly modes of operation.

Swiss citizens over the age of 18 not only have the right to take part in parliamentary elections, but they may also launch and sign so-called popular initiatives and referenda regarding federal matters, and they can participate in votes (*Volksabstimmungen*) at the federal level.

- *Popular initiative* (main form): By signing a formal proposition, 100,000 citizens can demand a modification of the Federal Constitution (Article 139 Federal Constitution). The Federal Parliament recommends its approval or its rejection, or it may submit its own counterdraft. In all these cases, a popular vote on the proposition will inevitably take place unless the group that launched the popular initiative withdraws its proposition.
- *Mandatory or obligatory referendum:* All proposals for a revision of the Federal Constitution and some very important international treaties must be submitted to the vote of the People and the Cantons (Article 140 Federal Constitution). A proposal is only accepted if both a majority of the voters (*Volksmehr*) and a majority of the cantons agree with it (so-called *Ständemehr*[15]). Mathematically, in this situation, the vote of 1 person in Appenzell Inner Rhodes equals that of 40 persons in Zurich.
- *Optional referendum*: Federal Statutes (*Bundesgesetze*) and certain international treaties are submitted to the vote of the people at the request of 50,000 citizens within 100 days of a decree's publication. Moreover, a majority of those voting on the question is needed to decide whether the bill or treaty is approved or rejected.

These direct-democratic people's rights (*Volksrechte*) are regularly used. The Swiss citizens are invited to go to the polls three or four times a year to vote on about 10 to 20 popular initiatives and referenda at the federal level.[16] Whereas the referendum is described as a brake applied by the people, the popular initiative is regarded as the driving force of the Swiss political system.

The specific people's rights have important direct and indirect effects on the way the political system functions. In political practice, the direct-democratic instruments are often used by groups that are not directly represented in the national parliament, like action or interest groups, or that have a weak parliamentary position. Thus, the direct-democratic rights serve as a political instrument for parties in opposition, but also for other kinds of minorities.

The political process regularly starts long before the Federal Parliament begins to discuss a topic in detail. It is characterized by a permanent search for broad compromises, as a political consensus is sought among all groups that are able to launch a referendum or an initiative, in order to avoid a popular vote. Beyond this, there is a strong tradition of proportional representation. Swiss unwritten rules require a proportional representation of the linguistic communities on all important boards, commissions, and committees. In general, the minorities are even over-represented.

Due to the existence of direct-democratic rights, all the main political parties have over time been integrated into a broad all-party-coalition (*Allparteienregierung*). Since 1959 the Federal Council has been composed of two Radical-Democrats, two Christian-Democrats, two Social-Democrats, and one member of the Swiss People's Party. The proportion 2:2:2:1 is called *Zauberformel*—the magic formula. Currently, the four main political parties occupy 175 seats (87.5 percent) in the National Council (*Nationalrat*) and 46 seats (100 percent!) in the second chamber (*Ständerat*). A parliamentary opposition in the usual sense does not exist. This fact is called consensus democracy or consociational democracy (*Konkordanzdemokratie*) by Swiss and foreign political scientists.[17] Opposition comes from outside (popular rights) and from inside—from the members of the governmental parties, sometimes even a governmental party as a whole—fighting the proposals of the Federal Council.

The political systems of the cantons differ from each other as well as from the federal system. But they all comprehend even more specific political rights than the one at the federal level—for example, popular initiative concerning statute law or optional referendum against certain parliamentary decisions concerning cantonal spending. And the minority-friendly phenomenon called consensus democracy or consociational democracy, which is based on the idea of integrating the minorities through political participation, can be generally observed at the cantonal level as well.

An attentive British observer of the Swiss system, Jonathan Steinberg, once noted:

> Whereas the British and American systems produce winners, the Swiss prefer to protect the losers. Where other systems strive to generate a powerful majority, which can govern, the Swiss opt for complex formulae that produce coalitions. All political machinery in Switzerland has a provisional quality because the "Sovereign," "the people," is really sovereign and may exercise its power to change this or that instrument of its will.[18]

SUBNATIONAL CONSTITUTIONS AND THEIR RELATIONSHIP TO THE NATIONAL CONSTITUTION

The Swiss federal system is of the integrative type (i.e., previously independent entities coming together[19]). Twenty-six subnational units called cantons (*Kantone, cantons, cantoni, chantuns*) compose the Swiss

Confederation nowadays. They are enumerated in Article 1 Federal Constitution. Article 51 Federal Constitution obliges the cantons to adopt written constitutions.

The cantonal constitutions are quite different from each other—first of all owing to their date of origin. The constitutions of nine cantons date from the nineteenth century: Geneva (1847),[20] Fribourg (1857), Zurich (1869), Appenzell Inner Rhodes (1872), Lucerne (1875), Basel-City (1889), Grisons (1892), Zug (1894), and Schwyz (1898). The adoption of the present constitution of Valais took place in 1907. In general, cantonal constitutions can be amended quite easily, and amendment is frequent. Since their adoption, the constitutions mentioned here have all been repeatedly amended in parts. For example, the constitution of Zug was revised more than 30 times in a period of 100 years.[21] Consequently, despite their age, these constitutions are not necessarily antiquated.

The cantons of Nidwald and Obwald produced totally revised constitutions in 1965 and in 1968; the newly established canton of Jura adopted its constitution in 1977. Since the 1980s, 13 cantons have adopted totally revised, modern constitutions: Argovia (1980), Basel-Land (1984), Uri (1984), Solothurn (1986), Turgovia (1987), Glarus (1988), Berne (1993), Appenzell Outer Rhodes (1995), Ticino (1997), Neuchâtel (2000), St. Gall (2001), and the cantons of Schaffhausen and Vaud in 2002.

The recently revised constitutions are quite similar in structure and content.[22] In fact, it is clear that it was not the intent of the cantonal sovereigns to reinvent constitutionalism. Additionally, the later constitutions were influenced by the prior constitutions and by the draft for the new federal constitution of 1977 and the one of 1996.

Furthermore, the constitution of Appenzell Outer Rhodes (1995) is in parts modeled on the Bernese constitution (1993), but the similarities of these two constitutions should not be overestimated. Each cantonal constitution contains some particularities and shows an individual character, especially in the field of the organization of the authorities and the political process, in particular, direct-democratic rights. Therefore, one cannot say that the cantonal constitutions were generally modeled on each other. This reflects not only the vast cantonal autonomy regarding constitutional questions, which is guaranteed by the Federal Constitution in Article 51, but also the fact that the Swiss cantons have been able to develop and to maintain their own identity.

Despite their differences, there is one point in common: The cantonal constitutions, at least the recent ones, can be considered as complete constitutions (*Vollverfassungen*). These constitutions try to name all functions of a modern constitution. Hence, it is obvious that they do not merely establish the cantonal authorities, define their competences, and organize the legislative process. They also limit power, especially by guaranteeing fundamental rights, and they address the most important duties as well as the tasks of the respective canton—for example, in the fields of education, cultural affairs, public health, protection of the environment, police, roads, taxes, and so on.

Article 51 of the Federal Constitution provides that every canton "shall adopt a democratic constitution."[23] In this context, *democratic* means that each canton must have a parliament elected directly by the people, and the cantonal constitution must respect the principle of separation of powers. Furthermore, Article 51 Federal Constitution requires that cantonal constitutions be approved by the people and that these documents be subject to revision if a majority of the people requires so. The cantonal constitutions must be guaranteed by the Confederation. This guarantee is given by the Federal Parliament, if the reviewed constitution is not contrary to any federal law (Article 49 and Article 51 Federal Constitution). At the end of the nineteenth century, rejections of cantonal constitutions were often pronounced, particularly because the cantons disregarded equal political rights.[24]

Beyond that, the Federal Constitution does not explicitly mention any requirements regarding the content of cantonal constitutions. It is the task of each canton to decide how it organizes its governmental branch. Although the Swiss cantons enjoy a considerable constitutional autonomy including the taxing power, one important limitation does exist: Both the cantonal constitutions and the cantonal law as a whole must respect the fundamental rights guaranteed by the Federal Constitution, especially with regard to minority rights—Article 8 Federal Constitution (equality before the law, prohibition of discrimination), Article 15 Federal Constitution (freedom of religion),[25] and Article 18 Federal Constitution (freedom of language).[26]

Regarding the processes for the adoption and revision of cantonal constitutions, we have to distinguish between total revision (*Totalrevision*) and partial revision (*Teilrevision*) of the constitution.[27] Some cantonal constitutions provide the appointment of a constituent assembly (*Verfassungsrat*) for elaborating the total revision of the cantonal constitution. In the other cantons the revision is the task of the cantonal parliament. Moreover, we must distinguish between the ordinary method of revision and revision by popular initiative. Normally, a change in the cantonal constitution is deliberated on by the cantonal parliament, and the revised part is then submitted to the vote of the people. In every canton a certain number of citizens can demand a modification of the cantonal constitution by signing a formal proposal. When this occurs, the cantonal parliament can approve or reject the proposal or submit its own counterdraft, but a popular vote must take place in any case unless the group that launched the popular initiative withdraws its proposal. Thus, every revision of a cantonal constitution in partial or in total must be approved in a popular vote. Therefore, it is always "the Sovereign" who decides, and in Swiss political discourse "the Sovereign"—"*der Souverän*"—means the citizenry as a whole.

In general, the politics associated with cantonal constitutional change are not significantly different from more ordinary cantonal politics. The attitude toward the constitutions is quite practical. Swiss constitutions are often revised; they are not sacrosanct pieces of parchment, but a form of running record of the decisions of the voters on more or less important issues. In case of a total revision, the discussions may assume a more fundamental character. However, constitutional provisions are, normally, less detailed than provisions in ordinary statute law.

The governmental structures of the Swiss cantons are similar to those at the federal level. Both the cantonal governments and the Federal Council do not depend on a parliamentary majority. The main differences include the following: The cantons do not have the bicameral system unlike the federal state system. In general, the size of the cantonal parliaments varies between 58 and 200 seats. The five or seven members of a cantonal government or an Executive Council (*Regierungsrat, Staatsrat*) are elected directly by the people and not by the parliament as at the federal level. In two small cantons, namely Appenzell Inner Rhodes and Glarus, an archetypal form of democracy has survived, the *Landsgemeinde*, an annual people's assembly, held outdoors, where the citizens express their political will[28] by a show of hands.

All the recent cantonal constitutions include a chapter in which the usual fundamental rights are guaranteed. Because the new Federal Constitution (adopted in 1999) lists a comprehensive catalogue of fundamental rights (Article 7 through Article 34 Federal Constitution), these cantonal "bills of rights" are generally of limited practical importance. However, some cantonal fundamental rights go beyond the federal standard. The Bernese constitution of 1993, for example, guarantees the right of the individual to consult all administrative documents, not only those concerning him- or herself, unless preponderant public or private interests justify keeping them secret (Article 17). The right to strike according to Article 20 of the constitution of Jura (1977) goes further, or, at least, seems to go further than the corresponding guarantee at the federal level (Article 28 Federal Constitution).

In general, it is possible to bring disputes concerning cantonal constitutional law to court. Three cantons (Nidwald, Jura, and Basel-Land) have established a constitutional court. In other cantons the administrative courts exercise, incidentally, constitutional jurisdiction, especially in cases concerning the violation of constitutional rights. A particular set of constitutional law disputes are solved by a majority decision of the cantonal parliament—for example, invalidation of popular initiatives in most of the cantons as well as contention of competence between the cantonal administration and the cantonal courts.[29] The Federal Supreme Court (*Bundesgericht*) in Lausanne decides on the authoritative interpretation of the cantonal constitutions in the final instance.

THE PROTECTION OF MINORITIES IN THE CANTONAL CONSTITUTIONS

Earlier, I emphasized that Switzerland is a land of minorities. Therefore, it is astonishing that the word "minority" appears only rarely and quite incidentally in the Swiss constitutional texts—if it is mentioned at all.[30] As an example, Article 70 Federal Constitution states that the traditional "indigenous linguistic minorities" shall be respected. The constitution of the canton of Grisons mentions the notion "minority" in the context of education (see Article 27). The new constitution of the canton of Berne, which entered into force in 1995, does include a particular provision concerning the status and the protection of minorities:

> Art. 4 Minorities
> (1) All cantonal authorities have to take into account the needs of linguistic, cultural and regional minorities.
> (2) To this end, minorities can be granted special rights.[31]

However, in the Swiss federal and cantonal legislation, there is no legal definition of the notion "minority."

Language and Religious Rights

Article 70 Sec. 2 Federal Constitution states: "The cantons shall designate their official languages. In order to preserve harmony between linguistic communities, they shall respect the traditional territorial distribution of languages, and take into account the indigenous linguistic minorities." The constitutions of the three bilingual cantons—Berne, Fribourg, and Valais (German-French)—and of the trilingual Grisons (German-Italian-Romansch) all include provisions laying down the official languages (*Amtssprachen*) at the cantonal level. The citizens have the right and are also obliged to communicate with the cantonal authorities in these official languages.

Additionally, the Bernese constitution also defines in Article 6 the official languages of its districts. In the Grisons, a canton with an old and strong tradition of communal autonomy and decentralization, it is up to the communes and districts to lay down the official language(s) and the school language(s).

Article 21 of the constitution of Fribourg provides that the use of German and French as the official languages is to be regulated by statute law in respect of the so-called territorial principle (*Territorialitätsprinzip* or *Sprachgebietsprinzip*). This principle defines the official language at the level of the districts and of the communes, which has to be used in respect of the traditional territorial distribution of languages.[32]

The equal treatment of German and French in legislation and administration is protected by the constitution of Valais in Article 12. Finally, it is also worth noting Article 15 of the Bernese constitution, which guarantees the freedom of language. So does Article 18 Federal Constitution now, too. Moreover, the Bernese constitution explicitly forbids all discrimination on the grounds of language (Article 10). The same provision can be found in Article 8 Sec. 2 Federal Constitution. Furthermore, the cantons have the competence to determine the official use of a language between public institutions such as public schools or courts and the citizen.[33]

According to Article 72 Federal Constitution, the relationship between the church and the state has to be regulated at the cantonal level. However, Article 15 Federal Constitution guarantees the freedom of religion and philosophy as a right of the individual, stating:

> All persons have the right to choose their religion or philosophical convictions freely, and to profess them alone or in community with others. All persons have the right to join or to belong to a religious community, and to follow religious teachings. No person shall be forced to join or belong to a religious community, to participate in a religious act, or to follow any religious teaching. (Sec. 2–4)

Freedom of religion also means confessional neutrality on the part of the state, especially in the field of education. Based on the constitutionally guaranteed freedom of religion, the Federal Supreme Court, in many decisions, has defended secularization and enforced confessional neutrality.[34] However, the Federal Constitution does not prevent the cantons from granting public law status (*öffentlichrechtliche Anerkennung*)—with considerable autonomy—to religious communities. Almost all cantons do so. An establishment clause along the lines of the First Amendment of the U.S. Constitution does not exist. Normally, this official recognition is granted to the two principal Christian confessions: the Roman Catholic church and the Evangelical-Reformed or Protestant church. A few cantonal constitutions also recognize the Christian Catholic church and/or the Jewish community—for example, Article 121 and Article 126 of the Bernese constitution. Several cantonal constitutions mention the possibility of granting public law status to other religious communities by statute law. Two cantons—Geneva since

1907 and Neuchâtel since 1941—have a system that almost completely separates the state from the church. The officially recognized churches are authorized to levy taxes on the income of the members who belong to the respective religious communities. This kind of taxation is called *Kirchensteuer*.

PARTICIPATION IN THE DECISION-MAKING PROCESS

Few provisions in cantonal constitutions grant minorities a specific participation in the decision-making process. Berne is the only canton that has created a specific institutional solution. According to Article 5 of the Bernese constitution, the three French-speaking districts of Courtelary, Moutier, and La Neuveville shall have a particular status (*besondere Stellung*), which allows them to preserve their linguistic and cultural identity and to participate actively in the process of decision-making at the cantonal level. The "Gesetz über die Verstärkung der politischen Mitwirkung des Berner Jura und der französischsprachigen Bevölkerung des Amtsbezirks Biel" (Law on the intensification of the cooperation of the region of Bernese Jura and the French-speaking population of the administrative district of Biel in political matters) of 1994 established a Regional Council that participates in the preparation of all important projects that concern the French-speaking parts of the canton in a particular way. Beyond that, the cantonal constitution includes in Article 84 Sec. 2 the obligation for one of the seven members of the cantonal government (*Regierungsrat*) to have her or his residence in one of the three French-speaking districts.

By defining three specific constituencies (*Kantonsteile*) the constitution of Valais provides for an adequate representation of the German-speaking minority in the five-member cantonal government (*Staatsrat*). One of these constituencies is formed by the five German-speaking districts (see Article 52). Each of them elects one member of the cantonal government. The fourth and fifth members of the government are elected in a constituency formed by the whole canton. In other cantons unwritten conventions guarantee a more or less balanced representation of the different cantonal regions and their population within the government. In such instances, the protection of minorities is a matter of political culture.

Generally, the districts are the constituencies for the election of the members of the cantonal parliament. The members of Parliament are usually elected according to the system of proportional representation. This solution ensures an adequate representation of the regional or linguistic minorities in the cantonal parliaments.

The far-reaching popular rights like the referendum or the popular initiative are quite effective instruments in defending the interests of minority groups at the cantonal level, too.

In conclusion, the protection of minorities is ensured by instruments of direct democracy, by granting fundamental rights such as freedom of language or equal protection at the federal level,[35] and by political culture and traditions. The contribution of specific constitutional provisions to the protection of cantonal minorities is, in general, quite modest.

AFFIRMATIVE ACTION

In Switzerland the minority protection policy by way of affirmative action has a certain tradition in the fields of language and culture. Affirmative action is generally a matter of statute law, and the contribution of cantonal constitutional law is modest. Some provisions are found in the constitutions of the bilingual cantons. For example, the constitution of Fribourg provides in Article 21 the duty of the canton to encourage understanding between the linguistic communities. The Bernese constitution includes a general provision on minority policy (see Article 4, mentioned earlier), and it provides that the canton shall take measures to strengthen the relationship between the French-speaking Bernese Jura as well as the other parts of the canton (Article 5). Article 92 states that an appropriate number of the civil servants employed at the central, or cantonal, administration must be French-speaking.

At the federal level, Article 70 Section 3–5 Federal Constitution provides:

> The Confederation and the cantons shall encourage understanding and exchange between the linguistic communities. The Confederation shall support the plurilingual cantons in the fulfilment of their particular tasks. The Confederation shall support the measures taken by the cantons of Grisons and Ticino to maintain and to promote Romansch and Italian.

A federal statute enables the granting of federal subsidies to the cantons of Ticino and Grisons for cantonal measures in favor of the Italian and Romansch languages and cultures. In 1999 the subsidies amounted 2.2 and 4.6 million Swiss francs, respectively. The Confederation established the foundation Pro Helvetia that, among other tasks, has to promote the interchange of cultural values between the four linguistic communities and cultures. Besides, the national Broadcasting Corporation (SRG/SSR) runs 10 radio channels, namely 3 in German, 3 in French, 3 in Italian, and 1 for the Romansch region, and six television channels—two channels in each of the three main languages. The radio and television fees are shared through a preferential key for the smaller linguistic communities: 43 percent for transmissions in German, 33 percent for transmissions in French, and 23 percent for transmissions in Italian.

OTHER PROTECTIONS

In 1997, Switzerland ratified the European Charter for Regional or Minority Languages, designating Romansch and Italian as "less widely used" official languages according to Article 3 of the Charter. In addition, the European Framework Convention for the Protection of National Minorities was ratified by Switzerland in 1998.[36]

Certain cantonal constitutions also include some measures in favor of the traveling community of the Jenish people, an indigenous minority of a few thousand people, also called the Fahrende in legal documents. The Jenish people are similar to Sinti and Roma. The canton of Basel-Land, for example, supports the Fahrende in finding some places to stay.[37] Zukunft für Schweizer Fahrende is a foundation established by the Confederation in 1994.

Finally, the creation of a new canton—the republic and canton of Jura—in 1978 deserves mention. The canton of Jura was formed by three French-speaking, Roman Catholic districts that formerly made up part of the mainly German-speaking, Protestant canton of Berne. In the plebiscite of 1974, these three North Jurassien districts voted for separation from the canton of Berne.[38] Three other South Jurassien districts of the Bernese Jura, although French-speaking, decided in 1975 to remain Bernese. Furthermore, in 1989 the German-speaking, but Roman Catholic district of Laufen determined to join the canton of Basel-Land. After 30 years of sometimes violent separatist activities, this cascade of plebiscites had been authorized by an amendment to the Bernese constitution (*Verfassungszusatz*), approved by the Bernese sovereign in a popular vote in March 1970. Afterwards in 1978, the Swiss People and Cantons approved the creation of the canton of Jura in a popular vote with a mandatory referendum. The Swiss People and Cantons approved the transfer of the district of Laufen to Basel-Land in 1993. And in 1996, the subsequent transfer of the commune of Vellerat with its 69 inhabitants from the canton of Berne to the canton of Jura took place. On this occasion the cantonal constitution of Berne played an important part in the process of the creation of the new canton of Jura, although its role was more similar to an instrument of policy (see the adoption of the *Verfassungszusatz* in 1970).

CONCLUSIONS

As we have seen, there are few constitutional provisions at either the cantonal or the federal level that mention explicitly the status or protection of minorities. Despite this almost total lack of minority-specific norms in Swiss constitutional law, the political system functions quite well. The explanation seems to be found in a combination of several important legal and nonlegal factors, including:[39]

- the highly decentralized structure of the political and administrative system.
- the acceptance of common basic values as mentioned in Article 2 Federal Constitution by members of the involved minorities.
- direct democracy at all levels and a political culture of compromise.
- proportional representation (often over-representation).
- the far-reaching cantonal autonomy within the federal state, and a considerable autonomy of the communes, sometimes of the districts, too, within the cantons.
- fundamental rights, especially equal protection, freedom of religion, freedom of language, guaranteed by the Federal Constitution as a corrective.
- experience with a long history in common with some religious wars in the sixteenth, seventeenth, and eighteenth centuries.
- the fact that the cantonal (political) boundaries and the linguistic and confessional boundaries do not coincide.

In summary: Switzerland relies on territory-based, not ethnic, solutions combined with self-government and fundamental rights; on general principles, not specific minority-protecting rules, plus pragmatism. The Swiss political system, of course, has its disadvantages—for example, innovation goes rather slow. But Swiss history and the economic prosperity show that Swiss federalism is quite successful in integrating minorities and in ensuring a peaceful coexistence.

NOTES

1. Schweizerische Eidgenossenschaft, Confédération suisse, Confederazione Svizzera, Confoederatio Helvetica.

2. The Confederation lost about 100 men, the Sonderbund fewer.

3. In comparison with other countries: Austria (8.1 million inhabitants / 83,000 sq km), Belgium (10.2 million / 30,000 sq km), Croatia (4.5 million / 55,000 sq km), Denmark (5.3 million / 43,000 sq km), the Netherlands (15.7 million / 41,000 sq km), Slovakia (5.4 million / 49,000 sq km); the German Länder Niedersachsen (7.8 million / 47,000 sq km), Baden-Württemberg (10 million / 36,000 sq km), Bavaria (12 million / 70,000 sq km); or Massachusetts (6 million / 21,000 sq km), New Jersey (7.8 million / 20,000 sq km).

4. The canton of Appenzell Inner Rhodes (172 sq km) has only 14,900 inhabitants (1.24 percent of the population of the canton of Zurich).

5. According to Article 70 Federal Constitution the official languages (*Amtssprachen*) of the Confederation (federal level) are German, French, and Italian. Article 70 further provides that Romansch shall be an official language for communicating with persons of Romansch language.

6. The roots of (Raeto-) Romansch date back to the Roman Empire, when the (latinized) Raetian people inhabited a large area from the Rhine to the Adriatic. The Swiss Raeto-Romansch is divided into three main written variants and some nonliterary dialects. In 1982 a uniform written language was created, the so-called Rumantsch Grischun, which is used now for official texts.

7. In Switzerland we usually distinguish between four cultures, but we think in terms of only one people; nobody in Switzerland would call our country a *Vielvölkerstaat*.

8. The results of the 2000 census are not yet available.

9. More precisely, the Swiss Germans *write* German, but they *speak* Schwyzerdütsch which stands for a large number of quite distinct German dialects belonging to the broad linguistic group of Alemannic.

10. Residents by mother-tongue. Other languages: 8.9 percent. In 1990, 65.4 percent of Swiss Germans declared themselves to be monolingual, but only 43.4 percent of Swiss French, 27.0 percent of Swiss Italians, and 20.3 percent of Swiss Romansch did so.

11. Christian Orthodox: 1.0 percent; Jewish: 0.3 percent; Christian Catholic: 0.2 percent; others: 1.5 percent; no confession: 7.4 percent; no declaration: 1.5 percent.

12. Article 150 Federal Constitution.

13. The canton of Glarus, for example, counts for 1 member of the National Council and for 2 members of the Council of States; the canton of Zurich for 34 members and 2 members, respectively.

14. At present, the Federal Supreme Court in Lausanne is composed of 18 German-speaking judges, 9 French-speaking judges, 2 Italian-speaking judges, and 1 Romansch-speaking judge.

15. *Stände* means the cantons as more or less sovereign political entities and members of the Confederation.

16. According to an inquiry in 1987, 40 percent of all national referenda held in the world between 1980 and 1986 were Swiss.

17. See Wolf Linder, *Swiss Democracy—Possible Solutions to Conflict in Multicultural Societies*, 2nd ed. (New York, 1998), 166–74.

18. Jonathan Steinberg, *Why Switzerland?*, 2nd ed. (Cambridge, 1996), 75.

19. Exception: the newly established canton of Jura.

20. This constitution is older than the Swiss federal state.

21. The Federal Constitution of 1874 was revised more than 140 times in 125 years.

22. Especially the chapters on fundamental rights.

23. Translation of this and other provisions of the Federal Constitution according to: "Switzerland's New Federal Constitution" (unofficial translation by Pierre A. Karrer) (Berne, 1999).

24. See Jean-François Aubert, *Bundesstaatsrecht der Schweiz*, Band 1, (Basel and Frankfurt on the Main: Helbling & Lichtenhahn Verlag AG, 1991), 235, n. 582.

25. Important cases (Federal Supreme Court): BGE 91 I 480 (1965), *Association de l'Ecole française*; BGE 100 Ia 462 (1974), *Derungs*; BGE 106 Ia 299 (1980), *Brunner*; BGE 121 I 196 (1995), *Noth*; BGE 122 I 236 (1996), *Jorane Althaus*.

26. Important cases (Federal Supreme Court): BGE 116 Ia 252 (1990), *Comune di Cadro*; BGE 118 Ia 46 (1992), *Verein Scientology-Kirche Zürich*; BGE 123 I 296 (1997), *X.*; BGE 125 I 300 (1999), *Abd-Allah Lucien Meyers*; BGE 125 I 369 (1999), *Verein Scientology-Kirche Basel*.

37. In Switzerland new or changed provisions are usually inserted into the current text of the constitution. Thus, there are no constitutional amendments of the U.S. American type.

28. Regarding legislative and other important issues; certain elections.

29. For example, Article 31 Cl. 4 of the constitution of Zurich, 18 April 1869; Article 79 Sec. 1 Cl. d of the Bernese constitution, 6 June 1993; Article 39 Sec. 1 of the constitution of Neuchâtel, 22 November 1999.

30. See, for example, the constitutions of the bilingual cantons of Fribourg and Valais.

31. "Art. 4: Minderheiten. (1) Den Bedürfnissen von sprachlichen, kulturellen und regionalen Minderheiten ist Rechnung zu tragen. (2) Zu diesem Zweck können diesen Minderheiten besondere Befugnisse zuerkannt werden."

32. Representatives of French, Italian, and Romansch areas generally prefer the territorial principle because it protects their linguistic integrity in the face of Swiss German, which is the dominant language in commerce, banking, and tourism.

33. See Andreas Auer, Giorgio Malinverni, and Michel Hottelier, *Droit constitutionnel suisse*, 2 vol. (Berne: Stämpfli, 2000), 462, n. 943.

34. Cf. BGE 116 Ia 252 (1990), *Comune di Cadro*; BGE 114 Ia 129 (1988), *M.*

35. See notes 25 and 26.

36. Stephan Breitenmoser and André Husheer, *Europarecht*, 2 vol., 2nd ed. (Zurich/Basel/Geneva: Schulthess, 2002), 748, n. 1496–1500. Describing the European Council in a few words, this forum sets up a minimum standard of minority rights protection with the mentioned documents although there is no possibility of sanctioning a defaulting member state. In case of breach of a convention, the European Council has only the right to point out the committed fault.

37. For example, paragraph 109 of the constitution of Basel-Land.

38. All residents of Swiss nationality were able to vote, not only the native Jurassiens.

39. See also Linder, *Swiss Democracy*, 8–38; Daniel Thürer, "National Minorities: A Global, European, and Swiss Perspective," in *The Fletcher Forum of World Affairs* 19 (winter/spring 1995), 61–69.

SUGGESTED READING

Auer, Andreas, Giorgio Malinverni, and Michel Hottelier. *Droit constitutionnel suisse*, 2 Vol. Berne: Stämpfli, 2000.

Basta Fleiner, Lidija R., and Thomas Fleiner (eds.). *Federalism and Multiethnic States: The Case of Switzerland*, 2nd rev. ed. Bâle, Genève, Munich: Helbing & Lichtenhahn, 2000.

Biaggini, Giovanni. *Föderalismus im Wandel: das Beispiel des schweizerischen Bundesstaates*. In Zeitschrift für öffentliches Recht (ZÖR) 57 (2002), 459–92.

——. *Verfassungsvergleichung im Dienst der Verfassungserneuerung*. In Materialien zur Zürcher Verfassungsreform (herausgegeben von Thomas Dähler, Alfred Kölz und Markus Notter), Band 2. Zürich: Schulthess, 2000, 105–24.

——. *Erste Erfahrungen mit der Kantonsverfassung des Kantons Basel-Landschaft von 1984*. In Kurt Jenny et al. (eds.), Staats- und Verwaltungsrecht des Kantons Basel-Landschaft. Liestal: Verlag des Kantons Basel-Landschaft, 1998, 9–76.

Bundesrat (Swiss Federal Council). *Erster Bericht der Schweiz zur Umsetzung des Rahmenübereinkommens des Europarates zum Schutz nationaler Minderheiten* (April 2001), Berne 2001 (also in French).

Fleiner, Thomas. *Minderheitenschutz im kantonalen Recht der Schweiz.* In Jahrbuch des öffentlichen Rechts der Gegenwart (JöR), Neue Folge, Band 40. Tübingen: Mohr, 1991/2, 45–57.

——. *Die Stellung der Minderheiten im schweizerischen Staatsrecht.* In Festschrift Werner Kägi. Zürich: Schulthess 1979, 115–28.

Häfelin, Ulrich, and Walter Haller. *Schweizerisches Bundesstaatsrecht*, 5th ed. Zürich: Schulthess, 2001.

Kälin, Walter, and Urs Bolz (eds.). *Handbuch des bernischen Verfassungsrechts.* Berne: Stämpfli, 1995 (French edition: Manuel de droit constitutionnel bernois). Berne: Stämpfli, 1995.

Klöti, Ulrich, et al. *Handbuch der Schweizer Politik*, 3rd ed. Zürich: NZZ-Verlag, 2002.

Linder, Wolf. *Swiss Democracy—Possible Solutions to Conflict in Multicultural Societies*, 2nd ed. London: Macmillan, 1998.

——. *Schweizerische Demokratie: Institutionen—Prozesse—Perspektiven.* Berne: Haupt, 1999.

Rhinow, René. *Die Bundesverfassung 2000.* Basel, Genf, München: Helbing & Lichtenhahn, 2000.

Steinberg, Jonathan. *Why Switzerland?* 2nd ed., Cambridge: Cambridge University Press, 1996.

Thürer, Daniel. "National Minorities: A Global, European, and Swiss Perspective." In *The Fletcher Forum of World Affairs* 19 (winter/spring 1995): 53–69.

Thürer, Daniel, Jean-François, Aubert, and Jörg Paul Müller (eds.). *Verfassungsrecht der Schweiz.* Zürich: Schulthess, 2001.

Index

About the Editors and Contributors

GIOVANNI BIAGGINI is Professor of Constitutional, Administrative, and European Law at the University of Zurich, Faculty of Law. He is the author of *Öffentliches Wirtschaftsrecht* (1998), with René Rhinow and Gerhard Schmid; *Theorie und Praxis des Verwaltungsrechts im Bundesstaat* (1995); *Verfassung und Richterrecht* (1991). His research interests include Swiss and comparative constitutional law, federalism, and the general theory of state.

ANNA GAMPER is Senior Researcher and Lecturer at the Institute of Public Law, Financial Law and Political Science at the University of Innsbruck (Austria). She is a former researcher at the Institut für Föderalismus in Innsbruck and, since 2001, the Austrian vice-representative in the Group of Independent Experts of the Institutional Committee (CLRAE, Council of Europe). Her main research interests include Austrian constitutional law, comparative federalism, and European regionalism.

KRISTIN HENRARD is Senior Lecturer at the University of Groningen where she teaches human rights, refugee law, and constitutional law.

Between 1995 and 1999 she also worked at the Constitutional Court of South Africa as researcher for Judge Kriegler and monitored the South African constitutional negotiations in 1996 for the Flemish government. Her main publications pertain to the areas of human rights and minority protection.

ARSHI KHAN is Senior Assistant Professor in the Centre for Federal Studies. He serves on the editorial board of the *Indian Journal of Federal Studies* at Hamdard University in New Dehli. He has published several papers in scholarly journals and edited books dealing with the federal issues in India.

JOSEF MARKO is Associate Professor of Comparative Public Law at the University of Graz (Austria) and Scientific Director of the Research Department "Minorities and Autonomies" of the European Academy of Bolzano. He is a former Judge of the Constitutional Court of Bosnia and Herzegovina and former Member of the Advisory Committee of the Framework Convention on the Protection of National Minorities, Council of Europe. His publications focus specifically on minority protection and constitutional developments in South East Europe.

FRANCESCO PALERMO is Associate Professor for Comparative Constitutional Law at the University of Verona (Italy) and senior researcher at the European Academy of Bolzano/Bozen. He has been a lecturer at the University of Trento and at Vermont Law School. His main research fields include comparative federalism, minority rights, and EU constitutional law.

WOUTER PAS is auditor at the Belgian Council of State and scientific collaborator at the Institute of Constitutional Law of the K. U. Leuven. His research interests include Belgian and comparative constitutional law and federalism.

EDUARDO J. RUIZ VIEYTEZ is Lecturer on Constitutional Law and director of the Human Rights Institute at the University of Deusto (Bilbao). He has published several books and articles, both in Spanish and English, on immigration law, national conflicts, minority rights, and related issues. He has been legal adviser to the Basque Ombudsman. He occasionally acts as an independent expert for the Council of Europe in relation to the European Charter for Regional or Minority Languages and is an active member of a Basque NGO working for the promotion of the human rights of immigrants in Spain.

G. ALAN TARR is chair of the Political Science Department at Rutgers University-Camden and director of the Center for State Constitutional Studies (www.camlaw.rutgers.edu/statecon/). He is the author of numerous books and articles dealing with subnational constitutions and federalism, including *Understanding State Constitutions* (1998), *Constitutional Politics in the States* (Greenwood Press, 1996), and *Federalism and Rights* (1996). He is currently heading a project focusing on the reform of American state constitutions.

NICOLE TÖPPERWIEN is a Senior Research Fellow at the Institute of Federalism of the University of Fribourg, Switzerland. Her main field of interest is comparative constitutional law and legal theory with primary focus on decentralization and institutional arrangements for multicultural societies.

NORMAN WEISS is Senior Researcher and Lecturer at the Human Rights Centre of the University of Potsdam (Germany). His publications focus on Human Rights Law, especially prohibition of torture and the death penalty, universal and regional mechanisms for the protection of human rights, and the prohibition of discrimination.

ROBERT F. WILLIAMS is Distinguished Professor of Law at Rutgers University School of Law, Camden, and Associate Director of the Center for State Constitutional Studies. He is the author of *State Constitutional Law: Cases and Materials* (3rd ed., 1999) and of *The New Jersey State Constitution: A Reference Guide* (rev. ed. 1997), as well as of numerous journal articles on state constitutional law. His research interests include American state constitutional law and subnational constitutional law in other federal systems. He is currently working on a study of the 1875 Constitutional Commission in New Jersey.

JENS WOELK is Lecturer and Researcher in Comparative Constitutional Law at the Law Faculty of the University of Trento (Italy) and Senior Researcher at the European Academy of Bolzano/Bozen (Research Deprtment "Minorities and Autonomies"). His current research focuses on federalism/regionalism, minority-group issues, and South-eastern Europe.